TAXATION, INFLATION, AND INTEREST RATES

TAXATION, INFLATION, AND INTEREST RATES

Edited by Vito Tanzi

International Monetary Fund • 1984

Washington, D.C.

ISBN 0-939934-32-9 (cloth)
ISBN 0-939934-33-7 (paper)

© 1984 by the International Monetary Fund

INTERNATIONAL MONETARY FUND
Washington, D.C. 20431

PRICE
US$20.00 (cloth)
US$15.00 (paper)

Foreword

The behavior of interest rates in major industrial countries affects capital movements and, consequently, exchange rates and trade flows. It may also influence the attitude of policymakers toward the growth of the money supply. The level of interest rates in these countries is a critical determinant of the cost of servicing the external debt of the developing countries. The Fund, in carrying out its purposes, is concerned with changes in interest rates, especially in connection with its surveillance over the exchange rate and debt policies of member countries. In support of the surveillance exercise through consultations under Article IV the Fund prepares a series of *World Economic Outlook* papers and, from time to time, it also undertakes analytical studies of interest rates in developing and developed countries.

During the past few years, interest rates in industrial countries have been higher and more variable than at any time over recent decades. Factors that have often been mentioned to explain this phenomenon are changes in inflationary expectations, taxation of interest income, deductibility of interest payments for tax purposes, and, of course, the effects of large fiscal deficits. Various research papers by the Fund staff have analyzed these issues, with particular emphasis on the roles of taxation and inflation in the determination of interest rates. In view of the importance of the subject to both policymakers and academicians, the Fund is making available the studies to a wider public audience through the present volume. It is my hope that they will contribute to an informed discussion of this important subject.

J. DE LAROSIÈRE
Managing Director
International Monetary Fund

July 1984

Acknowledgment

This volume has been prepared by the Fiscal Affairs Department of the Fund under the overall supervision of its Director, Vito Tanzi, with the assistance of Ved P. Gandhi, Chief of the Tax Policy Division. Its publication has been coordinated by Rasheed O. Khalid, Deputy Director.

Eight studies, attributed to specific authors, and an overview by the Fiscal Affairs Department comprise the volume. The overview represents a collective effort, with John H. Makin, Leif Mutén, Jitendra R. Modi, and Menachem Katz having contributed to it in addition to Vito Tanzi and Ved P. Gandhi. Furthermore, it has benefited from useful comments received from colleagues in other departments of the Fund. Of these contributors, Sheetal K. Chand, George F. Kopits, George von Furstenberg, Deena R. Khatkhate, and Vicente Galbis deserve special mention.

The manuscript has been put into publishable form and guided through all stages of production by Ella H. Wright, with assistance from Paul E. Gleason. The Graphics Section of the Fund made a substantial contribution in the design and production of the volume.

Special thanks are due to Sonia A. Piccinini and the secretaries of the Fiscal Affairs Department for numerous tasks cheerfully undertaken in connection with a succession of drafts which must have seemed interminable.

List of Papers

Contributors

Uri Ben-Zion is Professor on the Faculty of Industrial Engineering and Management at Technion-Israel Institute of Technology, Technion City, Israel. He holds a doctorate in economics from the University of Chicago. In the summer of 1982, Mr. Ben-Zion was a consultant to the Fiscal Affairs Department of the Fund.

Mario I. Blejer is a senior economist with the Fiscal Affairs Department of the Fund. He holds a doctorate in economics from the University of Chicago.

Menachem Katz is an economist with the Fiscal Affairs Department of the Fund. He holds a doctorate in economics from Columbia University.

John H. Makin is Professor of Economics at the University of Washington and a Research Associate with the National Bureau of Economic Research. He holds a doctorate in economics from the University of Chicago. In 1982–83 he was a consultant to the Fiscal Affairs Department of the Fund.

Vito Tanzi, Director of the Fiscal Affairs Department of the Fund, holds a doctorate in economics from Harvard University.

Introduction

VITO TANZI

To non-economists, economists may appear to be masters of a highly unified discipline. Economists themselves, however, like practitioners in other scientific fields, view their discipline as an archipelago in which each island is a different specialization. Thus, there are labor economists, monetary economists, fiscal economists, international trade economists, and so on. These specialists suffer from what is sometimes called the small-island syndrome: they come to know most of what goes on in their own area of interest but little of what goes on in others. Two groups of economists defy this characterization. One consists of generalists who use basic economic tools in their routine work but are often too busy to learn any one branch in depth. These economists do not have the time and/or the inclination to make professional contributions to economic literature. The second group consists of the giants of the field, who are able to make contributions to several branches but rarely acquire a detailed institutional knowledge of the various specializations, so that their contributions are predominantly theoretical.

The situation described above has obvious advantages: with specialization comes detailed knowledge and, thus, progress, as was so eloquently explained by Adam Smith two centuries ago. But there are costs, too. Some problems cannot be neatly assigned to one branch of economics, since they cut across various branches. These problems may go unnoticed and unsolved if each specialist continues to see the world myopically. This book deals with some problems that fall, so to speak, through the cracks between several specializations. More specifically, it deals with issues that are of mutual interest to fiscal economists, to monetary economists, and to specialists in international finance. The book explores some links among the three important branches of economics in which these specialists work.

The study of monetary-fiscal links in closed and open economies is a new and exciting area of research in economics. It is an area still occupied by few economists and one that the staff of the Fund can claim to have been among the first to explore. It is to be hoped that the papers presented in this book will be seen as a useful contribution. However, like other papers written by those who have explored new fields, these papers may raise more questions than they answer.

What are some examples of these monetary-fiscal links? A few are mentioned in this introduction. It is generally assumed that the market rate of interest is one of the independent variables that determine the quantity of money that individuals wish to hold; most quantitative, as well as theoretical, papers have utilized that rate. But what if interest income is taxed? Shouldn't one then adjust the market rate for the effect of the tax? After all, the opportunity cost of holding money in that case is the net-of-tax interest rate. What this means is that tax policy may have an immediate effect on the demand for money. As obvious and as important as this point is, no study done outside the Fund has yet paid attention to it. What if the rate of inflation raises the nominal interest rate, and thus the tax payments on interest income, to such an extent that the net-of-tax interest rate falls below the expected rate of inflation? Wouldn't one then witness a substitution between money and real assets or goods? Here is another example of a link between fiscal and monetary economics.

Several decades ago, Fisher theorized that, when there is inflation, the nominal rate of interest will increase by as much as the expected rate of inflation. But being essentially a monetary economist, Fisher ignored the effect of taxes. In the mid-1970s, three papers published at about the same time—one of which was written in the Fund— advanced the important hypothesis that, in such a situation, the nominal rate of interest would have to rise by more than the expected rate of inflation.[1] This Fisher-cum-taxes hypothesis is now generally accepted in the literature and has received recent empirical backing.

Finally, what happens if, because of a variety of factors. investors are more likely to have to pay taxes on interest income earned on domestic financial assets than on foreign ones? Or what happens if the tax treatment of interest income in different countries is different? This is, again, an important area that had received little attention (perhaps because it fell through the cracks between the three branches of economics) and one in which a good share of the work done so far has been done in the Fund. It is an area with obvious important implications, since it affects capital movements as well as theoretical conclusions reached when these tax effects are ignored, such as in-

---

[1] See Michael R. Darby, "The Financial and Tax Effects of Monetary Policy on Interest Rates," *Economic Inquiry* (Long Beach, California), Vol. 13 (June 1975), pp. 266–74; Martin S. Feldstein, "Inflation, Income Taxes, and the Rate of Interest: A Theoretical Analysis," *American Economic Review* (Nashville, Tennessee), Vol. 66 (December 1976), pp. 809–20; and Vito Tanzi, "Inflation, Indexation and Interest Income Taxation," *Quarterly Review*, Banca Nazionale del Lavoro (Rome), No. 116 (March 1976), pp. 64–76. The Tanzi paper was first issued as an unpublished paper in the Fund's Fiscal Affairs Department on February 14, 1975.

terest rate parity. These are just some of the issues discussed in this volume.

The volume is made up of nine studies, some dealing with purely theoretical aspects, others with purely empirical ones, and still others dealing with both. Part I consists of a rather lengthy paper that touches on many theoretical, as well as policy, issues arising out of the tax treatment of interest income and expense. In a way, all the other papers are inputs into this one. Thus, the busy reader who has to budget his time would be advised to read this paper. To my knowledge, this is the only published source in which information from many industrial countries on the legal treatment of interest income and expense has been compiled. Given the complexity of tax laws, this was not an easy task.

PART I. OVERVIEW

Part I includes four major sections. Section I is an introduction. Section II summarizes the main differences in the tax treatment of interest income and payments and of foreign exchange gains and losses among 16 industrial countries. These differences are shown to be substantial. For example, some countries allow unlimited deductions on interest paid on consumer loans; others do not. Some allow unlimited deductions for mortgage payments; others do not. If the Fisher-cum-taxes hypothesis has empirical validity, these different legal treatments are likely to result in different pressures on interest rates and, eventually, in capital movements. As it turns out, the U.S. tax treatment of interest expense is among the most generous. This treatment implies that U.S. borrowers are willing to pay higher rates than they would if there were a less generous treatment. Thus, interest rates may tend to be higher in the United States than elsewhere. Capital may therefore be attracted to the United States from other countries, and capital outflows may, in turn, raise interest rates in other countries. Although no firm conclusions can be drawn about the empirical significance of these effects, some educated guesses are offered.

Section III provides a detailed theoretical discussion of the Fisher effect. It argues that in the real world, the situation is not as simple as is assumed by the early literature on the Fisher effect, with or without taxes. In fact, the Fisher hypothesis is postulated under the assumption that the real rate of interest does not change over time or when inflationary expectations are changing. But this assumption cannot be maintained, as is indicated by several recent studies showing that factors such as changes in the rate of inflation itself, in economic activity, in the price of energy, in the productivity of capital, in the tax laws, in the variance of the rate of inflation, and so on may change the real rate of interest. Of course, if the real rate of interest changes, the simple one-to-one relation between the nominal rate of interest and the expected rate of inflation will not hold even when taxes are ignored. Section III also contains a brief discussion of proposals that would remove the tax effect of interest rates. Some of these are politically unrealistic, some administratively infeasible. One proposal that would seem administratively feasible and that might have a political chance is for nondeductibility of interest expense connected with consumer loans. This proposal would contribute to the reduction of the fiscal deficit in the United States, would have beneficial effects on capital formation, and would reduce interest rates. Its effect on the rate of interest might, however, not be very significant.

Section IV extends the discussion to an international setting. Differential tax treatment of interest income and expense is shown to affect the levels of interest rates and to induce capital flows across countries. The role of differential tax rates on foreign exchange gains and losses, as compared with interest income and expense, in determining nominal interest rate differentials is discussed. Other issues discussed include policies of monetary restraint and the volatility of interest rates since 1979. Section V summarizes many of the conclusions.

PART II. BACKGROUND PAPERS

Part II of the book is divided into three sections. The first is made up of two chapters that survey the literature. The second contains three chapters dealing with the American scene, and the third section contains three chapters dealing with the international scene.

The two literature survey papers concentrate, respectively, on a closed economy (Chapter 2) and an open economy (Chapter 3). Chapter 2 examines the recent contributions on the relationship between inflation and interest rates in a world with taxation. It surveys several extensions of the basic Fisherian theory, including real balance effects, substitution effects, personal income tax effects, and effects associated with corporate income taxes and capital gains taxation. It also describes a recent formulation of a general equilibrium model. Various empirical studies for the United States and other countries are surveyed. Overall, the studies surveyed point to the need for more explicit recognition of the fact that economic behavior of lenders and borrowers is governed by net-of-tax interest rates, prices, and incomes.

The paper concludes with an agenda for research which points toward the integration of tax policies into traditional analyses of effects of monetary policy.

Chapter 3 shows that although extensive literature exists on the interrelationship between inflation rates, interest rates, and exchange rates and on the effects of these three variables on international capital movements, most of this literature has not considered the impact of taxes and of differential taxation across countries. The few articles that have done so are reviewed. It is shown that taxes play a crucial role in the determination of capital mobility and that the assumptions regarding the tax treatment of foreign interest income are of particular importance.

The second section of Part II includes three studies, all of which deal with the United States. The first of these—Chapter 4—analyzes the factors that have affected the level and volatility of interest rates in the United States. The most important among these factors are the following: (a) expected inflation; (b) stage of the business cycle; (c) changes in the fiscal deficit; (d) unanticipated changes in the money supply; (e) tax treatment of interest income, interest expense, and depreciation; and (f) uncertainty about the rate of inflation. The role of each of these factors is discussed. It is argued that (a) a higher expected rate of inflation, (b) greater economic activity, (c) a larger fiscal deficit, and (d) an unanticipated fall in the rate of increase of the money supply unambiguously increase the rate of interest. The effects of taxes and inflation uncertainty are more ambiguous.

Taxation of interest income and exemption of interest expense from taxation both raise the interest rate. This impact is reduced, but not eliminated, by taxes on noninterest income. These taxes force an individual to invest a larger share of his loanable funds in financial assets, thus depressing his rate of return. It is concluded that taxes generally have a positive net effect on interest rates. Inflation uncertainty increases the rate of return expected by lenders, but it also decreases the demand for funds by borrowers. Therefore, the net effect of inflation uncertainty is ambiguous. The theoretical section also shows that tax effects magnify the volatility of nominal interest rates arising from fluctuations of expected inflation and real interest rates.

The paper develops an econometric model to test the results derived from the theoretical analysis. The rate of interest on treasury bills is correlated with expected inflation, economic activity, unanticipated changes in the money supply, and fiscal deficits. An extremely good fit is derived. The model is shown to explain well the behavior of interest rates from the early 1960s through the end of 1981. Previous studies have not been as successful at explaining the behavior of interest rates during the volatile period since October 1979.

Chapter 5 considers some equity aspects of the tax treatment of interest income and expense. It points out that income taxes are not proportional, but progressive. As a consequence, even if there should be a full adjustment of the interest rate to the effects of taxes and inflation (i.e., even if the Fisher-cum-taxes hypothesis were validated), the interest rate would adjust for some *average* tax rate. Therefore, it would be too high for some taxpayers (those with low marginal tax rates) and too low for others (those with above-average marginal tax rates). As lenders, the first group would gain, the second would lose. The results for borrowers would be exactly the reverse. Thus, to determine whether a given income class gains or loses during inflation, one needs to consider whether the class is a net lender or borrower. The analysis shows that the U.S. middle classes were the net gainers, since they were net borrowers. The paper also attempts to determine whether the government gained or lost from this tax treatment of interest incomes and expenses. It is shown that when inflation became very high, the government gained.

Chapter 6 deals with a theoretical issue that also has some practical relevance. This is the issue of whether the demand for money in a country such as the United States is affected only by the rate of interest, as is normally argued, or by both the rate of interest *and* inflationary expectations. The paper argues that in the absence of taxes on income and of institutional constraints on interest rates, only interest rates would be relevant, since the rate of interest would generally exceed the rate of inflationary expectations and would thus be the relevant opportunity cost of holding money. However, when, in the presence of inflation, interest rates are constrained, as they are in developing countries and/or when interest income is taxed, then inflationary expectations, rather than the rate of interest, may be the main variable influencing the demand for money. The paper emphasizes that, until recently in the United States, the net-of-tax rate of return on financial assets was often lower than the rate of expected inflation (a situation that has obviously changed). Therefore, it became convenient for people to get out of both money and financial assets and into real goods (gold, houses, etc.). The paper tests the hypothesis that inflationary expectations, rather than the rate of interest, were the major determinant of the demand for money in the United States over the past two decades. The empirical tests validate this hypothesis.

The third section of Part II includes three chapters, all dealing with international aspects. Chapter 7 attempts to test the Fisher hypothesis for eight industrial countries, using a consistent methodology for estimating inflationary expectations. It is shown that, generally, interest rates adjusted for expected inflation (as provided by the method used to determine it) but lagged behind actual price changes. Some evidence of tax effects on interest rates was also found.

Chapter 8, which is a purely theoretical paper, analyzes the relationships between inflation, interest rates, and exchange rates when the role of taxes is taken into account. It incorporates tax considerations into a unified analytical framework. The basic premise of the analysis is that the presence of taxes induces portfolio shifts aimed at restoring equality between the expected net returns on domestic and foreign assets. Four main results are obtained: (1) Identical rates of taxation across countries do not prevent capital flows and changes in real interest rates when inflation rates differ. (2) Differences in tax rates are conducive to differentials in real after-tax rates of interest. In general, higher tax rates result in lower real interest rates, even if rates of inflation are identical across countries. (3) Under purchasing power parity, increases in the inflation rate of the high-tax country result in a capital inflow and in a reduced real rate of interest. They may also induce two-way capital flows if exchange gains are taxed at a lower rate than interest income. (4) When the exchange rate is determined by interest parity, departures from purchasing power parity and the variability of the exchange rate are proportional to the differences between tax rates.

While Chapter 8 is a purely theoretical paper, Chapter 9 is a purely empirical one. It attempts to show how tax factors may have affected international capital flows. First, an analysis of seven industrial countries indicates that short-term foreign exchange gains may be effectively taxed at lower rates than long-term gains. If this empirical result is correct, it is somewhat surprising. Second, it shows how differential tax treatment by the United States of interest income and foreign exchange gains realized after 12 months can lead to simultaneous capital flows in opposite directions. However, this happens only rarely.

As was stated at the beginning, the book will probably raise more questions than it will answer. Some readers are likely to disagree with parts of it. However, they will find it difficult to disagree with two of the book's basic conclusions. First, the role of taxes in areas such as monetary economics and international finance cannot be ignored by economists working in those areas who seek to deal effectively with the real world. Too many monetary economists and specialists in international finance still go about their work as if they had never heard about taxation. Second, in a world where taxation is so predominant, the idea that inflation changes just nominal values, without affecting real values, is, as this book should make abundantly clear, a mere fiction. Unfortunately, one still sees much economic writing that perpetuates this fiction. It is to be hoped that this book will encourage a growing number of economists to concentrate on those areas where monetary economics, fiscal economics, and international finance intersect.

Contents

PART II. BACKGROUND PAPERS

Survey of the Literature

Chapter 2: **Recent Literature on the Impact of Taxation and Inflation on Interest Rates**.................. **Uri Ben-Zion**   **69**

PART I

OVERVIEW

1

Interest Rates
and Tax Treatment of
Interest Income and Expense

FISCAL AFFAIRS DEPARTMENT

In recent years the Executive Directors of the International Monetary Fund have expressed concern over the effects on the level and variability of interest rates arising from differential tax treatment of interest income and expense across countries. They have also expressed concern with respect to the effects of these and other related tax provisions on the effectiveness of policies of monetary restraint and on international capital movements. The Executive Directors therefore asked the Fund staff to assess the role of tax factors in the high levels of interest rates prevailing in 1981–82 in the United States and other major industrial countries.[1]

The situation has changed somewhat in the past year. Nominal interest rates have fallen considerably in the United States and elsewhere, but real interest rates have remained high. Some industrial countries have started taking a closer look at tax provisions relating to savings and capital formation. Attention has focused on the influence of taxation on the after-tax costs of investments and returns on savings, especially in an inflationary situation. Furthermore, the tax deductibility of interest payments unrelated to income-earning activ-

---

[1] Although the paper was a collective effort by Fiscal Affairs Department staff members, assisted by a consultant—Professor John H. Makin of the University of Washington and the National Bureau of Economic Research—specific individuals were responsible for certain parts. Section II was prepared mainly by Ved P. Gandhi, who also coordinated the preparation of the entire paper. The factual information on which that section is based was researched by Jitendra R. Modi, who was also responsible for the preparation of the three tables in Appendix III. Section III was written by John H. Makin and Vito Tanzi, with contributions by Ved P. Gandhi, Menachem Katz, and Mario I. Blejer. Section IV was mainly the work of John H. Makin, who also prepared Appendix II. The introductory and concluding sections were written by Ved P. Gandhi, John H. Makin, and Vito Tanzi, with Mr. Gandhi carrying a greater share of the burden. Leif Mutén wrote Appendix I.

3

ities (viewed by some observers as a "tax expenditure") has come under close scrutiny in the United States and other industrial countries.

Nevertheless, tax reforms have been slow. Different tax policies, frequently dictated by tradition and by the national goals of individual countries, continue to be the rule. Therefore, insofar as tax factors do affect significantly the level and volatility of interest rates in a closed (domestic) economy, and differential tax regimes affect exchange rates and international capital movements in an open (international) economy, the concern expressed by the Executive Directors remains valid and significant.

I. BACKGROUND

As tax factors have generally been given little importance in the literature on monetary theory and international finance, the professional body of knowledge in this area is limited. Theories of interest rate determination and of demand for money are often discussed in terms of pretax variables, and they omit reference to taxation of interest income or to deductibility of interest payments from taxable income. Similarly, the literature on theorems of interest rate parity and purchasing power parity has largely ignored the effects of tax factors. On the other hand, public finance literature has focused on the microeconomic (allocative) and equity (redistributive) effects of taxes and has ignored their macroeconomic effects.[2]

Limitations of the paper

As is often the case, the research effort involved in preparing the present study, while answering many questions, has raised many more and has made the Fund staff more aware of the many problems in this area.

(1) There is little unanimity among economists as to the determinants of interest rates and international capital movements. As a matter of fact, no single theory of interest rate determination that has been advanced is readily accepted by the majority of economists or can explain the unusually high levels of real interest rates in recent years.

---

[2] Surveys of recent works on the effects of taxation on interest rates and international capital movements have been carried out in the Fiscal Affairs Department; see the background papers by Ben-Zion in Part II of this volume. Other relevant papers prepared by the Department are included in the References. The present paper relies heavily on findings and conclusions contained in those papers.

(2) The interrelationship between nominal or market interest rates and their determinants, particularly expected inflation, has been unstable over time, so that no specific conclusions can be reached about the precise quantitative effect of inflation on interest rates.

(3) The available empirical evidence on the interrelationships between taxation, inflation, and interest rates is sketchy. For the United States and one or two other industrial countries, the evidence that does exist is often conflicting or ambiguous.

(4) The tax provisions bearing on interest rates and international capital movements of individual countries tend to be highly complicated and thus subject to a variety of qualifications and interpretations. (Some of these problems are discussed in Appendix I.) Furthermore, recent ad hoc legislative efforts aimed at adjusting the tax systems for inflation have created uncertainties of their own.

(5) Finally, little statistical information is available on the taxes actually paid by groups of savers and investors in individual countries. In addition, the existence of many possibilities for tax avoidance (e.g., tax allowances for savers and tax deferrals for investors) and tax evasion (resulting from shortcomings in national tax administration and the existence of tax havens abroad) makes the available legal information of doubtful usefulness (see Appendix I).

The research on the subject, carried out in the Fund's Fiscal Affairs Department and elsewhere, can therefore claim at best, to have reached, tentative conclusions subject to the above-mentioned limitations.

Outline of the paper

The paper focuses on the following questions:

(1) Does the tax treatment of interest income and payments differ markedly among major industrial countries? Do other tax provisions affecting interest rates and international capital movements also differ markedly?

(2) How does the tax treatment of interest income and payments influence the level and volatility of interest rates, especially in an inflationary environment? If there is an influence, what is the direction of the effects of these and other relevant tax factors?

(3) How do potential international movements of capital and related tax provisions alter the results of changes in tax treatment regarding interest income and expense initiated by a single country?

(4) What implications does the tax treatment of interest income and expense and related tax policies have for the impact of changes in the degree of monetary restraint?

(5) What are the consequences of tax policy for the volatility of interest rates and what are the procedures for changing tax policy?

Sections II, III, and IV attempt to answer these questions and to present the available empirical evidence. Section V brings together the major conclusions of the paper and states their implications for Fund activities.

Summary of major conclusions

Section II, supported by three tables in Appendix III, shows that, even though the taxation of interest income is nearly universal and that such income is generally taxed at ordinary income tax rates, the tax regimes of major industrial countries differ in major respects. The marginal rates of the income tax differ among industrial countries, and the tax allowances offered to savers by individual governments also differ markedly. Furthermore, the changes that have been made in income tax structures in response to inflation in most industrial countries have been ad hoc ones and have been incomplete. As a result, the effective tax rates for real interest income differ among industrial countries, although no estimates of these rates are available.

The differences in the tax treatment of interest payments are even more marked. Of the 16 industrial countries surveyed,[3] 7 offer deductibility from taxable income of *all* interest payments, including those for income-earning activities, mortgage payments, and consumer loans; 8 allow tax deductibility of interest payments for income-earning activities and for mortgages but none for consumer loans; and only one country does not allow any deduction for either mortgages or consumer loans.

The tax treatment of foreign exchange gains and losses also differs among industrial countries, although the legal provisions are more complex. In some countries, gains are treated as capital receipts and are thus subjected to capital gains taxes, which are generally levied at lower rates; in other countries, they are treated as current receipts and are subjected to the regular income tax.

Section III suggests that, even in the absence of income taxes, the one-to-one relationship between expected inflation and nominal interest rates (the basic Fisherian hypothesis) may not be valid for a variety of reasons. The existence of expected inflation may, in fact, lower the rate of return on real investment and, consequently, the

---

[3] Australia, Austria, Belgium, Canada, Denmark, France, the Federal Republic of Germany, Ireland, Italy, Japan, the Netherlands, Norway, Sweden, Switzerland, the United Kingdom, and the United States.

real rate of interest, thereby limiting the increase in nominal interest rates.

The taxation of nominal interest income and the tax deductibility of nominal interest payments, which typically exist in many industrial countries, can theoretically cause a more-than-proportional increase in nominal interest rates as a result of a given expected rate of inflation. But this increase is also limited by the existence of many other tax factors, including the tax treatment of other capital income and capital gains that limit the investor's capacity to avoid taxes, the tax depreciation allowances and inventory procedures that increase taxation on companies and thereby reduce their ability to pay higher interest rates, the existence of tax-exempt lenders and borrowers, tax evasion, tax havens, etc. Because of these many tax factors, the positive impact of the tax treatment of interest income and interest payments is likely to be somewhat reduced. The few empirical investigations covering this area tentatively suggest that, when all factors are taken into account, the nominal interest rate, on average, does not increase more than proportionately with expected inflation (e.g., see Section III, Table 1). However, this empirical result does not rule out the possible existence of tax effects.

Many proposals have been made to restrain the positive effect of the "typical" tax treatment of interest income and payments on nominal interest rates. In particular, these have included (1) a complete inflation adjustment of interest income and expense for taxation purposes, (2) the elimination of taxes on interest income simultaneously with the elimination of the tax deductibility of interest payments, and, finally, (3) limitations on the tax deductibility of interest payments. The discussion in Section III suggests that the first two proposals will have the greatest effect on interest rates but are unlikely to be adopted by many countries (and, because of capital flows, it may not be in the interest of large single countries to do so). The last proposal—limiting the tax deductibility of interest payments for nonbusiness purposes— seems, in reality, to hold the most promise; it is administratively feasible, it would reduce the fiscal deficits, and it would have beneficial effects on capital formation. Its effect on interest rates would, however, not be very significant.

Section IV considers some extensions and qualifications of the discussion in Section III. Differential taxation across countries is shown to affect the levels of interest rates and to induce international capital flows. In addition, tax rates on foreign exchange gains (and losses) that are lower than those on interest income would lead to an increase in the pretax nominal interest rate differential in order for an international equilibrium of credit markets to exist. A change in the tax treatment of interest income and expense through inflation adjustment would lower the effective tax rates on interest income for any single country taking such steps. As the nominal interest rates would also fall, some capital outflows would result. A new equilibrium nominal interest differential would thus emerge, based on the relationship between the new effective tax rate on nominal interest and the tax rates applied to foreign exchange gains and losses.

Economic theory and empirical evidence suggest that expected inflation causes a decline in after-tax real interest rates. When this relationship is considered in the context of policies of monetary restraint, it implies that real interest rates may stay high for some time after the initiation of monetary restraint. Initially, this may be due to negative liquidity effects when money growth is first slowed; then it becomes due to a rise in the real interest rate resulting from a combination of the wealth effect and tax policy.

Section IV also examines the causes of the higher volatility of interest rates since 1979 (see Section IV, Table 2). The tax treatment of interest income and expense, coupled with "bracket creep," has probably enhanced the impact of changing inflationary expectations on the volatility of interest rates in recent years. As interest rates are determined in forward-looking markets by investors and savers interested in future, after-tax, real returns, any event that tends to broaden the range of possible future outcomes for inflation, fiscal deficits, and the tax code itself also increases interest rate volatility.

Section V brings together the major conclusions of the paper and reflects on their implications for Fund activities. It argues for the use of opportunities offered by consultations under Article IV of the Fund's Articles of Agreement to review, especially in inflationary circumstances, important tax reforms in areas such as the tax treatment of interest income and expense and taxation of foreign exchange gains and losses. Control of inflation should be an important objective of all governments. If inflation cannot be controlled (and subject to budgetary and other constraints), the country should explore the possibilities for adjustment of income taxation for inflation, including the tax treatment of interest income and payments. Such an exercise should also simultaneously review the scope for (1) curtailing discretionary, and often distortionary, tax incentives given to the recipients of capital income, and (2) improving the efficiency of collection of income tax from such income so as to reduce the opportunity for tax avoidance and tax evasion. The possibilities for narrowing the differences in the tax treatment of foreign exchange gains and of interest income should also be explored.

Finally, interest is only one form of capital income; dividends, capital gains, business profits, and property rentals are other important forms. Ceteris paribus, the tax treatment of interest income and payments relative to the tax treatment of other capital income tends to have important allocative effects in an economy (Ben-Zion (1983)), and their differential tax treatments across countries can affect the form of international capital movements and the sectors to which the international capital will flow. This paper does not deal with these important and complex allocative questions, nor does it deal with the effects of taxes in developed and developing countries where most interest rates are regulated.

II. TAX TREATMENT OF INTEREST INCOME AND EXPENSE

The tax treatment of interest income and expense varies among major industrial countries.[4] The differences are due partly to historical reasons and partly to the different weights that policymakers attach to the objectives of tax policy—namely, revenue, equity, and efficiency. Prima facie, the differences among industrial countries in the taxation of income—and particularly in the tax treatment of interest income and payments—appear to be so large[5] as to defy generalization. However, on closer look, and subject to the problems discussed in Appendix I, some basic similarities are discernible.

Basic similarities

Almost all of the industrial countries have the following similarities:
    (1) They treat nominal interest income, including that received from abroad, as any other source of income and thus tax it at the progressive global income tax rate.[6]
    (2) They exempt interest income earned by certain institutional recipients, such as pension and retirement funds, selected financial institutions, certain government bodies, and most charitable and non-profit institutions (see Appendix III, Table 3).

---

[4] Section II is based on a survey of the tax systems of 16 industrial countries: Australia, Austria, Belgium, Canada, Denmark, France, the Federal Republic of Germany, Ireland, Italy, Japan, the Netherlands, Norway, Sweden, Switzerland, the United Kingdom, and the United States. See the tables in Appendix III for more detail.

[5] The tables in Appendix III show only major differences and are not comprehensive.

[6] In reality, withholding of income tax at the source for selected interest income can introduce a schedular element.

(3) They exempt, with or without limits, interest on certain debt instruments, such as specified government securities, deposits with selected savings institutions, and bonds of certain public enterprises (see Appendix III, Table 3).

(4) They often exempt specified amounts of interest and/or dividend income for administrative reasons or to promote savings (see Appendix III, Table 3).

(5) They allow full deductibility of interest payments on all borrowing for income-generating activities (see Appendix III, Table 4).

(6) They permit deductibility, with or without limit, of mortgage interest payments on at least one owner-occupied house (see Appendix III, Table 4).

(7) They generally tax interest paid to nonresidents at final withholding tax rates (frequently well below the typical marginal tax rates for individuals and corporations); nonresident taxpayers can generally rely on a foreign tax credit to avoid double taxation in their country of residence (see Appendix III, Table 5).

Major differences

Despite the similarities, there are major differences:

(1) While most countries tax nominal interest income at the normal income tax rates, Belgium, Japan, Italy, and France permit withholding taxes on them to become final taxes. Some of these rules are pragmatic measures to ensure compliance. The United Kingdom, on the other hand, has a supplementary tax of 15 percent, over and above the income tax, on all investment income, including interest income. In Belgium, too, a supplementary tax, ranging from 20 percent to 47 percent, is levied on interest and dividend income exceeding certain limits.

(2) While most countries exempt interest income earned on selected debt instruments within reasonably low limits, and sometimes subject to a ceiling on the taxpayer's total income (see Table 1; see also Byrne (1976)), the exemption of interest income is relatively generous in Japan (see Appendix III, Table 3). An exemption of interest on savings up to a cumulative nominal amount of US$56,000[7] is statutorily permitted to each household for bank deposits, postal savings deposits, certain government bonds, and savings for formation of employee's assets. In addition, in Japan there is no ceiling on the taxpayer's income to qualify nor is a taxpayer limited to having only

---

[7] Based on a rate of exchange of ¥ 250 = US$1.

one savings account. In the United States, too, there is no restriction on a taxpayer's holdings of state and local government bonds. The selected debt instruments (government bonds and savings deposits) on which interest tends to be exempt from taxation generally carry lower interest rates, when adjusted for risk, than taxable debt instruments of equal maturity.[8]

(3) While all countries allow tax deductibility of business-related interest payments, subject to few restrictions, only the United States, the Netherlands, Switzerland, and the Scandinavian countries permit the tax deductibility of interest payments on consumer loans and without any limit (Appendix III, Table 4). The degree to which consumer loans are readily available and the degree to which taxpayers habitually use them vary among these countries. The question of the imposition of some limits on this "tax expenditure," and even a complete elimination of it, has been raised at one time or another in the United States, the Netherlands, and the Scandinavian countries.

(4) While many countries allow tax deductibility of mortgage interest on owner-occupied housing (Appendix III, Table 4), they either tax the imputed incomes from housing or limit the amount of mortgage interest that can be deducted, or do both. The United States, the Netherlands, Switzerland, and the Scandinavian countries do not limit the tax deductibility of mortgage interest. Furthermore, Canada, France, Japan, Switzerland, the United Kingdom, the United States, and a few other industrial countries do not tax the imputed income from such owner-occupied housing.

(5) While most countries have withholding taxes on interest income,[9] Australia, Canada, the Netherlands, and the Scandinavian countries have no such taxes (Appendix III, Table 3). The United States also does not have a withholding tax on interest income and has recently rejected its introduction.

(6) While most countries tax long-term capital gains of individuals, either under a separate tax (e.g., the United Kingdom) or under the regular income tax after exempting a certain proportion of capital gains (e.g., Canada, Sweden, and the United States), most industrial countries apply lower tax rates on long-term capital gains than on ordinary income. The Federal Republic of Germany[10] and Japan, on the other hand, treat long-term capital gains in much the same manner

---

[8] In the United States, for example, the risk-adjusted difference in the interest rates on taxable and nontaxable bonds has historically been of the same magnitude as the average tax rate on interest income.

[9] The existence of withholding taxes often reduces the opportunity for tax evasion.

[10] Only when long-term capital gains arise from disposal of business assets.

as they treat ordinary income. The tax treatment of long-term capital gains realized by companies also differs among countries.

(7) While most countries tax interest earned by nonresidents, some countries provide for selective exemptions. For example, Belgium, France, Ireland, and the United Kingdom exempt interest earned by nonresidents on certain government securities, and the United States exempts interest earned by nonresidents from banks and other savings institutions, as also do Belgium and Denmark (see Appendix III, Table 5). If withholding taxes are imposed on interest payments to nonresidents, they are typically much lower than normal income tax rates, but they apply to gross payments rather than to net income and are often final tax payments in the source country. Capital gains of nonresidents are usually taxable, especially if they are related to real property or business, but France, the Federal Republic of Germany, and the United Kingdom exempt capital gains of nonresidents on all but a few assets. Such provisions can encourage foreign capital inflows for selected purposes.

(8) While most countries tax only the realized foreign exchange gains of their residents, legal provisions frequently tend to be complex and subject to different interpretations. Some industrial countries treat these gains as capital receipts and subject them to the tax rates for capital gains; others treat them as current receipts and apply the income tax rate. In most countries, the tax treatment becomes a subject for court decisions, and the case becomes law. The final outcome, though consistent with prevailing accounting practices in individual countries for tax purposes, tends to affect capital flows between countries.

State of inflation adjustment

To the extent that the bases of the income tax, corporation tax, and capital gains tax of industrial countries are not adequately adjusted for inflation, the effective tax rates on real amounts of interest income, corporate profits, and capital gains tends to rise. At the same time, the effective benefits from the tax deductibility of nominal interest payments and various tax incentives for savings and investment also rise. Although certain industrial countries have in recent years introduced some adjustment schemes, none of these countries seems to have fully adjusted its personal income tax and its corporate income tax for inflation.

The most comprehensive adjustment schemes for the personal income tax are found in Canada and the Netherlands, but even these schemes are limited to the adjustment of tax brackets and do not extend to the tax bases. In Canada, income tax brackets and personal allowances are automatically changed annually in accordance with changes in the consumer price index. In the Netherlands, income tax brackets are normally adjusted annually by a certain percentage of the increase in the consumer price index of the preceding year. Several other industrial countries (for example, Denmark, France, Sweden, and the United Kingdom) have also introduced adjustments for inflation. In France, such adjustments are discretionary and limited to years when the inflation rate exceeds 5 percent. The U.K. adjustments are also discretionary and have been limited to personal allowances and deductions. Sweden also has an automatic indexation of exemptions and bracket limits, but recent legislation has restricted application of the system. Legislation in the United States provides for the indexation of income tax brackets and personal exemptions to inflation beginning in 1985. Italy has also experimented with occasional adjustments of the tax bracket.

Selective information collected on changes in the income tax systems of eight industrial countries (Austria, Canada, France, the Federal Republic of Germany, Italy, Switzerland, the United Kingdom, and the United States) suggests that, since 1973, personal allowances (or tax credits) and income deductions have generally been adjusted by less than the rates of inflation in these countries.

With respect to taxation of capital gains, Ireland and the United Kingdom have made legal provision for adjustment of the cost of acquiring assets with reference to the consumer price index over the holding period of the asset. Sweden and France also have such a provision, but it is applicable only to certain categories of assets.

Tax provisions for a comprehensive adjustment of business and corporate profits for inflation do not exist in any industrial country, although a few industrial countries (e.g., Belgium, Japan, the Netherlands, and the United States) do allow use of the last-in, first-out method of inventory accounting. In all industrial countries except Denmark, depreciation of assets is still allowed on the basis of historical cost rather than replacement cost. Most countries, however, have liberalized their investment incentives (accelerated depreciation allowances, investment allowances, income tax credits, tax-free reserves, grants, free write-offs, etc.) in recent years,[11] often allowing more

---

[11] The conventional forms of accelerated depreciation are, however, inadequate substitutes for depreciation based on replacement cost; the larger the anticipated rate of inflation and the longer the life of the asset, the wider is the gap. Investment allowances and income tax credits, on the other hand, favor short-lived assets, because every time such assets are replaced the investor can take advantage of these incentives in addition to using full depreciation.

than 100 percent of the original cost of acquisition of assets, or have adopted other means of reducing the growth of the real tax burden on corporate entities. The value of such tax subsidies to capital varies from country to country; these subsidies seem to be more generous in Italy, the United Kingdom, and the United States and less generous in the Federal Republic of Germany and Japan (Kopits (1981)).

In conclusion, the tax regimes of major industrial countries are seen to be different, as a result of both different traditions and the mix of domestic objectives pursued by policymakers. Yet the taxation of interest income is nearly universal, and practically everywhere interest income is taxed on nominal rather than real magnitudes. The changes made in response to inflation in the structure of income taxes (e.g., the rates, income brackets, personal allowances, and one or more personal deductions) have been both ad hoc and incomplete. The effective tax rates on interest income, therefore, have tended to differ among industrial countries as a consequence of differences in legal provisions, in degrees of tax compliance, in rates of inflation, and in degrees of exemption accorded to interest income.

The tax treatment of interest expense differs even more markedly among industrial countries. Some countries offer deductibility from taxable income of all interest payments (for business, home ownership, and consumer credit), while others allow it only for income-earning activities and still others allow it for business purposes as well as home ownership (the latter generally in a restricted fashion). But nearly everywhere the deductions for interest payments reflect nominal amounts, making the tax benefits of available deductions differ even more significantly from country to country, depending on the rate of inflation.

Interest payments to nonresident taxpayers are subject to withholding taxes in most industrial countries, but foreign exchange gains and losses are not treated uniformly. In some countries, they are treated as capital receipts and are subjected to (lower) capital gains taxes while in other countries they are treated as current receipts and are subjected to (relatively higher) regular income taxes.

The possible implications of these and other differences in tax regimes on (1) the level and variability of interest rates and the effectiveness of monetary restraint in a given economy and on (2) interest rate differentials between countries and international capital movements are discussed in Sections III and IV.

III. EFFECTS OF TAXES AND INFLATION ON INTEREST RATES

In an inflationary environment, the typical tax treatment of interest income and expense—taxing nominal interest received and allowing a deduction for nominal interest paid—can have a significant impact on the level of interest rates and can also affect their volatility. As inflation distorts the base for the tax on interest income and increases the effective tax rates on income in general, this impact is likely to be magnified over time as long as the rate of inflation continues to be high. The tax treatment of interest income and expense may also alter the redistributive impact of monetary restraint and may affect capital flows across countries.

The survey of taxation of interest income in Section II indicates that the industrial countries generally (1) tax nominal interest income without allowing any adjustment for its inflationary component, (2) allow a deduction for interest expense, again without any adjustment for the inflationary component, (3) permit the issuance of tax-free financial assets by public bodies, and (4) do not tax the income received by certain institutions (such as charitable, educational, and religious ones).

However, these generalizations hide important differences, which are set forth in Section II and in Appendix III. For example, (1) France, Italy, and Japan collect withholding taxes, levied at lower rates than marginal income tax rates, that become final taxes (for taxpayers with high taxable incomes, this is an advantage that may induce them to supply loanable funds at lower rates than they would otherwise do); (2) Japan provides more generous exemptions for interest income than other countries do, again potentially reducing the offer price (the interest rate demanded) for funds; and (3) the Netherlands, the Scandinavian countries, Switzerland, and the United States permit tax deductibility of interest payments on consumer loans and also do not limit the tax deductibility of mortgage payments.[12] Thus, it would be expected that the rate of interest would be higher in the latter countries and that a potentially larger share of investment would go toward these tax-advantaged investments.

In recent years, the potential effect of taxation on the level of interest rates in an inflationary situation has attracted the attention

---

[12] For fiscal year 1984, the tax revenue loss from deductibility of interest on consumer loans in the United States is estimated at about $8 billion. The revenue loss from deductibility of mortgage interest on owner-occupied houses is estimated at about $28 billion.

of some economists. Two major conclusions have come out of the resultant literature.

In a situation where there is inflation and the income tax is imposed on nominal interest income while nominal interest payments are deductible expenses, taxation should have a positive effect on the nominal rate of interest. To the extent that part of the interest received is not taxed or part of the interest paid is not tax deductible, this tax effect would naturally be reduced.

As the rate of inflation is likely to be negatively correlated with the real rate of interest (for reasons given below), the positive effect on interest rates associated with the existence of taxes may not be apparent in simple quantitative analysis.

Effects of inflation on interest rates in the absence of income taxes

For convenience, the discussion here is organized around the Fisher equation, which simply states that the nominal (or market) rate of interest, i, equals the sum of the expected real rate, r, and the expected rate of inflation, π. That is,

$$i = r + \pi \tag{1}$$

In the absence of expected inflation, the real rate of interest and the nominal rate of interest will be the same. As expected inflation acquires a positive value, the Fisherian hypothesis asserts that, if the expected real rate is constant and therefore independent of expected inflation, each percentage point rise in the expected rate of inflation results in a percentage point rise in the nominal rate of interest. This hypothesis is usually expressed as

$$i = r + \beta\pi, \text{ where } \beta = 1 \tag{2}$$

It must be emphasized, however, that equation (2) represents a quite rigid or extreme view of how inflation is likely to affect interest rates.[13] In reality, there are several reasons why β would not be equal to unity. (It should be stressed that the existence of taxes is still being ignored.)

Real balance effect

The real balance effect, associated with Robert Mundell and James Tobin, postulates a negative relationship between the real rate of interest (r) and the expected rate of inflation (π). In Tobin's formu-

---

[13] Fisher himself is reported to have had doubts about this extreme version of his theory.

lation, a rise in expected inflation causes a shift out of money balances and into real capital, thereby depressing the marginal product of capital and the equilibrium real rate of interest. In Mundell's formulation, a rise in the expected rate of inflation reduces the real cash balances of individuals, making them feel poorer. They react by raising the steady-state level of saving, thus pushing down the real rate of interest.

Liquidity effects

As additional money is injected into the economy, individuals may for a time experience excess liquidity, particularly if the increase in the money supply is not fully anticipated. Thus, before prices and inflationary expectations fully adjust upward, the impact of excess money may, as Keynes argued long ago, lead to a lowering of the rate of interest. However, when the money increase is fully anticipated, as it would be when the rate of inflation has stabilized, this effect disappears. In an economy where inflation has been rampant for some time, this liquidity effect is not likely to be significant. By the same token, the real rate of interest may increase if there is a drastic but not fully anticipated decrease in the growth of the money supply.

Economic activity effect

Various nominal rates of interest can be associated with the same inflationary expectation, provided that the level of economic activity varies. The demand for loanable funds is likely to be lower during recessions or during periods of low economic activity, when many investments are postponed; on the other hand, it is higher during booms, when optimism is prevalent and investment is high. Thus, a slowdown in economic activity is likely to pull the rate of interest below the level that, ceteris paribus, would exist if economic activity remained at a "normal" level. This effect might be reflected in insufficient adjustment of the nominal rate for the expected rate of inflation.

Institutional constraints

There is probably no country where all interest rates are completely free to adjust to the level determined by the market. To varying degrees, the movement of interest rates is constrained by legal or institutional limitations, so that the observed rates may be lower than the rates that would prevail in the absence of any limitations.

Money illusion

Although economists have become increasingly skeptical about the existence of money illusion, there must be at least some individuals who, especially when the rate of inflation is low or when inflation is a new phenomenon, confuse nominal interest rates with real interest rates. As long as some hold this illusion, the nominal rates may tend to increase by less than expected inflation.

Fiscal deficits

Fiscal deficits can influence the rate of interest in various ways. If they change the level of economic activity in the country, they will affect the rate of interest in the same way as described above. If they change the supply of money in the economy, they will affect the expected rate of inflation, π, and may also influence the rate of interest through the liquidity effects described above.[14] However, a more direct effect is through the demand for loanable funds. As the government sells bonds to finance the deficit, the supply of bonds, ceteris paribus, increases. The price of bonds falls, and the rate of interest rises. If these fiscal deficits occur during a recession, when private sector borrowing is depressed, the effect of the deficit on the rate of interest may not be obvious. If the fiscal deficit continues into a boom, its effect on interest rates may become more evident, as public borrowing will be added to the higher level of private borrowing, thus pushing upward the total demand for loanable funds.

Uncertainty

Empirical evidence indicates that higher inflation tends to be associated with a greater variance in relative prices. As investments are essentially commitments to a given set of future realistic prices, it is implied that the risk factor associated with investment rises. This rise in the risk factor induces a negative shift in the borrowing schedule which, per se, implies a lower real rate of interest. On the other hand, similar considerations also reduce the willingness of lenders to lend, thus bringing about a negative shift in the lending schedule. It is thus an empirical question whether, on balance, uncertainty reduces or increases the real rate of interest.

---

[14] If people expect that the fiscal deficits will be monetized in the future even though they are not monetized in the short run, the fiscal deficit may keep long-run rates high, which in turn, through arbitrage, may also keep the short-run rate high.

To summarize, the most basic theory of the behavior of interest rates in an inflationary situation is that the nominal rate of interest increases pari passu with the expected rate of inflation; that is, the real rate of interest does not change. However, recent amendments to that theory indicate that (even in the absence of income tax) the Fisherian hypothesis of a close correspondence between expected inflation and nominal interest rates may not be valid. For several reasons, when the expected rate of inflation is increasing, nominal interest rates are likely to adjust by less than the expected rate of inflation.[15] It is therefore implied that, in terms of equation (2), the coefficient of π (β) will be less than unity. In other words, a rise in expected inflation is likely to reduce the real rate of interest. Only when a substantial fiscal deficit coexists with a strong boom does the nominal rate of interest increase by more than the expected rate of inflation. Or, alternatively, only when the rate of inflation decelerates significantly does the real rate of interest increase.

In a period of accelerating inflation and in the absence of income taxes, borrowers, ceteris paribus, face lower real costs of borrowing (and lenders face lower real rates of return) than during a period of price stability. But, as inflation is likely to affect the efficiency of the economy, the rate of return on real investment is also lower.

Effects of inflation on interest rates in the presence of income taxes

Within the framework outlined above, it is now assumed that nominal (rather than real) interest income is fully taxed at a marginal rate equal to τ and that nominal (rather than real) interest expense is fully deductible from the taxpayer's income before the tax is assessed on his taxable income. This is in conformity with the tax laws of most of the countries surveyed in Section II under which there is no distinction between real and nominal values of interest income and expense.

It becomes necessary to make a distinction between a before-tax real rate of interest, r, and an after-tax real rate of interest, r^*. For simplicity, it is assumed that the tax rate, τ, is the same for all taxpayers—that is, the income tax is a proportional tax.[16] If, given the tax rate, τ, the net-of-tax expected real rate of interest, r^*, is to remain unchanged in the face of a rise in the expected rate of inflation, π, the nominal rate of interest must rise by more than π. More specif-

---

[15] And, by the same token, when the expected rate of inflation is falling, the nominal rate is expected to fall by less than the rate of inflation.

[16] See Tanzi (1977) for a discussion of the implications of progressive taxes.

ically,[17] the Fisher equation must be modified and rewritten as follows:

$$i = r + \frac{\pi}{1 - \tau} \tag{3}$$

In this equation, the effect of π on i is magnified by the existence of taxes. The higher τ is, the greater is the impact of π on i; τ can range between 0 and 1. In the United States, in recent years, the tax rate on interest income has been close to 40 percent. Adjusting for exemptions and tax evasion, the effective tax rate may be closer to 25 percent. It is therefore implied that, ceteris paribus, a 1 percentage point increase in the expected rate of inflation would result in a 1.33 percentage point increase in the nominal rate of interest. And it also is implied that a 1 percentage point fall in the rate of inflation would result in a 1.33 percentage point fall in the nominal rate of interest. This example shows how taxes can potentially increase the volatility of the nominal rate of interest in situations where inflationary expectations are rapidly changing.

In considering the combined impact of expected inflation and income taxation, it is assumed that (1) lenders and borrowers agree on a 4 percent real interest rate, r, in the absence of inflation; (2) the effective income tax rate is 25 percent[18] and the real rate of interest is independent of expected inflation; and (3) expected inflation rises from 0 percent to 6 percent. Equation (3) implies that the nominal rate of interest would have to rise to 12 percent in order to maintain the purchasing power of a 4 percent interest rate without expected inflation. To be more specific, the lender is paid 12 percent, of which he pays one fourth, or 3 percent, in income taxes and "loses" another 6 percent to inflation. He is thus left with an expected after-tax real interest rate of 3 percent, which is the same as he would have received in the absence of inflation but in the presence of income tax. The same after-tax real interest rate will also result for a borrower expecting the same inflation rate and paying the same tax rate. Obviously, a lower income tax rate would lead to a lower increase in the nominal rate of interest, while a higher inflation rate would lead to a higher nominal rate.

The theoretical example above gives an exaggerated view of the expected change in the nominal rate of interest when income taxes are present and when the expected rate of inflation is positive. The various factors that make the nominal rate of interest less responsive

---

[17] See, in particular, Tanzi (1976).
[18] Thus, the net-of-tax real interest rate is 3 percent.

to changes in expected inflation than would be expected from equation (2) were discussed earlier in this section. Some tax-related factors reduce further some of the magnification effect implied by $\pi/1-\tau$ in equation (3). These are described below.

Taxes on other assets

Equation (3) implies that alternative and untaxed channels of investment are available to the lender, so that he is willing to lend the same amount as before only if he does not suffer any reduction in his net-of-tax real interest income. But suppose alternative uses of his funds, i.e., real or other financial investments, are also taxed, even though at lower rates. (Some of these other taxes may simply be the capital gains taxes on realized gains from real property or from bond holdings.) In this case, the lender's options are limited, and he may be willing to accept a lower rate of return on all his financial investment. It would therefore be implied that the effect of π on i would be less than $\pi/1-\tau$. If the average tax rate on all other operations is indicated by θ, then the effect of π on i is $\dfrac{\pi(1-\theta)}{1-\tau}$.

If θ is equal to zero, the situation would revert to that described by equation (3). If $\theta = \tau$, then there is no tax effect. In general, θ would be lower than τ but higher than zero.

Taxes on borrowers

The theoretical result of equation (3) must also be qualified to take into account the fact that the borrowers themselves may experience tax increases associated with expected inflation that reduce their willingness to pay the nominal rate shown by equation (3). For example, if depreciation is estimated on the basis of historical cost, and if inventories are evaluated on the basis of first-in, first-out accounting methods, as is the case in most industrial countries, corporations will find their tax burden increased during an inflationary period. Therefore, they will not be willing to pay the nominal rate implied by equation (3). Thus, again, the nominal rate of interest is likely to be lower.

Tax-exempt lenders and borrowers

As all financial markets frequently include many lenders who do not pay taxes on interest received and many financial instruments that, because of the nature of the issuers, pay tax-free interest (see

Appendix III, Table 3), the impact of taxes on interest rates is reduced. It is unlikely that tax-free institutions are marginal lenders;
nevertheless, this factor again reduces the role of taxation in interest
rate determination. In the United States in 1976, the latest year for
which this information is available, the proportion of tax-exempt income to total interest income was 15.

Tax evasion

The tax systems of all countries require interest income to be taxed.
In reality, however, owing to the absence of withholding provisions
in the tax systems of many countries (including the United States),
the existence of bearer's shares, and the inability of the tax authorities
to ascertain all interest income paid, some interest income is not reported to the tax authorities. Thus, the potential effect of taxation
on interest rates may be reduced by tax evasion. Here, again, it must
be realized that it is the tax treatment of the marginal lender (and
borrower) that is significant. But, to the extent that tax evasion brings
about a rightward movement in the supply schedule of funds, it reduces the nominal rate of interest.

Capital inflows

If taxes magnify the effect of inflation on nominal interest rates in
a given country, these rates could become attractive to foreigners,
especially if the latter can avoid being taxed in their own countries
and are not taxed in the country in which they invest their money.
Furthermore, as capital flows in from "tax-haven" countries, it exerts
a downward pressure on the interest rate, which helps to make the
rate diverge from the theoretical results of equation (3).

To sum up, the presence of income taxes—that is, the taxation of
interest income and the tax deductibility of interest expense—tends
to magnify the effect of inflation on interest rates. Many economists
have therefore come to expect that $\beta > 1$. In reality, many tax-related
and nontax-related factors (listed in this section) tend to dampen the
value of β. Consequently, the fact that an increase in the expected
rate of inflation does not always increase the nominal rate of interest
more than proportionately cannot be taken to mean that tax factors
do not matter; it could simply be that the positive impact of the tax
treatment of interest income and expense may be partially or fully
neutralized by the other factors mentioned above.

Empirical investigations

Empirical investigations of interest rates have improved the level of understanding about their determinants but have not yet fully explained the behavior of real rates of interest. In addition, economists attempting empirical investigations of interest rate behavior have struggled with the very difficult problems of accurately measuring expected inflation and expected real interest rates in terms of observable variables. Their efforts have progressed through three stages.

The first stage of concerted empirical investigation of interest rate behavior in the period after World War II was centered on the simple Fisher equation (equation (2) above). The approach was to regress nominal interest rates on various measures of expected inflation. Thus, most investigators were testing a joint hypothesis of market efficiency, whereby a percentage point rise in expected inflation would result in a percentage point rise in nominal interest, conditional on the hypothesis that the expected real rate was independent of expected inflation. As with all empirical investigations of interest rate behavior, it was also necessary to assume that behavior of expected inflation was being accurately measured. Many of these investigations conducted during the 1960s and early 1970s found a less-than-proportional impact of expected inflation on nominal interest; that is, the estimated values of β were found to be persistently below unity.[19]

The second phase of empirical investigation of interest rates, begun during the late 1970s, incorporated the taxation of interest income and deductibility of interest expense into a modified Fisher equation (equation (3) above) and hypothesized a greater-than-proportional rise of interest rates to changes in expected inflation. Given the persistence of a less-than-proportional response of interest rates to expected inflation, the gap between theory and reality was widened even further.[20] This forced investigators to re-examine the hypotheses of constancy of real interest rates and their independence from expected inflation.

The third phase of empirical investigation of interest rates derived expressions for nominal interest rates from more comprehensive models. This approach enabled investigators to incorporate into interest rate equations those variables, other than expected inflation, that theoretically should help to determine the behavior of real rates.[21]

---

[19] It must be recalled that this was generally a period of rising inflation.

[20] This led some researchers to argue that there may have been monetary as well as fiscal illusion at work during the period.

[21] For an example of such an approach, see the background paper by Makin and Tanzi in Part II of this volume (Chapter 4).

A number of these variables are discussed above. This broader approach also indicated more clearly the precise nature of the relationship between interest rates, expected inflation, and variables such as taxes, real balance effects, economic activity, and uncertainty, all of which determine the real rates of interest.

The comprehensive approach to modeling interest rates has also helped to resolve the paradox arising from consideration of tax treatment of interest income and expense only in the context of the simple Fisher equation. The incorporation of tax treatment of interest income and expense into the analysis of the relationship between nominal interest rates and expected inflation suggested a magnified impact of the latter on the former (that is, $\beta > 1$). Failure to discover such a magnified impact led some analysts to conclude that the effective tax rates on interest income and interest expense must be very low, but this interpretation was questionable for at least three reasons: (1) empirical results usually find a coefficient of 0.7 to 0.9 on anticipated inflation and, even if effective tax rates were only 10 percent, the coefficient should be about 1.1; (2) information on the holdings of tax-exempt financial assets or of tax-exempt interest income suggests that, in the United States, such tax-exempt securities constitute only 10–15 percent of total holdings; (3) and most important, a comprehensive framework of interest rate determination has also yielded a value for the coefficient on anticipated inflation, β, in the 0.7 to 1.0 range.

A recent paper by the Fiscal Affairs Department has investigated the relationship between interest rates and inflation (simple Fisher equation) and the effects of taxation on this relationship (modified Fisher equation) for a sample of eight industrial countries.[22] Subject to various limitations that are set forth, the paper investigates the extent to which interest rates have responded differently to changes in expected and actual inflation rates in countries with different legal tax treatments of interest income and payments.[23]

The eight countries were divided into three groups according to the degree of taxability of interest income and the deductibility of interest payments. The first group consisted of Canada, the Netherlands, and the United States, all of which treat interest income and payment literally in a way that would imply a relatively high value of

---

[22] See Chapter 7, background paper by Katz in Part II of this volume. The eight industrial countries are Canada, France, the Federal Republic of Germany, Italy, Japan, the Netherlands, the United Kingdom, and the United States.

[23] These differences refer to the legal treatment alone, since differential possibilities of tax evasion could not be assessed. Furthermore, the capital gains taxes that determine the value of θ are assumed to apply to realized gains on a yearly basis.

β (greater than unity). The second group consisted of France, the Federal Republic of Germany, Italy, and the United Kingdom, all of which have a more moderate tax treatment of interest income and payment. The third group consisted of Japan, which has a more generous tax treatment of interest income and an implied low value of β (smaller than unity).

The estimation results for 1971–81 presented in Table 1 indicate that the response coefficients of nominal short-term interest rates to *actual* inflation, adjusted for changes in real interest rates, were not significantly different from unity for Canada, France, the Federal Republic of Germany, and the United States. The estimated response coefficients were found to be more moderate for Italy and Japan, low for the Netherlands, and insignificant for the United Kingdom.

For nominal short-term interest rates, the response coefficients to *expected* inflation were significantly greater than unity for Japan but not significantly different from unity for the other seven countries.[24]

For long-term interest rates, the response coefficients to *expected* inflation were about unity for the United States, moderate for France, and low for all other sample countries (see Table 1). The response

Table 1. Eight Industrial Countries: Impact of Taxation on Adjustment of Interest Rates to Inflation, 1971–81[1]

Country	$\dfrac{1}{1-\tau}$	$\dfrac{1-\theta}{1-\tau}$[2]	β (of π^e)[2]	β(of π)[3]
Canada	1.176	0.906	0.991	0.879
France	1.493	1.120	1.022	0.973
Germany, Fed. Rep. of	1.515	0.970	0.991	1.050
Italy	1.429	1.072	1.030	0.505
Japan	1.075	0.860	1.162	0.818
Netherlands	1.299	—	0.984	0.283
United Kingdom	1.316	0.921	0.997	0.061
United States	1.299	0.909	0.993	0.968

Source: Background paper by Menachem Katz, "Inflation, Taxation, and the Rate of Interest in Eight Industrial Countries," in Part II of this volume (Chapter 7), Table 4.

[1] The average income tax rate applicable is denoted by τ and the capital gains tax rate is denoted by θ.

[2] The tax rates used here are given in Table 15 of the Katz paper (see Source). The difficulties of calculating the effective tax rates are well known; hence, it was necessary to adopt a variety of approaches for estimating these rates. The method used, as well as its limitations and the biases it creates, is explained in the Katz paper (see Source).

[3] The coefficients β (of π^e) and β (of π) represent, respectively, the Fisher effect for expected and actual inflation rates.

---

[24] This is puzzling because the tax effect should have been lowest in Japan.

coefficient of long-term interest rates to *actual* inflation was found to be well below unity for Canada, France, Italy, the Netherlands, and the United States, and insignificant for the Federal Republic of Germany, Japan, and the United Kingdom.

In general, while some variation occurs across countries in the value of β, none of the coefficients is significantly above unity. This situation suggests that the positive impact of typical tax treatment of interest income and interest expense is perhaps frequently neutralized by the impact of many other factors, as mentioned above at the beginning of this section. This inference can be treated as no more than a tentative hypothesis at this stage; further empirical work will be required to establish its validity.

Policy implications

In the preceding discussion, it is argued that high effective taxes on interest income and liberal tax deductibility for interest payments can, at least theoretically, have a significant impact on the level and variability of interest rates. To reduce this potential tax effect, three alternative policies have been suggested at one time or another: (1) Tax only real interest income and allow a deduction only for real interest expense. This implies the removal of the inflation component from both interest income and expense; (2) For individuals, at least, eliminate from income taxation all interest income and, at the same time, do not allow any deduction for interest expense;[25] (3) Reduce the range of deductibility of interest expense at least for consumer loans and possibly for mortgages on owner-occupied houses. Some of the implications of these policies are discussed below. On the basis of existing technology, it is not possible to give robust or reliable estimates of the effects of the above changes on the levels of interest rates. However, on the basis of a few plausible assumptions, some guesses can be made. Some of these are derived from a simple theoretical loanable fund model, outlined in Appendix II.

Inflation adjustment of interest income and expense

The distortions created by the typical tax treatment of interest income and interest expense in an inflationary environment are due

---

[25] This policy has recently been introduced in Iceland. The basic justification for this policy change seems to be the fact that interest rates in Iceland have approximated the inflation rate for most years, implying that real interest income and expense have been close to zero.

primarily to the taxation of nominal, rather than real, magnitudes. Full inflation adjustment would require that the inflation rate be subtracted from the nominal interest rate received by lenders before calculating the taxes due. It would also require that the inflation rate be subtracted from the interest rate paid by borrowers before a deduction for interest expense could be claimed.

Such a correction would shift the demand and supply schedules of loanable funds in ways that would result in lowering the equilibrium nominal interest rate associated with a given rate of inflation. The supply of funds schedule would shift to the right as lending became more attractive. The demand for funds schedule would shift to the left as borrowing became less attractive. In the numerical example discussed earlier in connection with equation (3), a nominal interest rate of 12 percent was required to yield an after-tax real rate of 3 percent, given a tax rate of 25 percent and an expected inflation rate of 6 percent. If the expected rate of inflation is equal to the actual rate of inflation and if the tax applies only to the *real* rate of interest, a 10 percent interest rate will now yield the same after-tax real rate of 3 percent. Thus, in this extreme example, the nominal rate of interest could fall by 2 percentage points.

Realism would require that (1) the negative impact of expected inflation on interest rates be recognized, and (2) the qualifications discussed in the preceding subsection on the effects of inflation on interest rates in the presence of income taxes be taken into account. When this is done, perhaps the reduction in the nominal rate of interest would be less than 2 percentage points. However, even if the fall in the nominal rate was only 1 percentage point (a figure that can be considered conservative), it would still have important effects. It would, for example, by reducing interest cost on the public debt, reduce the U.S. fiscal deficit by $8 billion, and it would reduce the cost of borrowing for developing countries by considerable amounts. Furthermore, the reduction would benefit disproportionately more those borrowers (including losing enterprises, low-income taxpayers, and developing countries) that had not been in a situation whereby they could deduct their interest expense from taxable income.

Not all the effects from this policy change would be positive. A few potentially negative effects are mentioned below.

(1) Inflation adjustment of taxable interest incomes would reduce tax receipts on interest earnings; however, this impact would be partly or totally offset by the gain in receipts, owing to the deductibility of (lower) real interest payments rather than (higher) nominal interest payments from taxable income. The net effect would depend on the average tax rates of lenders versus borrowers, with the net revenue

impact being positive if the average tax rate of borrowers exceeds that of lenders.[26]

(2) The results would also be affected by enactment or nonenactment of inflation adjustment in other developed countries. If only one country—even one as large as the United States—adopted such a change, the downward pressure on interest rates would be significantly reduced by capital outflow to markets where the absence of full adjustment of interest taxation continued to keep the interest rates higher.

(3) Inflation adjustment of the tax treatment of interest income and payments that lowered equilibrium nominal interest rates would confer windfall gains on lenders holding loans contracted at the fixed nominal interest rates that were required in the preindexing environment and would invoke windfall losses on the borrowers issuing such contracts.

(4) Even after indexation of interest income and payments for tax purposes is carried out, some distortions will still remain. The unindexed tax treatment of inventory and depreciation allowances, for example, will continue to affect the after-tax profitability of investment, inducing negative shifts in the investment schedule and, as a consequence, reducing the equilibrium rates of interest. Furthermore, indexation to reduce distortions in the after-tax costs and benefits of financing by means of debt will also have considerable effects on domestic equity markets as well as on the flow of debt and equity capital abroad.

(5) Finally, and most important, the indexation of interest income and expense for tax purposes would create nightmares for income tax administration. No country has adopted or even attempted complete indexation of interest income and payments, despite the theoretical attractiveness of the proposal. Thus, it would be utopian to expect that countries would agree to such a change just for its effect on interest rates.

Eliminating taxes on interest income and tax deductibility of interest payments

Total elimination of taxation of interest income, together with the total elimination of deductibility of interest payments, is the easiest solution administratively. It would be a desirable policy from the standpoint of lowering nominal interest rates. In fact, the reduction

---

[26] An empirical study for the United States has shown that gains and losses would approximately balance out. See Tanzi (1977).

in nominal interest rates associated with this policy would most likely exceed that associated with the taxation of real interest rates, as discussed above. Such a policy would produce a zero net impact on tax revenue in countries where the level of domestic borrowing and lending and the tax rates applicable to borrowers and lenders are equal. If it was carried out by all countries, it would also equate effective real interest rates in different countries, assuming the equality of expected inflation rates.

Yet such a policy is unlikely to be adopted by many countries. It will convert the existing global income tax system, under which all sources of income are treated equally, into a schedular income tax system. With the exemption from taxation of interest income, pressures would be created for the exemption of other capital income as well, on the grounds that such a policy distorts the flows in the financial and capital markets. Such a policy might be seen as unjust and inequitable between earners of labor income and capital income, especially at present when the real rates of interest and thus the income associated with financial assets are very high. In any case, the principal justification for this policy—that the rate of inflation is about equal to the nominal rate of interest—is clearly not valid at this time for many of the large industrial countries. Thus, the policy could be justified in certain countries but not in others.

Limiting the tax deductibility of interest expense

A realistic proposal would be to eliminate, or at least limit, the deductibility of interest payments for particular purposes, namely, interest on consumer credit and mortgage interest payments by households. To what extent this would result in a drop in the equilibrium nominal interest rate in a given country would depend on the elasticity of the supply of funds and the demand for funds. Because the elimination of the deductibility of household interest payments would cause a downward shift in the demand for funds, the downward pressure on interest rates would be correspondingly higher as the ratio of supply elasticity to demand elasticity is lower. No estimates of these elasticities are available; however, on certain hypothetical assumptions, it appears that the nominal interest rates would not fall by a large amount.[27]

---

[27] Assuming that (1) households account for roughly 40 percent of total borrowing, (2) the elasticities of the supply and demand schedules vary between 0.2 and 0.8, respectively, (3) the expected real rate of interest is 3 percent, and (4) the expected rate of inflation is 6 percent, it can be estimated by the model in Appendix II that such a policy change would reduce the nominal rate by less, and in most cases by much less, than 1 percentage point.

If deductibility of interest payments from home mortgages was preserved and only the deductibility of interest on consumer credit was eliminated, the impact would be even smaller. In the United States, mortgage borrowing, while volatile, usually constitutes well over half of total household borrowing. A policy that eliminated only nonbusiness and nonmortgage interest payments from deductibility would hardly reduce the equilibrium interest rate.

The elimination of nonbusiness and nonmortgage interest deductibility, despite its relatively small impact on the equilibrium level of nominal interest rates, would still produce significant effects on resource allocation, since more resources would be directed toward capital formation. It would also have some revenue effects that would produce a moderate reduction in fiscal deficits. The effect on revenue enhancement of such a policy change for the United States is estimated to be about $8 billion a year. In addition, a 0.5 percent drop in interest rates could also lower the annual U.S. debt service by about $4 billion annually. An overall reduction in the fiscal deficit for the United States of up to $12 billion annually would thus be possible.

In conclusion, inflation adjustment of interest rates for tax purposes or the nontaxation of interest income would have the largest effect on interest rates. The other, more modest, policy discussed above would still have some effect, but it would be somewhat more moderate. Implementation of such policies by any single economy, while helpful, would result in capital outflows. Even if prevention of such flows was considered desirable, it would be difficult to achieve in view of existing statutes in most industrial countries and in view of extensive arbitrage opportunities offered in the Eurocurrency markets.

The elimination of deductibility of interest payments for nonbusiness and nonmortgage (consumption) household purposes seems, in reality, to hold the most promise. It would produce beneficial effects in the form of enhanced capital formation and some moderate reduction in fiscal deficits, but it probably would not have a significant impact on interest rates in any country.

IV. EXTENSIONS AND QUALIFICATIONS OF THE ANALYSIS

This section considers some extensions and qualifications of the analysis in Section III. First, consideration is given to the implications for open economies of tax policies pursued by single countries and to the effects of introducing explicitly the tax treatment of foreign exchange gains and losses. Second, the implications of tax policies for the impact of monetary restraint are discussed. Finally, consideration is given to implications of tax policy on volatility of interest rates and to the related uncertainty regarding expected after-tax real interest rates.

Role of international differences in tax regimes

Insofar as capital is able to move between countries, both domestic and foreign tax policies with respect to interest income and expense will affect the level of interest rates in any given country. Further, as foreign exchange transactions are involved in arbitrage among many international financial assets, taxation of foreign exchange gains and losses will also play an integral role in determining the level of interest rates. To the extent that a country's capital market is isolated, by controls or other means, from world capital markets, cross-country differences in tax policies are obviously less relevant.[28]

Perhaps the best method of considering the international implications of the differential tax treatment of interest income and expense is to examine the impact of different tax policies on the after-tax interest parity condition, which states that, in equilibrium, the difference between after-tax interest rates must be equal to the after-tax gain (loss) from expected appreciation (depreciation) of domestic against foreign currency. In the absence of tax considerations, and if exchange rates are determined mainly by purchasing power parity, interest parity can be approximated by an interest differential equal to an expected inflation differential.

Suppose initially that interest parity holds under conditions where countries experience the same rate of inflation and, therefore, the expected change in the exchange rate is set at zero, effective tax rates are equal, and both domestic and foreign governments tax interest receipts and allow full deductibility of interest payments. If, for example, the domestic economy now exempts from taxation all or part of the interest income of households and no longer allows a deduction for all or part of the interest expense, the direct result is to lower the equilibrium nominal interest rates in the domestic economy.[29] As a consequence of this fall in interest rates in the domestic economy, capital begins flowing abroad, thus mitigating the initial drop in interest rates and inducing a reduction in the interest rate of the foreign country.[30]

---

[28] For a discussion of the effects of financial market taxation on international capital flows, see the background paper by Blejer in Part II of this volume (Chapter 8).

[29] As argued in Section III, this tax-induced fall in interest rates may not be very large.

[30] The degree of reduction in the interest rates in the domestic country and the increase in the rate in the foreign country is determined by the relative size of both countries.

The flow of capital from domestic to foreign markets will continue until the after-tax interest rates are again equalized, although at some lower level. These effects would be accentuated in an inflationary environment if, for example, the taxpayers in the foreign country experienced bracket creep while the taxpayers in the domestic country avoided it through indexation. This configuration would produce a steady upward drift in borrowing and lending schedules. Equilibrium would require an ever-increasing flow of capital from domestic into foreign markets.

So far, expected changes in the exchange rate have been set at zero by assuming equal inflation across countries or, alternatively, a system of fixed parities. When this condition is relaxed, and *expected changes in exchange rates are allowed*, tax policy regarding foreign exchange gains and losses becomes relevant in determining the levels of equilibrium interest rates and exchange rates. Assume that tax rates applied to such gains and losses are below the tax rates applied to interest income.[31] Such a tax policy would allow interest differentials to exceed expected appreciation or depreciation of currencies. Suppose, for example, that domestic currency is expected to depreciate against foreign currency at a 3 percent annual rate and the domestic interest rate is also 3 percent higher than the foreign rate. If the tax rate applicable to domestic residents on their expected foreign exchange gain is below that applicable to their interest income (regardless of its source), the tax liability to domestic investors on their foreign exchange position would be lower than the income tax liability incurred on their positive interest position. It would, therefore, induce capital outflows. As a result, the equilibrium after-tax interest differential that would not induce further capital movements would have to be above the pretax level. If, say, the capital gains tax rate was 20 percent while the income tax rate was 50 percent, a 3 percent pretax interest differential would have to be matched by a 4.8 percent after-tax interest differential (a factor of 1.6, derived as $(1 - 0.2)/(1 - 0.5) = 1.6$).[32]

An alternative to achievement of an after-tax equilibrium by means of interest rate changes would be a reduction in expected depreciation

---

[31] This assumption approximates the conditions in Canada, the United Kingdom, and the United States, where realized foreign exchange gains and losses are treated as capital gains and losses and the returns on assets held longer than a statutory minimum period are taxed at lower rates than interest earnings, which are taxed as ordinary income.

[32] The size of the actual gap between tax rates is exaggerated here for purposes of illustrating the impact. In practice, a very small expected return on an after-tax basis can generate large flows of capital.

of the domestic currency or a rise in the domestic spot price of foreign currency. That is, if the spot currency rate rose by enough to cut expected depreciation to 1.875 percent, the initial 3 percent pretax interest differential would not be altered by the differential tax treatment, because $3 = 1.6 (1.875)$. It should be noted, however, that a reduction in the expected rate of devaluation without changes in the underlying interest differentials would imply a deviation from purchasing power parity that had been caused by differential tax treatment of interest income and foreign exchange gains.

Actual equilibrium would probably result from a combination of a change in the interest differential and a change in expected depreciation of currency, if both were accompanied by some capital movements. Whatever the mode, the basic conclusion is that, like tax policy on interest income and expense, tax policy on foreign exchange gains and losses can significantly affect the equilibrium levels of interest rates and exchange rates.

This effect on equilibrium interest and exchange rates of tax policy on foreign exchange gains and losses could be removed by taxing foreign exchange gains and losses and interest income at equal rates. Given the widespread tendency to treat interest as ordinary income, as indicated in Section II, this tax policy would require treating foreign exchange gains and losses as ordinary income as well.[33]

The realization that neutrality of tax policy calls for a tax treatment of exchange gains and losses similar to that of ordinary income suggests an important asymmetry regarding after-tax interest parity. Consider the example given above and designate as Country A the case in which a 3 percent interest differential satisfies only pretax equilibrium and a wider interest differential (or a smaller currency depreciation) is required when lower (20 percent) tax rates are applied to foreign exchange gains and losses. If Country B applies, from its perspective, equal tax rates (50 percent) to both interest income and foreign exchange gains and losses, the 3 percent differential constitutes an after-tax as well as a pretax equilibrium. The equilibrium interest differential that will emerge in this circumstance would probably result in simultaneous movements of capital in opposite directions between Countries A and B. At anything above a 3 percent interest differential or its exchange equivalent, capital will flow out of Country B into Country A. At anything below a 4.8 percent interest differential or its exchange equivalent, capital would flow out of Country A into Country B. Any equilibrium between 3 and 4.8 percent would result

---

[33] This practice is followed in the Federal Republic of Germany, France, Japan, and some other industrial countries.

in two-way capital flows. If the situation persisted long enough, equilibrium could eventually be achieved by means of an adjustment of relative real interest rates through changes in the stock of real capital. The burden of adjustment would fall more heavily on the smaller economy.

Operation of the phenomenon just described may be manifested in the unexpected strength of Country A's currency against that of Country B. Given Country A's tax policies, equilibrium would be analogous to the 4.8 percent interest differential, while Country B's tax policies would imply an equilibrium analogous to the 3 percent interest differential. The result would be a flow of capital from Country B to Country A. Even a drop in Country A's rates would not necessarily stem the flow (and therefore the pressure on the currency of Country B to depreciate against the currency of Country A) unless an analog of the 3 percent equilibrium differential for Country B was reached. The asymmetry could be eliminated by alignment of tax policies whereby both countries would treat foreign exchange gains and losses as ordinary income.

To sum up, differential tax regimes between countries can result in either an increase or a decrease in the pretax equilibrium interest rate differential. Ceteris paribus, countries introducing policies that imply a lower taxation of interest income and a lower deduction for interest expense, in isolation, would have lower interest rates relative to countries that have higher tax rates. However, the negative impact of such policies on interest rates would be mitigated by capital outflows. For small countries acting singly, this impact could be eliminated completely. Finally, countries levying taxes on foreign exchange gains lower than the taxes levied on interest income are likely to experience a greater after-tax differential in interest rates vis-à-vis other countries. Clearly, different combinations of tax treatment result in different outcomes, but a central issue is that real interest rates may also be affected by differential tax policies through their effects on capital flows.

Implications of tax policy for the effectiveness and international impact of monetary restraint

Abrupt application of monetary restraint operates for a time to depress aggregate demand for domestic output through the positive impact on real interest rates as outlined in Section III and through the impact on the real exchange rate. In the absence of taxes applied to nominal interest rates, the result of abrupt and unanticipated monetary restraint would be to raise the market interest rate by the amount of the increase in the real interest rates as long as the initial impact of abrupt monetary restraint does not affect inflationary expectations. Since the full increase in the nominal interest rate would typically be taxed, attempts at preservation of the higher expected real, after-tax rate of return on the part of lenders would require market interest rates to rise by more than the increase in the real rate. The increase may be more easily accepted by borrowers, provided that they can fully deduct interest payments from taxable income. Such a magnification effect is analogous to that displayed in response to a change in expected inflation in the tax-adjusted Fisher equation (equation (3)) discussed in Section III.

However, owing to a somewhat interest-elastic demand for funds by borrowers and the depressing effect of monetary restraint on overall economic activity, the increase in nominal interest rates may be somewhat dampened. Still, the taxation of interest income and the deduction of interest expense would produce a larger positive impact of monetary restraint on interest rates than would otherwise have occurred.

Viewed in this way, the effect of a typical tax policy on interest income and expense is not to reduce the effectiveness of monetary restraint per se as much as to require that a large rise of market interest rates would result from a given monetary restraint if aggregate demand is to be reduced. Tax policy does have implications for the effectiveness of monetary restraint across income tax brackets, however. Households, enterprises, and nations facing effective tax rates below the average tax rate that has been incorporated in the level of interest rates would experience a sharp rise in their after-tax real interest rates relative to borrowers facing above-average tax rates. In sum, the effectiveness of monetary restraint is enhanced by tax policy for individuals and enterprises facing below-average tax rates and is reduced by tax policy for those facing above-average tax rates.

Tax policy regarding interest income and expense in a country applying monetary restraint would also have international implications, particularly if the country concerned is large. If a large country, which has relatively high tax rates for financial market participants—that is, which fully taxes interest income and allows liberal deductions of interest payments—applies monetary restraint, there will be a relative increase in after-tax real interest rates. Countries where investors (including the public sector) have access to international capital markets and where interest incomes are domestically taxed at lower rates or interest expenses are less liberally deductible would suffer as well. This result would be signaled by capital flows into the country applying the monetary restraint. Such inflows are a normal response to monetary restraint, but they are enhanced by differential tax policies on interest income and expense.

As noted above, the discussion up to this point has focused on the initial impact of monetary restraint, prior to any reduction of expected inflation. Once expected inflation begins to fall, the effect of tax treatment of interest income and expense is, symmetrically, to magnify the negative impact on interest rates. As the drop in interest rates reflects the average tax rates, after-tax real interest rates faced by those in above-average tax brackets will rise relative to after-tax real interest rates faced by those in below-average tax brackets. Likewise, countries that experience a relative increase in after-tax real interest rates as a result of monetary restraint will experience a relative reduction in after-tax real interest rates, once lower inflationary expectations begin to reduce interest rates.

The overall implication is that the fluctuations in after-tax real interest rates resulting from changes in monetary policy tend to be exacerbated for domestic and foreign borrowers and for lenders in lower tax brackets, given the differences in tax policy regarding interest income and expense.

The corollary for international capital flows is an enhanced outflow and inflow pattern for countries whose capital markets are closely tied to those of the country executing a policy of monetary restraint. Depending on the degree of intervention, exchange rates may be expected to be somewhat more volatile as well, in view of the tax policies under discussion here. Overall, differential tax policies regarding interest income and expense may increase the volatility of interest rates, exchange rates, and international flows of capital in the wake of application of monetary restraint in a large economy.

The sudden easing of monetary restraint would produce exactly opposite results compared with those caused by the sudden imposition of monetary restraint. Given the taxation of interest income and the deduction of interest expense, a greater fall in interest rates would result from monetary ease if aggregate demand is to increase. The initial liquidity effects of monetary ease would lower the after-tax real interest rates for those who are subject to below-average tax rates relative to those who are subject to above-average tax rates. Subsequent expectations effects would cause a relative increase in after-tax real interest rates for those in lower tax brackets, with the net result that those in below-average tax brackets (including borrowers in developing countries) are likely to experience more volatility in after-tax real interest rates, given either the easing of monetary restraint or its imposition.

A qualification to the analysis of the impact of monetary restraint or ease is called for in the light of possible effects of tax policies beyond those concerning interest income and expense and the empirical evidence of a negative relationship between expected inflation and real rates. The effect of tax policies taken as a whole and the associated phenomena may be to mitigate the negative pressure on nominal interest rates arising from a drop in inflationary expectations. A large body of empirical evidence suggests that the expected after-tax real interest rate may be negatively related to the level of expected inflation. This result implies that the initial rise in real interest rates attendant upon the effect of constrained liquidity may be prolonged at a later time when monetary restraint begins to result in lower inflationary expectations. Conversely, the initial drop in real interest rates resulting from monetary ease may be prolonged if the appearance of higher inflationary expectations is coupled with a drop in real interest rates. The exact timing and stability of such relationships is not understood, but the view is consistent (although crudely) with the recent U.S. experience with the imposition and relaxation of monetary restraint.

Volatility of interest rates

Discussion by the Fund's Executive Board has often included expressions of concern regarding the particularly high degree of volatility in interest rates and exchange rates since the late 1970s. An effort is made here to explore the possible role that tax policy and its administration may have played in the increased volatility of interest rates, with the implied increase in exchange rate volatility being taken for granted.

Interest rates are determined in forward-looking markets for assets that represent a claim on a nominal stream of interest payments and return of principal over some future period of time. Interest rate volatility at some mean level during a period of time (the variance of interest rates) reflects the volatility in the outlook for inflation and for the expected after-tax real rate of interest. A high volatility of expected inflation or of the expected after-tax real interest rate means that a wide range of possible future outcomes for these variables is contemplated. This is a formal characterization of uncertainty. An increase in such uncertainty entails risks for savers and investors for which they must be compensated. Viewed in this way, increased uncertainty attendant upon increased volatility of interest rates represents an additional cost of capital formation that lowers productivity growth and growth of real output and, in turn, enhances inflationary pressures. In view of such costs and their relationship to interest rate volatility, it is useful to consider the sources of increased volatility of interest rates.

It is clear from Table 2 that, in addition to reaching historically high levels since 1979, U.S. interest rates have been more volatile. This phenomenon has appeared in varying degrees in most industrial countries. The increased volatility has a number of sources. The two proximate determinants of interest rates—namely, expected after-tax real rates and expected inflation—have been unusually volatile, while the former have probably dominated the volatility of the latter in its impact on interest rates. Volatility of real interest rates in the United States may have been further increased by the volatility in the un-anticipated portion of money growth associated with the change in the conduct of monetary policy in October 1979, the imposition and removal of credit controls during 1980, and the implementation of a new policy mix under the new administration during 1981. Another factor that may have exacerbated the volatility of real interest rates is increased uncertainty about fiscal deficits and a wide range of tax provisions associated with debate over the passage and the modifi-cations of the Economic Recovery Tax Act of 1981 and the Tax Equity and Fiscal Responsibility Act of 1982.

Increased volatility of interest rates, like the level of interest rates, can be partially attributed to tax treatment of interest income and expense. The simplest approach, which parallels the discussion in Section III of the effects of these policies on the level of interest rates, is to derive an expression for the variance of nominal interest rates based on the tax-adjusted Fisher equation. Such an expression, which is found in Appendix II as equation (8), describes the variance of nominal interest as a weighted sum of the variances of after-tax real

Table 2. Level and Volatility of U.S. Interest Rates

(Monthly data)

Sample Period	Treasury Bill		Medium-Term Government Bond		Long-Term Government Bond	
	Mean	Standard deviation	Mean	Standard deviation	Mean	Standard deviation
1964–69	4.79	1.09	5.20	1.06	5.00	0.77
1970–74	5.95	1.68	6.69	1.02	6.83	0.79
1975–79	6.67	2.01	7.79	1.25	8.31	0.66
Jan. 1980– Jan. 1983	12.02	2.73	12.88	2.01	12.62	1.48

Source: United States, Federal Reserve System, *Federal Reserve Bulletin* (Washington), various issues.

interest rates and expected inflation plus a covariance term. The weights rise with the effective tax rates faced by borrowers and lenders. In effect, if two countries experience identical levels of volatility of after-tax real interest rates and expected inflation, the country with the higher tax rates will experience more volatility of nominal interest rates. If bracket creep raises the effective tax rates in a given country, that change alone, ceteris paribus, will increase the volatility of interest rates.

A more comprehensive approach to interest rate determination—one that takes into account open-economy effects (after-tax interest parity) and a wide range of tax policies that result in inflation-induced changes in real incentives to work, save, and invest—would reveal a more pervasive basis for tax policy to affect interest rate volatility. A given array of effective tax rates on all forms of income (including interest, labor income, profits, capital gains and losses, and foreign exchange gains and losses) is what determines the impact on nominal interest rates of changes in expected inflation and other variables. An environment of high or volatile rates of inflation, given the taxation of nominal values, results in numerous and frequently unpredictable changes in effective tax rates, which actually contribute to the volatility of after-tax real interest rates as well as nominal interest rates. In addition, ad hoc efforts to address tax-policy-induced distortions that are magnified in an inflationary environment increase the uncertainty attached to the future path of interest rates, owing to the volatile political process to which such proposals must be subjected.

V. CONCLUDING REMARKS

This section draws some conclusions from the study and discusses their implications for Fund activities.

Conclusions of the study

While tax regimes of major industrial countries vary widely with respect to the specific rules governing treatment of interest income and expense, some subsidy to consumption that is implicit in the liberal deductibility of household interest payments is prevalent—policies of the United States being among the most liberal and those of Japan being among the least liberal. These and related tax policies may have significant effects, not only on the level and variability of interest rates and the effectiveness of monetary restraint in a given country but also on exchange rates and international capital movements. Although there has been some empirical research on these subjects, a large amount of work remains to be done. This work should help to provide a fuller understanding of the behavior of real and nominal interest rates since 1979 and should allow a better quantification of a full range of effects arising from changes in tax policy. The simulation methodology required for a comprehensive analysis of the effects of changes in tax policies is just being developed.

Despite these qualifications, it is useful to set out two basic conclusions that emerge from this study.

(1) Full inflation adjustment, by developed countries acting as a group, of interest income to be taxed and of interest payments to be deducted from taxable income probably constitutes the single most effective tax policy measure for lowering nominal interest rates in developed countries and for lowering effective real interest rates in developing countries. However, inflation adjustment of interest income and expense is administratively very difficult for any country. It is thus unlikely that a concerted action of this type will take place.

(2) Elimination of deductibility of interest payments for some or all household consumption borrowing by developed countries would lower equilibrium interest rates and the gap between effective real interest rates in developed and developing countries, but by much less than full inflation adjustment. It would, however, result in removal of a consumption subsidy, with effects on resource allocation akin to those of increases in taxes on consumption. Some enhancement of revenue and some reduction in fiscal deficits would result, depending on the share of household borrowing considered ineligible for tax deductibility.

The corollary to the first proposition is that all of its desirable aspects can also be achieved by eliminating or at least reducing inflation and with it the distortionary effects on after-tax incentives to save and invest in both developed and developing countries. Viewed in this way, the reduction in inflation and inflationary expectations in the United States from the 11–12 percent level prevalent at the end of 1980 to the 3–5 percent level prevalent during the first half of 1983 has helped a great deal to reduce distortions arising from tax treatment based on nominal instead of real interest rates. Still, it is necessary to recall that, since interest rates are set in forward-looking markets, it is the outlook for future inflation rates and related variables, coupled with the knowledge that potential distortionary effects of taxing and deducting nominal interest rates remain in most tax systems, that produces continued uncertainty regarding the outlook for effective after-tax real interest rates. In sum, it might still be desirable in the current environment to contemplate changes in tax policy aimed at reducing the *potential* of tax systems to magnify the impact on interest rates of further possible changes in the level of inflation. But it must be recognized that tax policy is pursued for other objectives. The effect of tax policy on interest rates has been ignored in the past, and it is not likely that it will be given much attention in the future.

Implications for Fund activities

While tax policies of most countries are determined by domestic considerations, the present study suggests that they may have important international implications as well, especially for exchange rates and international capital flows. In addition, they may also have implications for real debt service burdens of developing countries. The Fund may, therefore, have a role to play in making national authorities more aware of the implications of their domestic tax policies for the international economy. The Fund's surveillance activity and Article IV consultations provide valuable opportunities to review important tax provisions in areas such as the tax treatment of interest income and expense and the taxation of foreign exchange gains and losses.

In particular, if the aims in an inflationary situation are (1) to dampen the effects of taxation on the level and volatility of interest rates and (2) to alter the redistributive impact of monetary restraint, adjustments may have to be made in the current tax treatment of interest income and payments, which typically ignores the existence of inflation. Any adjustments that may be carried out will need to ensure a "reasonable" after-tax real interest income to the lenders (i.e., will need to remove "excessive" taxation) and a "reasonable" after-tax real cost of interest payments to the borrowers (i.e., will need to remove "excessive" subsidy), without incurring severe budgetary consequences. This will call for removing many of the gaps in the tax base that exist in the form of exclusions, exemptions, and other tax incentives provided to interest income and payments and that are frequently justified on the premise that the tax system is not duly adjusted for inflation. A policy on inflation adjustment of taxable interest income and payments should go hand in hand with the elimination of special tax allowances for interest earners and interest payers. This general principle is valid not only for interest income and interest payments but also for the income and payments of all participants in the capital market and other taxpayers as well. In the final analysis, government budgets should rely more on the "fiscal dividend" of the rate of economic growth than on the rate of inflation in the economy. It is evident that the best solution is for governments to lower and stabilize inflation rates so that the need for the inflation adjustment of the tax system is minimized.

If the aim is to neutralize the effects of tax factors on international capital movements and exchange rates, indirect as they may be, adjustment of the tax treatment of foreign exchange gains and losses relative to the tax treatment of ordinary interest income also becomes relevant. Differences between the tax treatment of the former relative to the latter, wherever they exist, should be discouraged. Simultaneously, neutralization of these effects will also call for adoption of measures and tightening of administrative machinery in individual countries to improve the tax compliance of individuals and enterprises having income earned on international operations.

Finally, the tax treatment of interest income and payments relative to the tax treatment of other forms of capital income and payments tends to have important allocative effects. This paper has dealt with these important questions only in a very limited way and has not attempted to analyze the effects of taxes in countries (many of which are developing countries) where interest rates are regulated.

Appendix I

Tax Treatment of Interest Income and Interest Payments: An International Survey

Current analyses of money market developments and the use of interest rates as instruments of economic policy tend to include one or more aspects of taxation. One example is the tendency (shown by Makin and Tanzi in their paper in Part II, Chapter 4, of this volume) of a typical tax regime for interest income to exacerbate the interest rate fluctuations induced by inflation. Another example, of a more institutional kind, is how withholding taxes imposed by some countries on interest paid to recipients abroad may affect the Eurocurrency market and similar markets. A third example, and seemingly one of growing interest, is how the interest rate affects the behavior of savers and borrowers.

Taxes may also influence interest rate structures inasmuch as certain types of interest may be exempt, wholly or partly, from tax, certain groups of investors may be exempt from tax, and (on the opposite side) certain types of interest expenditure may be deductible within certain limits or without limits.

Any analysis of these issues, based on available information on the tax systems, necessarily suffers from three serious shortcomings. One is the interpretation problem often aggravated by language difficulties, as well as the institutional differences and deviations between the law as practiced and the statutes as published. Another is the quantification problem; while some few countries, the United States among them, have detailed statistics based on representative samples of tax returns, other countries have no statistics at all or have only vague estimates of the revenue importance of particular features of their tax laws. Finally, there is the question of how national differences in tax compliance may affect the effectiveness of the provisions of the law. To take just one example: if individual interest income in a country is notoriously underreported, to a point where few if any taxpayers care to comply, a mandatory withholding tax, even if it is imposed at a relatively low rate and is final, may imply a higher effective taxation on interest income than before. This may occur even though an analysis of the legal provisions may lead the innocent reader to believe that the change meant relief.

Taxation of interest

Exemptions for certain types of income

Interest income, as a general feature, forms part of the income tax base. This is self-evident in tax systems based on a global income concept. Systems developed from schedular systems may occasionally retain a final withholding tax on certain interest income as a remnant from the schedular system.

One type of exemption is mainly a *de minimis* rule. In countries applying pay-as-you-earn types of income tax, it is seen as desirable to avoid deviations from the withholding tax, particularly if the system is based on the premise that the pay-as-you-earn tax is final and no tax return is necessary in the majority of cases. Similarly, interest on postal savings bank accounts and accounts in similar institutions may be exempted, usually up to some maximum level; the background may well be that the interest rate on these accounts is low and that the tax exemption somehow compensates for this while at the same time the rule simplifies the tax system. The same motive can play a role for exempting interest on savings bonds issued to small savers.

There is, however, no clear distinction between this type of *de minimis* exemption, and those exemptions offered as measures to promote savings. Often the latter take the same legal form—that is, an exemption for a given amount of interest earnings (legally defined as gross earnings or net earnings after interest deduction, depending on other features of the system) or, alternatively, an exemption for interest on particular types of investment.

If it is sometimes difficult to distinguish between *de minimis* provisions and savings promotion schemes, the picture is further blurred by exemptions based on constitutional grounds, such as the exemption in the United States from federal income tax for interest on state and local government bonds. The constitutional issue might not be the only consideration; the exemption for interest on these bonds is more often than not seen as a means (of disputable effectiveness) of subsidizing the local governments or the activities the bonds are issued to finance.

Exemptions for certain recipients of income

More often than not, the institutional investors playing the major part in the bond market are social security institutions, pension funds, and the like, working under tax rules exempting them from tax on interest income. The exemption may be construed as a deferral rule: pension funds are allowed to be tax exempt, but beneficiaries will be taxed once they receive their pension payments. Or the institutional investor may be regarded as part of the government, exempt from tax under the somewhat dubious assumption that a government should not pay tax to itself. Other institutional investors may be insurance companies; their interest income may be subject to a lower tax than the usual corporate income tax rate under the assumption that the interest is accruing in the interest of policyholders and should be taxed at their representative average income tax rate or perhaps at a preferential rate aimed at stimulating insurance savings.

Whereas the institutional investors may benefit from preferential tax rules of this kind, they might well have to pay a price in the form of compulsory placement rules. There are many countries where the bond market, or at least the market for government bonds, is limited de facto to institutional investors that are forced by law to invest their funds in gilt-edged securities. If such rules are used to keep the market bond rate down at an artificial level, the tax exemption may be an insufficient compensation for the loss of potential investment income caused by the compulsory placement rules.

Other tax-exempt recipients of interest income are charities. Whereas tax laws often provide for income tax to be paid on business profits arrived at in competition with fully taxable subjects, there is a general tendency to allow charitable trusts and foundations to enjoy interest income without paying tax. Once again, the existence of important investors in this category tends to dilute the effects that a more general tax might have on the security market.

Finally, there are vast discrepancies in the treatment of interest paid to recipients abroad. Some countries abstain from any claim to such tax, presumably under the assumption that the tax withheld on foreign interest payments would be shifted to the domestic borrowers. Other countries impose withholding taxes on some or all interest payments, presumably under the assumption that the interest income has its source in the country and hence legitimately forms part of its tax base; there might also be a secondary argument that an exemption would make foreign borrowing too cheap and affect the relative prices of capital and labor in a direction that is undesirable, at least in countries with substantial unemployment. Attitudes toward these withholding taxes are affected by the existence of banking centers in tax havens and elsewhere that can be used to circumvent the interest withholding taxes of other countries; for competition's sake, countries are often unwilling to introduce withholding taxes, even if it is argued that in their absence the field is open for international investors to evade tax altogether. A certain moderation in withholding taxes on interest is dictated also by another reason: it is argued that a with-

holding tax levied on gross interest income may easily exceed a reasonable level if it is related to the actual net income of an investor
who himself has borrowed some or all of the capital lent.

Discrimination

Interest income may also be given less lenient treatment than other
income. One traditional method of doing this is by applying earned-
income relief to other types of income, such as salaries and wages,
but denying the same relief to interest income and other unearned
income. The U.K. tradition in this respect is old. The United States
formerly applied a maximum marginal tax rate of 50 percent to earned
income only, while allowing the top marginal rate to go higher for
unearned income. The basic effect is the same.

Other countries achieve the same purpose by net wealth taxes. In
a country subjecting interest income to preferential treatment, the
interest-bearing bank accounts may at the same time form part of the
taxable net wealth. The former provision may be aimed at promoting
savings, the latter at redistributing net wealth. The effectiveness of
net wealth taxes in this respect is not great, however. Carried too far,
net wealth taxes may channel savings into unproductive outlets of a
type difficult to tax, such as art, jewelry, and stamps, or they may give
an incentive to spend the money rather than to keep it.

Death duties also form part of redistributive taxation. For both these
duties and the net wealth taxes (and the two taxes are often seen as
substituting for one another), there is a conflict between the redistributive purpose of the law and the potential undesired consequences
in the form of dissaving or escape into tax-exempt assets or assets
difficult to tax. It is conceivable, though difficult to quantify, that the
propensity to save in interest-bearing instruments may be affected by
these taxes.

Deductibility of interest payments

Some concepts of taxable income include interest payments as an
element of negative income, deductible from the positive income in
order to arrive at the proper tax base. The argument may be one of
pure theory, referring to the periodical nature of the interest payments; more often, it seems as if this type of deduction is granted
with respect to the reduction of the taxpayer's disposable income—
and hence the ability to pay. Some may also have argued that, lacking
tax relief for negative net wealth, debt-ridden taxpayers should at
least have the benefit of a deduction for interest.

Other concepts of taxable income put interest payments on a level with other expenses. In other words, a deduction for interest is granted when the debt has been incurred to acquire or maintain an income-generating investment and is refused when the debt has been incurred to cover costs of living or investment in assets not generating any income. The implications of this approach vary considerably with what is understood by "income-generating" investment. Typically, the most important deduction for individual taxpayers is mortgage interest. If the imputed income of the taxpayer's own residence is assessed as an income item, the residential investment is obviously income generating and the mortgage interest should be deductible, according to the basic principle. However, even in many countries assessing imputed income of this kind, it is felt that the assessment value is not equal to the market value. Hence, a limit might apply to the mortgage interest deductible, either at a level preventing the home investment from rendering a deductible net deficit or at a level representing a maximum for what is seen as normal. It is noteworthy that a country such as the United States, while not taxing imputed income of residences, offers unlimited deduction for mortgage interest, whereas several of the European countries that impose income tax on imputed income nevertheless apply limitations to the deduction for mortgage interest.

A common problem in applying this type of rule is the proper allocation of loan interest to the corresponding investment. A rule attaching the debt to the collateral and refusing a deduction for home mortgage interest would prevent a homeowner from deducting interest paid on a mortgage taken up, say, to finance his business. On the other hand, requirement of specific information about the original purpose of a loan, while often possible, might lead to incorrect conclusions if the loan was originally taken to finance an income-generating investment but repayment has been postponed in order to use the money for other purposes. Finally, it is often argued that the nondeductibility of interest on consumption loans or mortgages discriminates against those of limited means, who must borrow, and favors those who can draw upon their income-generating assets in order to finance their consumption or their home investment. The former get no tax relief; the latter enjoy a reduction in income tax.

When the debtor is a corporation, the deduction for interest payments creates a considerable difference in treatment of the yield of an investment between equity and debt capital. Dividends are very rarely a deductible item for corporation tax; on the contrary, there is often a double discrimination against dividends, inasmuch as there is not only no deduction for the dividends but they are often also subject to a higher withholding tax, when paid to foreign recipients, than interest payments. With regard to this preferential treatment of debt, many countries have therefore been compelled to set up rules against "thin capitalization," treating loans from shareholders or from creditors affiliated with them as disguised equity, the interest on which should be treated as dividends.

Interest income and capital gains

Most countries offer either tax exemption or a more favorable tax treatment for capital gains than for ordinary income. The definition of what is a capital gain as distinct from ordinary income varies, however, with a tendency for the capital gains concept to be wider in countries taxing capital gains while the concept of current income tends to be wider in countries exempting capital gains.

One such definitional problem concerns interest. Inasmuch as bonds are issued at a discount, the effective interest may exceed the nominal interest. In some countries, issuers of bonds have used the capital gains tax treatment for bond discounts to obtain a favorable tax treatment. Legislative measures have been taken to stop this type of abuse by redefining interest to include bond discounts. There is still a problem, however, insofar as bonds are marketable and can be sold to some exempt entity at a gain representing the discount; if the gain on the sale is defined as a capital gain, the transaction may be a successful avoidance scheme. As is usual in this area, legislation reflects taxpayers' inventiveness only after some delay.

Interest income and foreign exchange gains

If a loan transaction affects two countries with different currencies, there is the possibility that repayment is offered at a different exchange rate than that prevailing at the time the credit was made. Depending on whether the creditor or the debtor has given or taken up the credit in a foreign currency, he may stand to gain or lose, respectively, depending on the foreign exchange rate.

In a great number of countries, the tax rules governing foreign exchange gains and losses are in a state of flux. First of all, there may be a difference between credits taken up or given in the course of a taxpayer's business and nonbusiness investment transactions. Second, even within the business sector, some countries recognize a capital gain and loss sector, and there have been cases in which a court has found a taxpayer taxable on his foreign exchange gain on lending in a foreign currency that has appreciated, while at the same time he has been deprived of a compensating loss deduction for corresponding borrowing in the same currency! Even if this type of incongruity is rare, it is still conceivable that borrowing for investment purposes is regarded as a capital transaction, the foreign exchange loss being a capital loss, with the restrictions applied to its deductibility. In this respect, a distinction is often made between different lines of business.

Even in those cases where the business character of foreign exchange gains and losses is recognized, timing may be a crucial factor. The traditional accounting principles may prescribe a recognition of losses while at the same time prohibiting the immediate accounting for unrealized gains; this kind of incongruity has, however, caught the attention of the authorities in several countries, and efforts are under way to establish accounting rules satisfactory to both the accounting profession and the tax authorities. At present, it is difficult to say what the prevailing rules are, even for one particular country. An international comparison of the tax treatment of foreign exchange gains and losses is a forbiddingly complicated subject.

Appendix II

Financial Sector Framework for Determination of Interest Rates

Expression for the level of interest rates

This simplified framework equates borrowing and lending, each determined by expected after-tax real interest rates and solves for a nominal interest rate, i, in terms of an expected after-tax real rate, r^*, and expected inflation, π.

The negative impact of expected inflation on the borrowing schedule (indicated below by the negative λ_1 term) reflects a depressing effect of expected inflation on the level of investment—an effect that arises in turn from a number of sources, some of which are tied to tax policy. First, "excess" taxes result from the use of historical cost depreciation and first-in, first-out inventory valuation in an inflationary environment. With such methods in use, as they are in the United States, a rise in expected inflation results in a foreseeable reduction in after-tax profits, thereby depressing investment. Second, higher expected inflation has been found in the United States to be associated with elevated uncertainty about relative prices. In turn, relative price uncertainty results in reduced investment and a negative shift in the borrowing schedule since most capital is not adaptable to a multitude of uses. Investment really represents an increased commitment to a given set of relative prices and is therefore made more risky by increased uncertainty about relative prices. Finally, if a rise in expected inflation depresses the equilibrium stock of desired money balances, a negative wealth effect requires a lower equilibrium level of the after-tax real interest rate. These effects are discussed, along with others, in Section III of the paper.

With these considerations in mind, lending and borrowing schedules are written as

$$L_t = \alpha_0 + \alpha_1 \left(i_t(1 - \tau_L) - \pi_t \right) \qquad\qquad \alpha_0, \alpha_1 > 0 \qquad (4)$$

$$B_t = \beta_0 - \lambda_1 \pi_t - \beta_1 \left(i_t(1 - \tau_B) - \pi_t \right) \qquad \lambda_1, \beta_0, \beta_1 > 0 \qquad (5)$$

where $\beta_0 > \alpha_0$ and

t = time

L = log of lending

α_1 = elasticity of lending with respect to lender's expected after-tax real rate, $i_t(1 - \tau_L) - \pi_t$

τ_L = lender's tax rate

B = log of borrowing

λ_1 = elasticity of borrowing schedule with respect to expected inflation, which also captures all the other effects of taxation mentioned in Section III in the subsection on effects of inflation on interest rates in the presence of income taxes

β_1 = elasticity of borrowing with respect to borrower's expected after-tax real rate, $i_t(1 - \tau_B) - \pi_t$

τ_B = borrower's tax rate

Setting equation (4) equal to equation (5) and solving for i_t gives

$$i_t = \frac{1}{\alpha_1(1 - \tau_L) + \beta_1(1 - \tau_B)}\left[(\beta_0 - \alpha_0) + (\alpha_1 + \beta_1 - \lambda_1)\pi_t\right] \quad (6)$$

The simple, tax-adjusted Fisher equation can be derived from equation (6) by setting $\tau_L = \tau_B = \tau$ and

$$\frac{(\beta_0 - \alpha_0)}{(\alpha_1 + \beta_1)} = r^*, \text{ the expected after-tax real rate.}$$

With these conditions satisfied and where $(\alpha_1 + \beta_1) = 1.0$

$$i_t = \left(\frac{1}{1 - \tau}\right)[r^* + (1 - \lambda_1)\pi_t] \quad (7)$$

Expression for the volatility of interest rates

Equation (7) implies an expression for the variance of i (given $\lambda_1 = \tau$):

$$\sigma_i^2 = \left[\frac{1}{1 - \tau}\right]^2 \sigma_{r^*}^2 + \sigma_\pi^2 + \left[\frac{2}{1 - \tau}\right]\rho_{r^*_\pi}\sigma_{r^*}\sigma \quad (8)$$

As $(0 < \tau < 1)$ implies $[1/(1 - \tau)]^2 > 1.0$, the effect of taxation of interest income and deduction of interest expense is to magnify the impact on the variance of nominal interest, σ_i^2, of changes in the variance of r^*, $\sigma_{r^*}^2$. The variance of i_t is likely to be reduced by the negative covariance between r^* and π, $\rho_{r^*_\pi} < 0$, which arises in connection with wealth, tax, and uncertainty effects.

Appendix III

Table 3. Selected Industrial Countries: Aspects of Tax Treatment of Interest Income

Country	Tax Exemptions of Interest Income			Withholding Tax on Interest Income of Residents[1]		
	Tax-exempt debt instruments[1]	Tax-exempt recipients[1]	General tax exemptions	Whether interest subject to withholding	Withholding tax rates (in percent)	Debt instruments whose interest earnings are not subject to withholding
Australia	Certain government securities issued prior to 1968 Certain securities issued abroad	Municipal corporations; certain "trustee" savings banks; superannuation funds; life insurance company superannuation business; various categories of associations that are tax-exempt on all income; credit unions (on income derived from their members); nonresidents (in part)[2]	None	No	Nil	All debt instruments
Austria	Certain government bonds (in part)[3] Savings deposits (in part)[3]	State railways and monopolies; the national bank; postal savings bank; retirement and pension funds; nonresidents (in part)[2]	—	Yes	20	Corporate bonds; government bonds; ordinary loans; mortgage loans;[4] bank deposits

Belgium	Certain government loans Certain government-guaranteed debt issues[5] Savings deposits[5] Investments in cooperatives[5] Interest income in general (final withholding tax)[5]	Some social bodies;[6] nonresidents (in part)[2]	—	Yes	25	Mortgage loans[4]
Canada	—	Municipal and other bodies; public enterprises;[7] trusts and corporations for (a) profit-sharing plans, (b) pensions and retirement savings, (c) home-ownership savings, (d) education plans	Up to Can$1,000 (US$815)	No	Nil	All debt instruments
Denmark	Compulsory savings instituted by law	Cooperatives; building societies; certain banks; public utilities; certain superannuation funds;[8] mutual insurance societies; nonresidents	Up to DKr 3,500 (US$600) to persons over the age of 67[9]	No	Nil	All debt instruments
France	Certain government bonds Savings bank deposits (in part)[10] Certain bank deposits in foreign currency Special deposits[10] Long-term savings schemes[10]	Agricultural and mutual credit funds; cooperative building societies; investment companies; pension and superannuation funds (in part);[11] nonresidents (in part)[2]	F 3,000 (US$610) on French fixed-interest bonds	Yes	10–25[12]	State government bonds; ordinary loans; mortgage loans;[4] bank deposits

Table 3 (continued). Selected Industrial Countries: Aspects of Tax Treatment of Interest Income

	Tax Exemptions of Interest Income			Withholding Tax on Interest Income of Residents[1]		
Country	Tax-exempt debt instruments[1]	Tax-exempt recipients[1]	General tax exemptions	Whether interest subject to withholding	Withholding tax rates (in percent)	Debt instruments whose interest earnings are not subject to withholding
Germany, Fed. Rep.	Certain federal government bonds[13] Home-ownership savings[13] Employee savings schemes[13]	Federal railways; postal service; certain banks and financial institutions; pension funds; nonresidents (in part)[2]	DM 800 (US$340)[14]	Yes	25	Corporate bonds; government bonds; ordinary loans; mortgage loans; bank deposits
Ireland	Post office savings bank deposits (in part)[15] Commercial bank deposits (in part)[15] National savings bonds[16] Public sector bonds (govt., local authority and some public enterprise)[16]	Approved superannuation funds; savings banks; National Insurance Funds (health and unemployment); nonresidents (in part)[2]	—	Yes	35	Bank deposits; profit-sharing bonds
Italy	All government and nationalized enterprises' bonds[17] Certain post office bonds Some companies' debt instruments (usually according to particular times of issue)[18]	Corporations (including credit institutions) for holdings of public debt (in part); certain small cooperatives; Mezzogiorno Fund (in part); credit institutions for some loans to local authorities; nonresidents (in part)[2]	—	Only on nonexempt bonds, deposits, and some other debt instruments[18,19]	12.5, 15, 25	Government bonds; selected other instruments

Japan	Bank and savings deposits[20]; Certain bonds and debentures[20]; Certain central or local government bonds; Savings for formation of employees' assets[20]	Local governments; fully government-owned corporations (railways, etc.); qualified nonprofit corporations	—	Yes[19]	20, 35	None
Netherlands	None	Public utilities undertakings; all pension funds; unemployment and sickness insurance funds; investment organizations; nonresidents (in part)[2]	f. 700 (US$270)[21]	No	Nil	All debt instruments except those whose income is regarded as dividends, such as debt claims participating in profits
Norway	Deposits with domestic banks[22]; Deposits with certain savings institutions[22]; Government savings bonds[22]; Bonds issued by debtors[22]	Cooperatives; mutual insurance companies; building societies; savings banks (but subject to municipal tax); nonresidents	—	No	Nil	All debt instruments
Sweden	—[23]	Local authorities; pension funds; benefit (death, unemployment compensation, etc.) societies; nonresidents	Married couple: SKr 1,600 (US$275)[23] Single person: Skr 800 (US$138)[23]	No	Nil	All debt instruments

Table 3 (continued). Selected Industrial Countries: Aspects of Tax Treatment of Interest Income

Country	Tax Exemptions of Interest Income			Withholding Tax on Interest Income of Residents[1]		
	Tax-exempt debt instruments[1]	Tax-exempt recipients[1]	General tax exemptions	Whether interest subject to withholding	Withholding tax rates (in percent)	Debt instruments whose interest earnings are not subject to withholding
Switzerland	Savings deposits[24]	Social security; compensation and staff welfare or provident funds; transportation enterprises; nonresidents (in part)[24]	—	Yes	35	Ordinary loans; mortgage loans
United Kingdom	National savings certificates; National savings bank deposits (in part)[25]; Certain stocks and loan issues[26]; Contractual savings, SAYE[26]	Local authorities; savings banks; issuing departments of certain foreign central banks;[27] approved superannuation funds; nonresidents (in part)[2]	—	Yes	30	Bank deposits; profit-sharing bonds;[28]
United States	State and municipal government bonds; Savings certificates of certain depository institutions (in part)[29]	Pension plans; farmers' cooperatives; nonresidents (in part)[2]	US$400[30]	No[31]	Nil	All debt instruments[31]

Sources: United Kingdom, *Income Taxes Outside the United Kingdon* (London: H.M. Stationery Office), loose-leaf service; Tax Management, *Foreign Income Portfolios* (Washington), loose-leaf service relating to Austria, France, the Federal Republic of Germany, Italy, the Netherlands, and Switzerland; Price Waterhouse, *Information Guide* on doing business in the countries surveyed, except Austria (New York), latest editions; for *Sweden and Switzerland*: Harvard Law School, *World Tax Series* (Chicago: Commerce Clearing House, 1959 and 1976, respectively); for *Japan*: Yuji Gomi, *Guide to Japanese Taxes* (Tokyo: Zaikei, 1981); for *Australia*: E.F. and J.E. Mannix, *Australian Income Tax* (Sydney: Butterworths, 1981); International Bureau of Fiscal Documentation, *The Taxation of Private Investment Income*, Guides to European Taxation, Vol. 3 (Amsterdam), loose-leaf service. The rates of exchange of June 1982 (or the nearest month) published in *International Financial Statistics*, International Monetary Fund (Washington), are applied to derive the U.S. dollar equivalents in the table and footnotes.

[1] Tax exemption is defined broadly here. It also includes preferential tax treatment, such as partial tax exemption, reduced rate of tax, refund of tax, and tax credit. The "tax-exempt" recipients tabulated here are some of the major categories of recipients listed in the income tax codes of these countries and are (in addition to the charitable, social, and religious bodies) institutions of scientific research, cooperative societies, agrarian collectives, organizations for low-cost housing, etc., which, too, are generally exempt in most of these countries. Neither the list of tax-exempt debt instruments nor that of tax-exempt recipients is intended to be exhaustive. Withholding tax on interest is subject to tax credit in all countries except Italy and Japan (see footnote 19).

[2] The categories of interest income of nonresidents to which the exemption relates are shown in Table 5.

[3] Tax exemption applies to bond issues (including mortgage bonds) and local government loans of up to S 100,000 ($6,050) and to interest on savings deposits of up to S 7,000 ($425) per taxpayer in each case.

[4] But not mortgage bonds, which are subject to withholding.

[5] Guaranteed debt relates to some exceptional loans by public enterprises (telegraph and telephone, railways). Savings deposit interest of up to BF 50,000 ($1,100) and interest received from cooperatives up to BF 5,000 ($110) are exempt. Interest of up to BF 10,000 ($220) is exempt if the total taxable income does not exceed BF 350,000 ($7,700). Interest income in general is subject to a final withholding tax insofar as certain limits are not exceeded (limit for interest income: BF 1,110,000 ($24,420); limit for interest and/or dividend income: BF 316,000 ($6,952); limit for interest and/or dividend income: BF 20 percent to a maximum of 47 percent when interest and/or dividend income exceeds BF 3 million ($66,000). Above these limits, a supplementary progressive tax is levied, ranging from 20 percent to a maximum of 47 percent when interest and/or dividend income exceeds BF 3 million ($66,000).

[6] Exemption is in the form of a reduced rate of tax.

[7] Minimum required government ownership is 90 percent.

[8] In 1984, a tax is payable on real incomes of certain pension funds (in excess of 3.5 percent return) at the rate of 40.5 percent.

[9] Thirty percent of interest income of taxpayers with incomes below Dkr 50,500 ($8,620), maximum available deduction being Dkr 3,500 ($600) per annum. For taxpayers with higher incomes, tax-exempt interest is reduced by Dkr 50 ($8.50) for each Dkr 100 ($17) in excess of the specified limit (Dkr 50,500 or $8,620), which is adjustable annually in line with the price index.

[10] Limited to a maximum savings deposit of F 32,500 ($5,320); only one third of interest on special deposit with the nonagricultural mutual credit institutions is subject to income tax; limit in regard to the amount of long-term savings is up to F 20,000 ($3,310) or one fourth of the taxpayer's income, whichever is higher.

[11] At a reduced tax rate of 10 percent.

[12] Lower rate applies to issues after January 1, 1965.

[13] Mainly issues after World War II (1952–55); includes mortgage bonds and municipal government debentures. Preferential treatment in respect of home ownership and employee savings schemes is extended through the payment of limited amounts of tax-free bonuses by government to certain categories of taxpayers participating in these schemes.

[14] This exemption from tax applies only on income (joint return) from movable capital.

[15] Interest on commercial bank deposits up to £Ir 50 ($63) and from savings banks up to £Ir 120 ($150), with a total ceiling of £Ir 120 ($150).

[16] Exemption usually extends to bonds held by persons not ordinarily resident in Ireland.

[17] As expressly provided in the laws sanctioning their issue.

[18] Under various laws for encouraging sectoral or regional investment in agriculture, mining, industry, and low-cost housing.

[19] Withholding tax on interest is final in Italy and Japan — in Italy, on all debt instruments except ordinary and mortgage loans and in Japan whenever the taxpayer has opted for a final withholding tax at the rate of 35 percent.

[20] Interest exemption applies to interest received on bank deposits of up to ¥3 million ($11,950), on postal savings deposits of up to ¥3 million ($11,950), on national or local government bonds up to ¥3 million ($11,950), and on employee savings of up to ¥5 million ($19,920) deposited with banks or security dealers under a contract, the total tax-exempt savings being ¥14 million ($55,770).

Table 3 (concluded). Selected Industrial Countries: Aspects of Tax Treatment of Interest Income

	Tax Exemptions of Interest Income			Withholding Tax on Interest Income of Residents[1]		
Country	Tax-exempt debt instruments[1]	Tax-exempt recipients[1]	General tax exemptions	Whether interest subject to withholding	Withholding tax rates (in percent)	Debt instruments whose interest earnings are not subject to withholding

[21] Available only on excess of interest receipts over interest payments, not on gross receipts.

[22] Combined interest income from only these sources is exempt up to NKr 4,000 ($660) on joint return and half this amount on single return.

[23] Certain savings deposits, up to a maximum yearly savings of SKr 7,200 ($1,240) on joint return and maximum total savings of SKr 30,000 ($5,165), are exempt. Most government bonds bought by private investors in Sweden are premium (non-interest-bearing) bonds, winnings on which attract a flat-rate lottery tax of 20 percent.

[24] Exemption is from the income tax imposed by cantons (not the federal government) as provided in their respective legislation. Nonresidents are not subject to federal income tax except by way of withholding tax on bonds, debentures, and interest on bank deposits, which is generally final (not refundable).

[25] Up to £70 ($105) a year.

[26] The exempt interest relates only to payments received by persons not ordinarily resident in the United Kingdom. SAYE is a "save as you earn" scheme under which employees participate in a scheme to acquire shares at 70 percent of their value by contributing £20 ($36) per month to the scheme; indexed part of interest income is tax free.

[27] India and Pakistan.

[28] Interest on such instruments is treated as a cash dividend.

[29] Applies to tax-free savings certificates issued by certain depository financial institutions (banks, thrift institutions, and credit unions) between October 1, 1981 and December 31, 1982. Limit on interest earnings on a joint return is $2,000.

[30] This exclusion of dividends and interest income on joint returns for 1981 is now reduced to $200 and relates only to dividends. Starting in 1985, taxpayers will be able to exclude 15 percent of the net interest income up to $450, net income being net of nonbusiness, nonhome mortgage interest payments.

[31] Effective July 1, 1983 all interest earnings other than those specifically exempted from withholding, e.g., minimal interest payments (below $150), certain payments by qualified cooperatives, and payments to exempt individuals and institutions, are subject to a 10 percent withholding tax.

Table 4. Selected Industrial Countries: Tax Deductibility of Interest Expense of Individuals

Country	Owner-Occupied Housing			Income-Generating Investment	General Consumer Credit
	Whether imputed income taxable	Whether deductibility relates to interest payments, principal (or equivalent savings), or both	Whether deductibility limited	Whether interest payments deductible	Whether interest payments deductible
Australia	No	None[1]	—	Yes	No
Austria	No	Principal and interest[2]	Yes	Yes	No
Belgium	Yes[3]	Principal and interest[3]	Yes[3]	Yes[3]	No
Canada	No	Principal and interest[4]	Yes[4]	Yes[4]	No
Denmark	Yes	Interest	No	Yes	Yes
France	No	Interest[5]	Yes[5]	Yes[6]	No
Germany, Fed. Rep.	Yes	Savings or interest[7]	Yes	Yes	No
Ireland	No	Interest[8]	Yes[8]	Yes[8]	No[8]
Italy	Yes[9]	Interest	Yes[9]	Yes[10]	No
Japan	No	Principal and interest[11]	Yes[11]	Yes	No
Netherlands	Yes	Interest	No	Yes	Yes
Norway	Yes	Interest	No	Yes	Yes
Sweden	Yes	Interest[12]	Yes[12]	Yes[12]	Yes[12]
Switzerland	Yes	Interest	No	Yes	Yes
United Kingdom	No	Interest	Yes[13]	Yes[14]	No
United States	No	Interest	No	Yes[15]	Yes

Sources: United Kingdom, *Income Taxes Outside the United Kingdom* (London: H.M. Stationery Office), loose-leaf service; Price Waterhouse, *Information Guide* on doing business in various countries under review (New York), latest editions; Tax Management, *Foreign Income Portfolios* (Washington), loose-leaf service; Yuji Gomi, *Guide to Japanese Taxes* (Tokyo: Zaikei, 1981). Exchange rates for June 1982 (or the nearest month) published in *International Financial Statistics*, International Monetary Fund (Washington), are applied to derive the U.S. dollar equivalents in the footnotes.

[1] Mortgage interest deduction ceased to apply to interest accruing after November 1, 1978.

[2] Since 1980, the contribution includes interest on borrowing connected with the building of a house up to a maximum of S 20,000 ($1,215) for taxpayer and spouse and S 5,000 ($303) for each child. Taxpayers are further entitled to receive an allowance for "extraordinary burden" (S 15,000, or $910, on joint return) arising from home acquisition in the first year.

Table 4 (concluded). Selected Industrial Countries: Tax Deductibility of Interest Expense of Individuals

Country	Owner-Occupied Housing			Income-Generating Investment	General Consumer Credit
	Whether imputed income taxable	Whether deductibility relates to interest payments, principal (or equivalent savings), or both	Whether deductibility limited	Whether interest payments deductible	Whether interest payments deductible

[3] The occupation of his own property by the owner is treated as taxable income from real estate, but an exemption is given up to BF 120,000 ($2,840), to which BF 10,000 ($220) is added for each dependent. Further, if the exemption does not exhaust the taxable amount, this amount is reduced to half when the total taxable income does not exceed BF 950,000 ($20,900). When the total taxable income exceeds BF 950,000 ($20,900), the imputed income may not be raised by more than half of the difference between BF 950,000 ($20,900) and the total taxable income. Mortgage interest payments are tax deductible to the extent that the deduction does not exceed the total income derived from immovable property and from interest and/or dividends. The principal is only tax deductible when the loan relates to a social property or to private property having a market value below BF 2,500,000 ($55,000) (purchase) or BF 2,700,000 ($59,400) (building), to which 5 percent may be added for each dependent or 25 percent when the property is partly for professional use. The deductibility of the principal is subject to different conditions and limitations. The amount of the deductible principal is also limited depending on the taxable professional income and may not exceed a limit of BF 45,000 ($990), a limit to which deductible insurance premiums must also be imputed, but in addition a tax deduction of BF 11,250 ($245) or BF 13,500 ($297) is possible. Supplementary incentives are granted, such as supplementary interest deductibility up to BF 200,000 ($4,400) spread over three years for new construction, exemption of taxation on imputed income from owner-occupied property in 1984–95 for new construction, and limited deductibility of expense for renovation of buildings.

[4] Deductibility relates to annual contributions of up to Can$1,000 ($815) for a lifetime maximum of Can$10,000 ($8,150) paid to a Registered Home Ownership Savings Plan (RHOSP) for only one residential property, to be limited to 20 years. Interest on income-generating investment is tax deductible only to the extent of income generated. However, such restriction is not applicable to investment in equity of a private company and to borrowing incurred prior to the 1982 budget for acquiring rental property.

[5] On interest for the purchase, construction, and major repairs of a principal residence at the rate of F 7,000 ($1,145) plus F 1,000 ($165) per dependent, for a maximum of 10 years.

[6] The deduction against real estate income is on the entire amount of mortgage interest. On income from movable property the deduction relates to the purchase of certain domestic financial assets—for example, shares in investment companies, officially quoted domestic securities (mainly company shares), or interest in a private company.

[7] Housing is usually acquired by means of savings with building associations first and mortgage loans from it thereafter. Home ownership savings contributions are tax deductible, provided taxpayer does not claim housing bonus thereon. Such contributions are, however, a part of "special expenditures," which are tax deductible only up to maximum amounts specified in the tax law. Interest on subsequent borrowing from the loan associations is tax deductible but only up to the amount of imputed income of the house to the owner, the latter being in practice considerably lower than the former.

[8] Except in respect of interest connected with rental income and interest on loans to pay death duties, deductibility of interest payments for all other purposes (currently under review) is restricted to £Ir 2,400 ($3,550) per annum on single returns and double that amount on joint returns. However, effective March 25, 1982, the relief will apply only to interest on mortgage loans for the purchase, repair, or improvement of sole or main residence, and on an interim basis (through 1984/85) on loans then in existence. For new loans thereafter, interest on general consumer credit will be deductible only on loans within specified limits of £Ir 25,000 ($37,000) and £Ir 5,000 ($7,400) for couples. Deductibility of interest on income-generating loans is now available only for trading and rental income and for investment in companies engaged in such activities and in professional partnerships.

[9] Notional income for each cadastral unit represents imputed income. Interest of up to a maximum of Lit 4 million ($3,080) paid on mortgage loans.

[10] The deductibility is limited to the total amount of interest payments multiplied by the ratio of taxable to total income (the latter inclusive of 90 percent of the tax-exempt interest income).

[11] Two schemes are in existence: (1) an employee contributing to a savings scheme for residential housing for at least three years gets a tax credit of up to ¥ 50,000 ($205) a year; and (2) an annual tax credit equal to 7 percent of the repayment of borrowing with a limit of ¥ 17,000 ($70) to ¥ 30,000 ($125) (higher amount is available where loan is raised by a formal loan agreement) for three years, based on an income mean test (annual income of ¥ 8 million, or $33,000, and below). Scheme (1) is being abolished under 1982 Tax Reform, with reliefs for houses acquired prior to April 1982.

[12] Interest deductions, available on all borrowings, are restricted so as not to reduce the tax by more than 50 percent even if the marginal tax rate is higher.

[13] Interest deductions are limited to a mortgage of £25,000 ($44,750) for acquiring a dwelling and for improvements thereto.

[14] Subject to one of four conditions: (1) on commercial property, it must be on rent for at least six months in a year; (2) taxpayer applying proceeds of borrowing for acquiring a share in an enterprise must either have a material interest in it or act personally in the conduct of trade; (3) proceeds of borrowing are being applied to pay transfer tax or purchase a life annuity; and (4) borrowing is for purchasing or improving land.

[15] Interest on borrowings that are applied to the acquisition of tax-exempt investments (e.g., state and local government bonds) are not tax deductible. The deductibility of interest on all other borrowings is limited to the investment income generated. To the extent that such interest exceeds $10,000 (raised to $15,000 if investor is seeking to increase his minority stockholding in an enterprise to a majority), the excess may be carried forward and may be deducted in the subsequent year subject to the same limitations as in the initial year.

Table 5. Selected Industrial Countries: Aspects of Tax Treatment of International Flows of Interest Income

Country	Foreign Interest Income of Resident Individuals		Interest Payments to Nonresident Individuals	
	Taxable interest gross or net of tax paid in source country	Type of double taxation relief available	Withholding taxes applicable[1]	Tax exempt interest, if any
Australia	Gross[2]	Foreign tax credit	10	On certain bearer bonds
Austria	Net	Foreign tax credit (in part) and exemption (in part)[3]	0, 15[4]	On convertible bonds; on profit-sharing bonds; on borrowings on local real estate mortgage
Belgium	Net	Foreign tax credit or deduction	0, 10, 15, 16, 25	On bank deposits; on registered bonds of banks; on registered government bonds and debt; on registered government bonds and debt instruments
Canada	Gross	Foreign tax credit[5]	0, 15	None
Denmark	Gross	Foreign tax credit	Nil	All
France	Gross[6]	Foreign tax deduction or credit[7]	0, 15[7]	On certain government bonds
Germany, Fed. Rep.	Gross[5]	Exemption (in part);[8] foreign tax credit (in part);[8] deduction (in part)[9]	0, 10, 15, 25[10]	On bank deposits and loans that are not mortgaged by local immovable property
Ireland	Net	None[11]	0, 10, 15, 35	On certain government securities
Italy	Gross	Foreign tax credit[8]	0, 10, 12.5 15[7]	On public loans; on certain qualifying institutions' bonds; on certain bonds issued abroad; on certain public enterprises' bonds
Japan	Gross	Foreign tax credit or deduction	10, 15	None

Netherlands	Gross[12]	Foreign tax credit	Nil	All interest other than from loan mortgaged by local immovable property and from substantial interest company
Norway	Net	None[13]	Nil	All
Sweden	Gross	Foreign tax credit	Nil	All
Switzerland	Net	None[11]	0, 5, 10, 15	All interest except from bonds and certain registered loans
United Kingdom	Gross	Foreign tax credit[14]	0, 10, 15, 30	On certain government securities
United States	Gross	Foreign tax credit or deduction	0, 5, 10, 15, 30	On bank deposits

Sources: Same as in Tables 3 and 4. Also, International Bureau of Fiscal Documentation, *Corporate Taxation in Europe* (Amsterdam), loose-leaf service; and Coopers and Lybrand International Tax Network, *International Tax Summaries* (New York: John Wiley, 1982).

[1] The rates given in the table apply only to interest flows from countries with which a given country has a double taxation treaty agreement. Almost all countries covered here have double taxation treaties with each other, and the rates vary in each case depending on provisions of the treaty with specific countries.

[2] Under treaty provisions. For nontreaty countries, interest income that is already taxed in source country is no longer taxable in taxpayer's country of residence.

[3] Exemption of interest on mortgage loans from some specific countries.

[4] Withholding tax applies only to interest on profit-sharing bonds.

[5] Foreign tax credit is available only to the extent that interest earnings are subject to domestic income tax.

[6] With treaty countries; for other countries, on a net basis and no tax credit is granted.

[7] Foreign tax relief is usually by means of deduction of foreign tax paid, but foreign tax credit often applies under tax treaties. Withholding tax applies to interest on loans.

[8] Under some tax treaties, foreign income is exempt from taxation. Credit against domestic tax is prorated to the ratio of domestic tax due to the total taxable income (both foreign and domestic).

[9] At taxpayer's option, foreign tax paid may be deducted from the computation of tax liability in the country of taxpayer's residence.

[10] Only on interest on bonds and mortgage loans.

[11] However, if taxpayer had spent less than ten years in the foreign country from which interest income was derived, he may be allowed some foreign tax credit.

[12] With treaty countries and nontreaty developing countries; for other countries, on a net basis and no tax credit is granted.

[13] Exceptions: (1) interest on mortgage loans, on foreign sites, on immovable property on which tax reduction may be granted on a pro rata basis as stated in footnote 8; and (2) all of specified interest from some specific countries.

[14] Extends even to the applicable highest marginal tax rate.

References*

Ben-Zion, Uri, "Impact of Inflation and Taxation on the Level, Allocation, and Financing of Investment: A Survey of Recent Literature" (unpublished, International Monetary Fund, February 24, 1983).

————, and J. Weinblatt, "Purchasing Power, Interest Rate Parity and the Modified Fisher Effect in the Presence of Tax Agreements" (unpublished, August 1982).

Byrne, William J., "Fiscal Incentives for Household Saving," *Staff Papers*, International Monetary Fund (Washington), Vol. 23 (July 1976), pp. 455–89.

Darby, Michael R., "The Financial and Tax Effects of Monetary Policy on Interest Rates," *Economic Inquiry* (Long Beach, California), Vol. 13 (June 1975), pp. 266–74.

Feldstein, Martin S., "Inflation, Income Taxes, and the Rate of Interest: A Theoretical Analysis," *American Economic Review* (Nashville, Tennessee), Vol. 66 (December 1976), pp. 809–20.

Gandolfi, Arthur E., "Inflation, Taxation and the Interest Rates," *Journal of Finance* (New York), Vol. 37 (June 1982), pp. 797–807.

Hartman, David G., "Taxation and the Effects of Inflation on the Real Capital Stock in an Open Economy," *International Economic Review* (Osaka, Japan), Vol. 20 (June 1979), pp. 417–25.

Howard, David H., and Karen H. Johnson, "Interest Rates, Inflation, and Taxes: The Foreign Connection," *Economics Letters* (Amsterdam), Vol. 9, No. 2 (1982), pp. 181–84.

Kopits, George F., "Taxation and Multinational Firm Behavior: A Critical Survey," *Staff Papers*, International Monetary Fund (Washington), Vol. 23 (November 1976), pp. 624–73.

————, "Fiscal Incentives for Investment in Industrial Countries," *Bulletin for International Fiscal Documentation* (Amsterdam), Vol. 35 (July 1981), pp. 291–94.

Lahiri, Kajal, "Inflationary Expectations: Their Formation and Interest Rate Effects," *American Economic Review*: (Nashville, Tennessee), Vol. 66 (March 1976), pp. 124–31.

---

* In addition to the background papers in Part II of this volume, the references listed here were important sources in the preparation of this overview.

Levi, Maurice D., "Taxation and 'Abnormal' International Capital Flows," *Journal of Political Economy* (Chicago), Vol. 85 (June 1977), pp. 635–46.

———, and John H. Makin, "Anticipated Inflation and Interest Rates: Further Interpretation of Findings on the Fisher Equation," *American Economic Review* (Nashville, Tennessee), Vol. 68 (December 1978), pp. 801–12.

Modi, Jitendra R., "Survey of Tax Treatment of Investment Income and Payments in Selected Industrial Countries" (unpublished, Fiscal Affairs Department, International Monetary Fund, May 27, 1983).

Mundell, Robert, "Inflation and Real Interest," *Journal of Political Economy* (Chicago), Vol. 71 (June 1963), pp. 280–83.

Nielsen, Niels Christian, "Inflation and Taxation: Nominal and Real Rates of Return," *Journal of Monetary Economics* (Amsterdam), Vol. 7 (March 1981), pp. 261–70.

Nowotny, Ewald, "Inflation and Taxation: Reviewing the Macroeconomic Issues," *Journal of Economic Literature* (Nashville, Tennessee), Vol. 18 (September 1980), pp. 1025–49.

Sargent, Thomas J., "Interest Rates and Expected Inflation: A Selective Summary of Recent Research," *Explorations in Economic Research* (New York), Vol. 3 (Summer 1976), pp. 303–25.

Steuerle, Eugene, "Is Income from Capital Subject to Individual Income Taxation?" *Public Finance Quarterly* (Beverly Hills, California), Vol. 10 (July 1982), pp. 283–303.

Summers, Lawrence H., "The Non-Adjustment of Nominal Interest Rates: A Study of the Fisher Effect," National Bureau of Economic Research (New York: Columbia University Press), Research Paper No. 836 (January 1982).

Tanzi, Vito, "Real, Fisherian, and Required Rates of Interest Under Inflationary Conditions: Theoretical and Empirical Results" (unpublished, International Monetary Fund (Washington), December 17, 1975).

———, "Inflation, Indexation and Interest Income Taxation," *Quarterly Review*, Banca Nazionale del Lavoro (Rome), No. 116 (March 1976), pp. 64–76.

———, "Inflation and the Incidence of Income Taxes on Interest Income: Some Results for the United States, 1972-74," *Staff Papers*, International Monetary Fund (Washington), Vol. 24 (July 1977), pp. 500–13.

———, "Inflationary Expectations, Economic Activity, Taxes, and Interest Rates," *American Economic Review* (Nashville, Tennessee), Vol. 70 (March 1980), pp. 12–21.

————, *Inflation and Personal Income Tax* (Cambridge: Cambridge University Press, 1980).

————, "Inflationary Expectations, Economic Activity, Taxes and Interest Rates: Reply," *American Economic Review* (Nashville, Tennessee), Vol. 72 (September 1982), pp. 860–63.

————, and Mario I. Blejer, "Inflation, Interest Rate Policy, and Currency Substitution in Developing Economies: A Discussion of Some Major Issues," *World Development* (Oxford, England), Vol. 10 (September 1982), pp. 781–89.

Tobin, James, "Money and Economic Growth," *Econometrica* (Evanston, Illinois), Vol. 33 (October 1965), pp. 671–84.

PART II

BACKGROUND PAPERS

2

Recent Literature on the Impact of Taxation and Inflation on Interest Rates

URI BEN-ZION

The effect of inflation on nominal interest rates, which was discussed extensively by Irving Fisher (1930), has received renewed attention in the economic literature since the early 1970s. The coincidence of rising inflation rates, rising nominal interest rates, and accelerating money growth that characterized much of the 1970s was difficult to explain without recourse to the Fisherian emphasis on the role of inflationary expectations in determining interest rates. Further, the exact way in which anticipated inflation affected interest rates was known to be important.

I. RECENT EMPHASIS IN THE LITERATURE

Without considering taxes, Fisher made it clear that if a unit change in inflationary expectations resulted in an equal unit change in nominal interest rates, it was possible to infer that the expected real interest rate, a crucial determinant of investment and saving behavior, would remain constant. In such a case, monetary changes that generated inflation and attendant inflationary expectations could be judged "neutral" or devoid of an effect on real economic activity or on relative prices. Empirical investigations in this area like those of Gibson (1972), Lahiri (1976), and Carr and others (1976) often reported estimated impacts of expected inflation proxies on nominal rates significantly below unity, suggesting that higher anticipated inflation was associated with lower expected real rates.

Two explanations for this result were put forward by those who expected to see some form of the neutrality condition emerge as the "true" result. The first group cited measurement error in the proxy for expected inflation. Such measurement error could bias downward the estimated coefficient on anticipated inflation. Others, including Sargent (1972) and Levi and Makin (1978), pointed to the Mundell effect, whereby one would expect a rise in anticipated inflation to depress the expected real rate, thereby causing a less-than-unitary impact of anticipated inflation on nominal interest.

The question as to possible nonneutral effects of anticipated inflation and attendant monetary behavior became even more intriguing when a number of authors began to point out that after-tax real and nominal interest rates were what really affected economic behavior. (See Darby (1975), Feldstein (1976), and Tanzi (1976).) In particular, it was easy to show that as an income tax is levied on nominal interest earnings, if a rise in anticipated inflation is to leave constant the after-tax expected real interest rate, the nominal rate must rise by *more* than the rise in anticipated inflation. Specifically, the increase in the nominal rate must be $[1/(1-t)]$ times the rise in anticipated inflation, so that if t, the marginal tax rate on interest income, is 0.33, $[1/(1-t)]$ equals 1.5.

This discovery was both important and perplexing. It was important because a new neutrality criterion was established for independence from anticipated inflation of the expected after-tax rate. The estimated impact had to be well above the value of unity indicated by the Fisherian no-tax analysis. Investigators were perplexed because most estimates of that impact were already significantly below unity; and while the Mundell effect could account for results below unity, given an expected value of unity, it could not account for the size of the gap between estimates significantly below unity and the value around 1.5 anticipated with taxes in the analysis.

Late in the 1970s, another group of papers began to appear that took account of taxes and the Mundell effect. By casting the analysis in a general equilibrium framework, these studies were able to identify other variables that ought to have appeared, along with some measure of anticipated inflation in an estimated interest rate equation. Levi and Makin (1978, 1979) derived an interest rate equation from a simple general equilibrium model that suggested the presence of output growth and inflation uncertainty, along with anticipated inflation, in the interest rate equation. Tanzi (1980 b) included a measure of the stages of the business cycle and suggested that the rapid acceleration of inflation may have resulted in "fiscal illusion," whereby actions were based on perceived tax rates below those actually in effect as a result of growing differences between nominal market and real interest rates. Makin (1982, 1983) considered the impact of various measures of the U.S. fiscal deficit, surprise changes in the money supply, inflation uncertainty, and anticipated inflation.

The upshot of this latter work is to reveal difficulties implicit in omitting significant explanatory variables from an interest rate equation. Once relevant variables are included, the estimated coefficient of anticipated inflation is about unity or slightly above, which, given operation of the Mundell effect, is a plausible value in a properly specified after-tax model. Of course, explicit consideration of the role played by taxes in interpreting this result is crucial. Ignoring taxes on interest, the unitary coefficient on anticipated inflation would lead one to conclude, along with Fisher, that anticipated inflation does not affect the expected real rate of interest and that monetary changes and associated effects on anticipated inflation produce no real effects. With taxes explicitly considered, it is not possible to rationalize the coefficient around unity without recourse to the negative relationship between expected inflation and the (after-tax) expected real interest rate hypothesized by Mundell (1963).

The remainder of this paper presents a more thorough survey of the literature on the effects of inflation and taxation on interest rates. It also includes in the Appendix the effects of taxation and inflation on the real tax burdens on individuals and corporations and on the equilibrium interest rate. Other aspects of the effects of inflation and taxation on real variables are included in Chapter 3 of this volume. The survey starts with the theoretical analysis of interest rate determination and the classical Fisher effect and follows this with the derivation of the modified Fisher effect in a world with taxes. The theoretical section is concluded by a discussion of other variables that affect the relationship between inflation and interest rates in a more general model. Since the emphasis is on inflation, taxation, and interest rates, the survey is generally restricted to a partial-equilibrium analysis which centers on this relationship.

The major part of the empirical work in this area was done for the United States. This paper, therefore, deals separately with studies done for the U.S. economy and sorts this literature according to the various approaches to the problem. Empirical work with U.S. data led researchers to different theoretical conjectures about individual and market behavior based only on a sample for one country. For that reason, a comparison with empirical results for other countries is important, despite the fact that data on other countries may not be as detailed as those available for the United States. An implicit (or explicit) assumption of many U.S. studies is that interest rates are determined in an intervention-free competitive market. While this assumption is questionable for the United States, it is much more so for some other Western countries.

II. INTEREST RATE DETERMINATION AND
THE FISHER EFFECT

In a period of changing prices, one has to distinguish between the nominal market rate and the real interest rate. As mentioned by Lutz (1974), the first theory of the relationship between inflation and interest rates was developed by Thornton (1802). This theory was formalized in the works of Irving Fisher (1896, 1930).

Using the theoretical framework of the loanable funds approach, Fisher concluded that the expected real interest rate is constant and that the nominal interest rate is equal to the expected real interest rate plus anticipated inflation. This analysis leads to the well-known Fisher equation

$$i = r + \pi \tag{1}$$

where

i = nominal interest rate
r = expected real interest rate
π = expected rate of inflation

If a rise in π leaves r unaffected, it will result in an equal rise in i. This is the Fisher effect. The assumption that the expected real rate was independent of expected inflation was questioned by Mundell (1963) and Tobin (1965). Mundell's argument is based on the negative impact of expected inflation on desired real money balances. Higher anticipated inflation reduces desired money balances. The resulting decline in wealth reduces consumption and stimulates increased saving. As a result, the equilibrium between higher savings and investment must occur at a lower expected real rate of interest, which induces real investment to rise to equal higher real savings.

Karni (1972) extends Mundell's analysis to the long run by assuming that the long-run marginal efficiency of capital is constant and independent of real balances. As a result, he shows that the equilibrium obtained by Mundell holds only in the short run and that in the long run the real rate of interest tends toward its original stationary-state level.

Tobin's (1965) analysis is also related to the effect of inflation on real money balances, with an emphasis on the cost of holding money balances as a liquidity premium for money. As inflation increases the nominal interest rate and the cost of holding money, it leads to a switch from money to bonds and other assets in individuals' portfolios. This increases savings and reduces the real interest rate.

III. EFFECT OF TAXATION ON THE FISHER EQUATION

The incorporation of taxation into the relationship between inflation and interest rates was suggested independently by Darby (1975), Tanzi (1976), and Feldstein (1976). Darby assumed arbitrarily that the liquidity effect and the income effect, which operate through the demand function for nominal balances, acted to exactly cancel in their effect on the real interest rate, so that the nominal interest rate increases in final equilibrium by exactly the increase in the rate of inflation. On the basis of this simplifying assumption, Darby restricts his analysis to the Fisher equation (1) and incorporates an income tax by assuming that borrowers and lenders are interested in a real after-tax interest rate and that the latter variable is maintained constant in the equilibrium solution. He assumes (as in the U.S. system) that interest receipts are taxable and interest payments are deductible. Assuming further the same marginal tax rate, t, on borrowers and lenders, Darby obtains a modified Fisher equation

$$i(1-t) - \pi = r^*$$

where r^* denotes the expected real after-tax interest rate, which is assumed to be constant and π is the expected rate of inflation.

Thus, the modified Fisher effect for a world with a simple income tax is given as

$$i = [1/(1-t)] (r^* + \pi) \tag{2}$$

Tanzi (1976) approaches taxes on nominal interest as one form of excess taxation that is owing to the nominal characteristic of the U.S. tax system (as well as the tax systems of many other Western countries). Tanzi shows that if one extends the Fisherian assumption—namely, that the required after-tax interest rate is constant—to a world with a tax, then the nominal interest rate will increase with inflation according to

$$i = [1/(1-t)] (r^* + \pi)$$

which is the same as the modified Fisher effect derived by Darby. Tanzi also shows that indexation of the tax system will lead to Fisher's classical results.

Feldstein's (1976) analysis starts with a model of a growing economy with inflation and an income tax wherein he observes that inflation and taxation tend to affect the equilibrium capital stock per capita. He considers implications of different tax rates on nominal and real income, as well as different tax rates for individuals and corporations.

However, for the U.S. corporate tax system, which incorporates no indexation, Feldstein approximates the impact of anticipated inflation on nominal interest as

$$di/d\pi = 1/(1-t) \tag{3}$$

which is identical to the conclusions of Darby (1975) and Tanzi (1976) and is larger than $di/d\pi = 1$ suggested by the Fisher equation for $1 > t > 0$.

Gandolfi (1976) developed a model of loanable funds that determines the equilibrium interest rate and places emphasis on investment decisions by firms. He recognized that while the imposition of a tax on profits has no effect on the Fisher equation when investment is financed by debt, a proportional income tax will cause a divergence between the after-tax real rate received by savers and the real rate paid by firms. In the latter case, Gandolfi derived the Fisher effect with taxes

$$di/d\pi = 1/(1-t)$$

He suggested also that this effect should be somewhat modified to take account of the Mundell real-balance effect on saving.

The firm can compensate the investor by more than the rise in the expected inflation rate because, owing to the tax deductibility of interest payments, the net marginal cost of interest to the firm increases only by

$$(1-tc)di/d\pi = (1-tc)\pi/(1-t)$$

where the corporate tax rate tc is equal to the personal tax rate t. Viewed alternatively, the net increase in the cost of capital as a result of inflation equals the rate of inflation in equilibrium. This also equals the nominal increase in the net marginal return on investment. Formally, this equilibrium condition can be written as

$$1 + r^* (1+\pi) = 1 + i(1-t) \tag{4}$$

where r^* denotes the real net marginal product of capital and t denotes the corporate tax rate, which is assumed to be the same as the personal tax rate t. The equilibrium solution is

$$[1/(1-t)] (r^* + \pi + r\pi) \tag{5}$$

The first term is the real rate of return in a world with tax rate t in the absence of inflation, while the second and third terms are the modified Fisher effect (where the third interaction term is often omitted for simplicity).

The results above are modified if the nominal capital gains created by inflation are taxed at the capital gains tax rate h. In this case, the basic equation (4) changes to

$$[1 + r^*] [1 + \pi(1-h)] = 1 + i(1-t) \tag{6}$$

From the firm's point of view, equation (6) yields

$$i = [1/(1-t)] [r^* + (1-h)\pi + (1-h)r\pi] \tag{6'}$$

The correction for inflation thus depends on the capital gains tax rate as well as on the regular (corporate and personal) tax rate. The combined effect of capital gains tax and corporate (and personal) income tax on interest rates outlined above was discussed in Feldstein and Summers (1978), Nielsen (1981), and Gandolfi (1982). The latter paper also discusses the relationship between inflation and the interest rate under alternative tax systems that differ in their treatment of capital gains and depreciation.

The intuitive interpretation of these results is that if a capital gains tax results in some reduction in returns to real assets because of inflation, the equilibrium rise required for returns on financial assets will be less.

It should be noted that the tax rate itself tends to affect the constant term in the Fisher equation, which is often viewed as the expected real rate. Properly specified as in equation (6'), the constant term becomes the expected after-tax real rate. It may not be appropriate to view it as a constant term if tax rates vary. Significant changes in tax brackets of representative investors (see the discussion of "bracket creep" in Feldstein and Summers (1978)) deserve careful attention in empirical work.

IV. GENERAL EQUILIBRIUM ANALYSIS OF INFLATION, INTEREST RATES, AND TAXATION

Darby's (1975) analysis, which leads to the modified Fisher effect, was based on a restricted partial-equilibrium analysis in the loanable funds market. The analysis was extended in a general-equilibrium framework in the recent works of Levi and Makin (1978, 1979) and Makin (1982, 1983).

The main characteristic of Levi and Makin's analysis is that investment (and possibly saving) depends on the real after-tax interest rate, while demand for money depends on the nominal market rate. (It should be noted, however, that the relevant interest rate is the after-tax, rather than the pretax, interest rate.) Using the above model (with the error mentioned), Levi and Makin derived a more complicated expression for the relationship between inflation and the interest rate, and were able to suggest a range for the marginal effect of expected inflation on the interest rate ($di/d\pi$) ranging between 0.857 and 1.333, compared with values of 1.0, suggested by the Fisher equation, and 1.5, calculated by the modified Fisher equation (assuming $t = 0.33$).

In a subsequent empirical paper, Levi and Makin (1979) extended the model by including inflation uncertainty σ, which is allowed to depress real investment and real income and, thereby, savings. They found that the negative impact on real investment is dominant; estimation reveals a significant negative relationship between inflation uncertainty and nominal interest.

Levi and Makin extended their analysis by adding the Phillips effect—positive relationship between inflation and growth. Assuming that inflation was not fully anticipated, they also considered the Friedman effect—the positive relationship between the amount of inflation and uncertainty about inflation (measured by standard deviation of the distribution of inflation).

On the basis of their theoretical analyses, Levi and Makin suggested a modification of the simple relation between nominal interest and inflation as

$$i = \beta_0 + \beta_1\pi_t + \beta_2\dot{y}_t + \beta_3\sigma_t + e_t \qquad (\beta_1 > 0; \beta_2, \beta_3 < 0)$$

where $\dot{y}$ denotes income growth in period t, σ_t denotes inflation uncertainty, and e_t is an error term. Making some reasonable assumptions about parameter values, the authors concluded that estimating the simple relationship between the interest rate and expected inflation (and omitting the two other variables) leads to a misspecified model in which the coefficient is underestimated. Empirical tests tended to confirm the effects hypothesized by Levi and Makin.

V. EMPIRICAL TESTS OF THE FISHER EFFECT IN THE UNITED STATES

An early empirical test of the Fisher effect was done by Fisher (1930) in conjunction with the development of his theory. More recent empirical works were initiated by Ball (1965) for the United Kingdom and Sargent (1972) for the United States.

Most early testing of the Fisher hypothesis concentrated on identifying alternative measures of anticipated inflation upon which to regress nominal interest rates. Investigations include those by Sargent (1972), Yohe and Karnosky (1969), Gibson (1970, 1972), Fama (1975), Carlson (1977 a, 1977 b), and Nelson and Schwert (1977). As all these investigations have ignored the role of taxation, they will not be surveyed in detail here. Some further discussion of these papers may be found in Roll (1972) and Sargent (1976).

The role of taxes in empirical testing of the Fisher hypothesis was first cast in a general-equilibrium framework by Levi and Makin (1978). They drew on the important earlier papers of Darby (1975), Feldstein (1976), and Tanzi (1976), which made explicit the economic fact that the behavior of investors depends upon expected after-tax real rates. When this reality was combined with a general-equilibrium framework that determined interest rates—as well as prices, output, and employment—Levi and Makin (1978) were able to demonstrate that a coefficient of unity describing the impact of anticipated inflation on nominal interest was both plausible and reasonable in a world where taxes were considered. Implications of the model that indicated a need for inclusion of additional explanatory variables, as well as anticipated inflation, were supported by results reported in Levi and Makin (1979). These additional explanatory variables included output, growth, and inflation uncertainty, as discussed earlier. More recently, surprise money growth and unanticipated fiscal deficits have also been shown to enter significantly into interest rate equations by Makin (1982, 1983).

Tanzi (1980 b) also includes explicit recognition of the role of taxes, together with roles played by explanatory variables and anticipated inflation, in explaining the behavior of interest rates. First, he compares alternative models describing formation of inflationary expectations with the Livingston survey[1] series on expected inflation. Next, he substitutes alternative series on expected inflation into the Fisher equation and finds coefficients of about 0.6 on anticipated inflation with the interest rate on a six-month treasury bill as dependent variable. For the interest rate on 12-month treasury bills, estimated coefficients on anticipated inflation are smaller and less robust.

Next, Tanzi suggests that important variables may have been left out of the regression indicated by the simple Fisher equation. He interprets the results in the context of the existing U.S. tax system and concludes that the results indicate possible "fiscal illusion" by

---

[1] This survey is conducted by the *Philadelphia Inquirer* under the guidance of Joseph Livingston and compiled semiannually by the Federal Reserve Bank of Philadelphia.

individual investors in the market. According to this view, individuals are compensated enough to keep the real, pretax interest rate constant, but the effect of income taxes in reducing the net-of-tax expected real rate of interest is ignored. In a competitive market, this assumption of fiscal illusion should also apply to borrowers, in particular those in the corporate sector, in order to explain the nonadjustment of interest to inflation. The effect of fiscal illusion would be inadequate changes in nominal interest rates relative to those required to keep constant the expected after-tax real rate in the face of a change in anticipated inflation.

Makin (1978) presents a model of an open economy in a world including taxes and flexible exchange rates that considers equilibrium in the market for labor, commodities, foreign exchange, and money. Using the equilibrium conditions in these markets, Makin derives the relationship between interest rates and expected inflation as

$$di/d\pi = 1/[(1-t) + \alpha]$$

where the added term α represents a set of parameters including elasticities of the demand for money, the demand for imports, and the supply of labor.

Using reasonable assumptions regarding those parameters, Makin finds that the term α is positive and thus concludes that it reduces the effect of expected inflation on nominal interest rates, compared with the modified Fisher effect. Viewed in this way, openness may help to account for findings of lower-than-anticipated effects of expected inflation on nominal interest rates. Further, the open-economy term can be expected to vary from country to country, as can the tax effect, which will depend, in turn, upon differences across countries in taxation of interest earnings, as well as upon differences in tax treatment of foreign exchange gains and losses.

The effect of inflation on long-term interest rates was estimated by Feldstein and Summers (1978). They first formulated a model of long-run inflationary expectations by estimating a Box-Jenkins autoregressive integrated moving average (ARIMA) model of the inflation rate.[2] Using the expectation derived from the model, they found that a 1 percent change in expected inflation increased the interest rate by 0.94 percentage point. Feldstein and Summers express the view that this result, which is not consistent with the modified Fisher model, is brought about by excess taxation of business in a nominal tax system that overstates profits by valuing inventory at historical costs and by

---

[2] ARIMA models explain inflation in terms of its own past history.

basing allowed depreciation allowances on historical costs. (See the Appendix for a full discussion of the effects of inflation on effective rates of taxation on individuals and businesses.) It should be noted that the Feldstein-Summers results are not robust under alternative estimation procedures, and the criticism that is sometimes directed at the use of full-sample data to generate a model of expectations for use within a sample applies to the ARIMA model used in the paper. (See Makin (1982) for a full discussion of such criticism.)

Summers (1982) presents a comprehensive study of the relationship between interest rates and inflation. Using data on interest rates and inflation for 1860–1979, he demonstrates that the real rate of interest fluctuates significantly. The average real interest rate ranged from 19.8 percent in the 1870s to −4.6 percent in the 1940s. It is not surprising that R^2 in the regression between interest and inflation is very low. Using data prior to World War II and a band spectral technique, Summers finds also that there is a very weak relationship between the interest rate on commercial paper and the long-term interest rate.

For the postwar data, Summers finds a significant positive association between interest rates and inflation, but the coefficient is much lower than the predicted coefficient of 1.33, which is derived in a world including taxes. In summarizing these results, Summers also concludes (p. 39) that "perhaps there is some unmeasurable variable which is correlated with inflation, and which affects required real returns." This conclusion is consistent with those of Fama (1981), Tanzi (1980 b), and Makin (1982, 1983). Summers also suggests the possibility of some form of money illusion in the financial markets. This idea of money illusion (or fiscal illusion) is consistent with analyses by Tanzi (1980 b) and by Modigliani and Cohn (1979).

VI. STUDIES ON THE RELATIONSHIP BETWEEN INTEREST RATES AND INFLATION IN OTHER COUNTRIES

As is true for most U.S. studies, a majority of investigations for other countries find a coefficient on anticipated inflation close to or below unity, indicating that in some cases nominal interest rates do not adjust sufficiently to maintain expected after-tax real rates in the face of faster anticipated inflation. Part of this result may be due to the varying degrees of openness alluded to by Makin (1978).

An early empirical investigation of the relationship between inflation and interest rates was done for the United Kingdom by Ball

(1965). Ball examined the relationship between a long-term interest rate and (l) a measure of liquidity (the ratio of money to income) and (2) expected inflation measured as a Koyck-type distributed lag on past rates of inflation. While the liquidity effect on the interest rate was negative and significant, the estimated effect of expected inflation was not significantly different from zero. It was negative for the prewar period (1921–39) and positive for the postwar period (1947–61). It is interesting to note that Ball viewed the rate of inflation as the price of holding money and tested this price effect on the interest rate. He did not consider the issue of real and nominal interest rates that was addressed in later works.

Tests of the tax effect and inflation on interest rates in Canada were performed by Carr and others (1976). In a test of the modified Fisher effect for Canadian data for 1959–72, these authors measured expected inflation using both a distributed-lag model and a synthetic prediction based on the rational-expectations hypothesis. Their results for alternative models indicate that the regression coefficient of anticipated inflation on both long-term and short-term interest rates tends to be about unity.

In a study of the Fisher effect for the Federal Republic of Germany, Siebke (1976) assumed a distributed-lag relationship between interest rates and inflation and estimated the impact of expected inflation on interest rates using, alternatively, the Koyck transformation approach and the Almon-lag procedure. Both results indicated a long-run coefficient of unity. The partial effect of inflation declined, however, when it was included along with the real changes in money supply.

In estimating the effect of price expectations on interest rates in the Federal Republic of Germany, Neumann (1977) developed a more general macroeconomic model that included several markets—namely,

(a) demand and supply for money
(b) demand and supply for domestic credit
(c) demand for foreign financial assets
(d) identifying restrictions to complete the model

Neumann found that for 1960–72 the coefficient of anticipated inflation on the interest rate (in a reduced-form model) was less than unity in the short run.

An interesting finding reported by Neumann is that the Deutsche Bundesbank (the central bank of the Federal Republic of Germany) was active in the market, and the discount rate set by the bank was adjusted to anticipated inflation, as well as to the adjusted foreign interest rate (which represented an alternative investment (loan) opportunity to German savers (borrowers)). Furthermore, the foreign interest rate appeared to have an independent positive effect on the domestic interest rate in the Federal Republic of Germany.

While Neumann's results were calculated in a period of fixed exchange rates, his findings may have implications for the recent periods of flexible exchange rates. His results and his discussion of central bank policy may also be relevant to other countries.

In a recent study of interest rates in Japan, Kama (1981) used a distributed-lag regression between interest rates and prices. He found (p. 26) that a 1 percent increase in the consumer price index in a given month increased the call money rate by 0.24 percentage point after 18 months. The effect on the bond rate was even lower.

In a recent study of Argentina for 1964–76, Leiderman (1979) followed Fama's version of the Fisher hypothesis by regressing the inflation rate on the interest rate. He obtained a coefficient larger than unity, which indicated that the interest rate adjusted only partially to inflation, with an implied coefficient of 0.5.

Testing the efficiency of the financial market, however, Leiderman could not reject the null hypothesis of market efficiency in the sense that the interest rate used all the information about subsequent prices that was available in the form of past price data. (Note that Nelson and Schwert's (1977) criticism of Fama (1975) regarding the power of such a test also applies here.)

Finally, in a recent comparative study for nine industrial countries, Mandelker and Tandon (1981) extended Fama's approach to test interest rates as predictors of inflation for 1966–79. The results indicated that some of the coefficients were on the order of unity for most of the countries, particularly when the regression was restricted to periods with no wage-price controls. These results led Mandelker and Tandon to conclude that movements in short-term interest rates can serve as proxies for changes in anticipated inflation. The results also indicated that the constant term, which they interpreted as an estimate of the real interest rate, is not significantly different from zero, and often is negative. The results suggest also that for the Netherlands there is no relationship between the interest rate and inflation. In Japan, the interest rate adjusts only partly to inflation; while in the Federal Republic of Germany, the implied coefficient of the interest rate on anticipated inflation is about 2.

The results for Japan, with an implied adjustment coefficient of 0.6, are consistent in direction with the findings of Kama (1981), while the results for the Federal Republic of Germany are different from those reported by Neumann (1977) for an earlier period. Since the inflation in Germany was lower than for other countries, it is possible that the Mandelker-Tandon results reflect the Deutsche Bundesbank's policy of raising its discount rate in response to higher foreign interest rates. If this is true (a proposition that was not tested), it is consistent with the policy described by Neumann.

VII. VOLATILITY OF INTEREST RATES

The increased volatility and variability of interest rates in the United States in recent years has led economists to study their determinants and their impact on the behavior of economic units (see, for example, Friedman (1982) and Walsh (1982)). An interesting and relevant question for this paper to address is the effect of inflation and taxation on the variability of the interest rate. This effect is analyzed by Makin and Tanzi (see Chapter 4 of this volume), and their arguments are reproduced below. When taxes are considered, recall that the aim is to define as the investor's objective an after-tax real rate r^*, written as

$$r_t^* = i_t (1 - \tau) - \pi_t (1 - \tau') \tag{7}$$

where τ denotes the perceived marginal tax rate on interest income i_t and τ' denotes a representative perceived marginal tax rate on returns from alternative (to interest-bearing) assets that is assumed to equal, on average, the expected inflation rate π_t. Transposing equation (7) to place i_t on the left-hand side gives

$$i_t = [1/(1 - \tau)] [r_t^* + (1 - \tau')\pi_t] \tag{8}$$

Turning to the question of interest rate volatility, an expression for the variance of interest rates, based upon equation (8), is given by

$$\sigma_i^2 = (1/1-\tau)^2 \, \sigma_{r^*}^2 + [(1-\tau')/(1-\tau)]^2 \, \sigma_\pi^2$$
$$+ 2[(1-\tau')/(1-\tau)]^2 \, \theta_{r_\pi^*} \, \sigma_{r^*} \, \sigma_\pi \tag{9}$$

where σ_x^2 denotes the variance of variable x ($x = r^*,\pi$) and $\theta_{r_\pi^*}$ denotes the coefficient of correlation between r^* and π. Notice that when taxes are ignored, as in equation (1), the variance of i is written as

$$\sigma_i^2 = \sigma_{r^*}^2 + \sigma_\pi^2 + 2\theta_{r_\pi^*} \, \sigma_{r^*} \, \sigma_\pi \tag{10}$$

The effects of considering tax rates are evident from comparing equations (9) and (10). Ignoring the effects of possible correlation between r^* and π ($\theta_{r_\pi^*} = 0$ for now), the volatility of after-tax real rates unambiguously produces *more* volatility of i, since for any $\tau > 0$, $[1/(1-\tau)]^2 > 1$. (As an example, given $\tau = 0.35$, $[1/(1-\tau)]^2 = 2.37$; or, given an average tax rate of 35 percent on interest income, a rise of 1 percent in the variance of the after-tax real rate increases the variance of i by 2.37 times the effect of an increase in the variance of the real rate when taxes are ignored, as in equation (10).) Furthermore, the higher is τ, the greater will be the volatility of i, ceteris paribus. Of course, this argument assumes that there is no fiscal illusion, so that tax effects are fully recognized by investors. Uncertainty over future tax policy can have a powerful impact on the observed volatility of i. Equation (9) suggests also that the effects of a rise in the variance of expected inflation upon the observed variance of i will be magnified as long as τ', the marginal tax rate on alternative assets, is below τ, the marginal tax rate on interest income.

Since theoretical considerations (the Mundell-Tobin effect) suggest that there is a negative correlation between anticipated inflation and the real interest rate ($\theta r_\pi < 0$), there will be some dampening of the effects of changes in variance of real rates and in variance of anticipated inflation in both tax and nontax cases, but the dampening effect will be reduced, for almost any conceivable values of relevant parameters, when tax effects are considered.[3]

It is interesting to note that since empirical studies suggest a positive relationship between the rate of inflation and the variance of inflation, an increase in the average rate of inflation will lead to greater volatility of interest rates, which will be further increased by the presence of taxes on interest earnings.

VIII. CONCLUDING COMMENTS

The paper summarizes the theory concerning the relationship between expected inflation and interest rates in a world with taxation, following the initial framework developed by Fisher. Several extensions of the basic theory are discussed, including the Mundell real-balance effect, the Tobin substitution effect, formulations of a general-equilibrium model from which one can derive an interest rate equation as a reduced form, and an extension to an open economy.

The earlier postwar empirical studies discussed focus largely on a positive relationship between nominal interest rates and expected inflation. Later studies attempt to control for movements in the expected after-tax real rate. In general, empirical studies have reported apparent underadjustment of nominal interest rates to changes in anticipated inflation, especially in the light of the impact of taxes on

---

[3] The effect of a rise in $\sigma_{r^*}^2$ upon σ_i^2 (where, for convenience, $\sigma_{r^*}^2 \approx \sigma_\pi^2$) is given by

$$\partial\sigma_i^2/\partial\sigma_{r^*}^2 = \frac{1+(1-\tau')[2\theta r_\pi^* + (1-\tau')]}{(1-\tau)^2}$$

when tax rates are considered and, ignoring taxes, by

$$\partial\sigma_i^2/\partial\sigma_{r^*}^2 = 2(1 + \theta r_\pi^*)$$

For $\tau = 0.35$, $\tau' = 0.25$, and $\theta r_\pi^* = -0.25$, the first of these equations equals 2.81, while the second equals 1.55. If $\tau' = 0$, the first equation equals 3.55; and if $\tau' = \tau$, it equals 2.6.

interest earnings. In some instances, indicated adjustments could only be rationalized by negative after-tax expected real rates during periods of accelerating inflation.

Resolution of the puzzle of apparent underadjustment of rates has been crucially related to the role played by introduction into the analysis of taxes on interest earnings. That step, which implied an adjustment coefficient of nominal interest rates to anticipated inflation of well above unity in the simplest case, prompted investigators to pursue other avenues, including the role played by taxes in rationalizing coefficients significantly below unity. The excessive gap between a theory that recognized the role of taxes and empirical findings led investigators such as Levi and Makin (1978) and Tanzi (1980 b) to expand theory in a manner that expedited identification of additional relevant explanatory variables in interest rate equations. Further progress in this direction has come in the wake of the Federal Reserve Board's new operating procedures, adopted in October 1979, and the emphasis they place on control of the money stock. After passage of the Economic Recovery Tax Act in August 1981, these procedures resulted in a "tight monetary and easy fiscal" stance for the United States. Makin (1982, 1983) investigates the role of fiscal policy variables and unanticipated money supply changes in affecting real, and thereby nominal, interest rates, while simultaneously allowing for taxation of interest earnings.

A number of other steps have been required to bridge the gap between theory and the actual behavior of interest rates. The role that tax considerations have played in this process has centered on allowing for tax treatment of capital gains and losses on alternatives to financial assets. This line of investigation is suggested by the work of Tanzi (1982 a and Chapter 6 of this volume) on money demand. Another topic worth investigating is the tax treatment of foreign exchange gains and losses, since, in an open-economy setting, interest rates and exchange rates are determined simultaneously. Work by Levi (1977) represents a promising start in this direction.

Another explanation, suggested by Feldstein and Summers (1978), for the nonadjustment of interest rates relates to the real effect of inflation on corporate profits owing to the tax treatment of depreciation of inventory and to depreciation that tends to result in overstatement of profits. Under such circumstances, inflation may reduce the firms' demand for loans by reducing their ability to repay, as well as their incentive to borrow money for investment projects. (See the Appendix for further discussion.) While the real cost of loans may decline with inflation, the real after-tax return from the use of a loan may also decline with inflation. This phenomenon may account for some apparent underadjustment of nominal interest rates to changes in anticipated inflation. The role of the negative relationship between inflation and corporate profits in affecting equilibrium and after-tax real returns merits further investigation.

A further explanation for underadjustment of nominal interest rates to changes in anticipated inflation, suggested particularly by Tanzi (1980 a, 1982 b) and Summers (1981), is the existence of "money or fiscal illusion" in the market. This illusion is said to decline over time as investors become accustomed to a change in the inflationary environment. This hypothesis is inconsistent with the notion that participants in financial markets are fully rational agents.

All of these considerations have been part of the rapid progress made in theoretical and empirical analysis of interest rate behavior. An important part of this progress has involved explicit recognition of the fact that actions of economic agents are governed by after-tax interest rates. What remains to be done is to include after-tax treatment of foreign exchange gains and losses along with interest rates (after-tax interest parity) in an open-economy, general-equilibrium setting. This approach will enable further analysis of the implications for the differential impact of monetary and fiscal policies pursued at home and abroad on alternative tax treatments of interest earnings and payments and foreign exchange gains and losses.

IX. AGENDA FOR RESEARCH

It is typical to observe taxes levied on nominal magnitudes, such as nominal interest rates, nominal capital gains, and nominal net profit flows. This fact implies that inflation or deflation results in significant and often unintended changes in the real, after-tax rates of return or relative prices that govern economic behavior. The classical assumption that monetary changes alter prices but produce no real effects may well be valid in a world without taxes, but it is invalid in a world with taxes. An agenda for research involves explanation of the roles played by taxes in economic behavior, in order to change (erroneous) ideas based upon analyses that ignore taxes. Specific questions that need further investigation include the following:

(1) How does the tax treatment of interest payments and receipts by individuals and corporations affect the real impact of aggregate monetary and fiscal policy measures at home and abroad?

(2) How might widely employed arbitrage-equilibrium conditions, such as interest parity, be affected by consideration of tax treatment of interest payments and receipts and of capital gains and losses by various governments?

(3) What are the implications for question (1) of incorporating answers to question (2) into a general-equilibrium, open-economy model designed to investigate effects of monetary and fiscal policy measures under alternative exchange rate regimes?

(4) What are the implications of taxes for the theory of exchange rate behavior?

(5) How might widespread use of indexed contracts in securities markets and labor markets alter the impact of inflation or deflation on real after-tax returns or relative prices?

Appendix

Impact of Inflation on Personal and Business Income Tax

Personal income tax

The personal income tax systems in most Western countries were defined until recently in nominal terms as far as personal deductions and tax tables were concerned. In this system, inflation tended to affect the real tax burden on the individual and his saving behavior. As discussed earlier, the taxation of nominal interest income at the personal level is one of the reasons given for the modified Fisher effect of expected inflation on interest rates.

A comprehensive analysis of the effects of inflation on the personal tax in an international context is presented in a recent book by Tanzi (1980 a). The book covers implications of the nominal tax system, discusses problems and solutions, and presents the experience of other countries with nominal tax systems. Several suggestions for adjustment and indexation are included in a conference volume on inflation and the income tax edited by Aaron (1976). Furthermore, discussions of the effects of inflation on personal tax burdens are included in a recent survey article by Nowotny (1980).

The Appendix will briefly present some aspects of the effects of nominally based personal taxes in inflationary periods and their possible effects on the supply of, and demand for, loans. For a more general framework, interested readers should see Tanzi (1980 a), Aaron (1976), and Nowotny (1980).

In a study of the U.S. economy for 1947–79, Steuerle and Hartzmark (1981) have shown that the average tax rate (including federal, state, and local taxes) increased during 1947–79 by 3.4 percentage points, from 10.1 percent to 13.5 percent. Furthermore, the percentage of returns paying a marginal tax of 22 percent or more increased from 10 percent in 1961 to 36 percent in 1979. These results may indicate that the recent tax rate reduction in the United States may partly compensate for increases in the rate during inflationary periods. A study of the United States by Joines (1981) indicates that the fraction of the labor force whose income was subject to taxation increased between 1953 and 1975 from 74.5 percent to 80.5 percent. Also, the marginal tax rate on labor income increased during that period from 21 percent to 27 percent.

Aggregate figures on the effects of inflation on effective taxation may be misleading. Nowotny (1980) refers to empirical studies for various countries that generally indicate that large family groups lost more than other groups because of the declining real value of exemptions. This change has tended to have a regressive effect on income distribution. A recent calculation for the United States by Arak (1976) indicates that low-income families have lost significantly owing to the fact that personal exemptions and maximum standard deductions are fixed in dollar (nominal) terms.

Important effects of inflation on the personal income tax depend on the taxation of nominal capital gains and the nominal interest rate. As Tanzi (1976) emphasized, taxation of the nominal interest rate tends to increase the real tax on interest income owing to a tendency for nominal interest rates to rise by an amount insufficient to maintain stable after-tax real returns. Similarly, with a nominal capital gains tax, individuals may face a tax liability even though the price of taxable assets has declined in real terms.

As suggested by Hendershott and Sheng Cheng Hu (1981), the treatment of interest costs as a deduction from taxable income for individuals, which is allowed in the United States and in some other countries, enables those individuals to benefit from the nominal aspect of the tax system. This is true in particular for individuals with large debt payments on their assets (e.g., homeowners with mortgages). The benefit from interest rate deductibility, in particular on housing, tends to increase the inequity of income distribution, since interest-rate deductions are more common among middle-income and high-income families. Furthermore, the exclusion of income in kind, in terms of housing services, from taxable income, which is a norm in many Western countries, has a regressive effect on the distribution of income. The deductibility of interest payments may, in addition, discourage other forms of saving in favor of home ownership. An empirical study by Tanzi (1977) for the United States showed that the main beneficiaries of the tax treatment of nominal interest income and deductions were the middle-income classes. Both higher-income and lower-income groups lost.

An important effect of inflation on the personal tax burden arises from taxation of nominal capital gains. As inflation increases the nominal value of assets, it creates a nominal capital gain, which often may be associated with a real capital loss if the price of the asset increases by a smaller percentage than the rate of inflation. Tanzi (1980 a) discusses this problem and also presents some alternative solutions and procedures used by different countries to correct the effects of inflation.

For the United States, an important component of the capital gains tax is the taxation of capital gains from the sale of corporate securities, while taxation of gains from the sale of housing can frequently be avoided. Feldstein and Slemrod (1978) claim that the capital gains tax on the sale of securities is excessive, since it is imposed on nominal gains that are largely caused by inflation—that is, real capital gains are much lower. Using a sample of income tax returns submitted to the Internal Revenue Service in fiscal year 1978, they calculated real capital gains using a consumer price index deflator and found that the tax liability of real capital gains was only $661 million, though the actual tax paid was $1,138 million. The excess tax paid was therefore $477 million, an increase of 70 percent over the inflation-adjusted tax. Feldstein and Slemrod also pointed out the randomness of the rate at which individuals with the same real capital gains are required to pay taxes on very different nominal gains. Their main recommendation was that individuals pay taxes only on real capital gains.

Feldstein, Slemrod, and Yitzhaki (1980) and Feldstein and Slemrod (1980) discussed and empirically estimated the effects of capital gains taxes when high capital gains taxes prevented individuals from realizing real capital gains on their portfolios. They also discussed the different effects of taxes on different assets, which led to misallocation of asset holdings and investment and welfare costs associated with the nonoptimality of this allocation.

Personal income taxes have an important effect on the supply of labor, since workers are interested in their after-tax income (see, for example, Macrae and Yezer (1976)). The inclusion of an income tax is important in theoretical derivation and empirical estimation of labor supply schedules and in determination of an equilibrium wage. The effects of inflation and taxation on the equilibrium wage were emphasized in a recent work by Tanzi and Iden (1981). The main idea is that in order to keep the same real wage in a period of inflation, the after-tax wage should increase by the rate of inflation. In a progressive tax system, when bracket creep is observed, wage rates must increase by more than the rate of inflation to compensate the individual for the increase in his marginal tax rate (for a given real wage and real income). This will lead to an increase in real (pretax) wage rates paid by employers.

Tanzi and Iden (1981) suggest that the response of wages W to inflation i depends upon the average and marginal tax rates—that is,

$$(\Delta W/W) = (i - ta)/(i - t_M)$$

where $\Delta W/W$ denotes the change in wage rate, ta denotes the average tax rate, and t_M denotes the marginal tax rate on the wage increase. This effect of a nominal progressive tax system may have important macroeconomic implications.

Effects of inflation and taxes on business income

Inflation also affects the real tax burden of corporations where the tax system is based on nominal values. This is true in most modern countries.

The problem of inflation accounting has attracted significant attention in accounting literature. In a summary of inflation-accounting issues, Vasarhelyi and Pearson (1979) present the basic taxonomy of the historically based accounting versus valuation- (or replacement-) based accounting, as well as a classification of the methods of research. Discussion regarding the reporting of inflation in the United Kingdom is given by Piper (1979), while a more general analysis of accounting treatments in continental Europe is given in Schoenfeld (1979). The survey of literature in this section deals with the economic implications of different accounting techniques rather than with the details of accounting methods.

On a theoretical level, it is shown by Stiglitz (1981) that the real effect of taxes on firms in an inflationary economy is created primarily by a tax system that is not fully indexed for inflation. In particular, Stiglitz (1973) claims that a fully indexed tax system will have a neutral effect on the firm. Stiglitz's condition for a neutral system is

(a) Depreciation must be at replacement cost and at the "correct" rate.

(b) Taxes on the interest rate must apply only to real interest rates, and only real interest rates are tax deductible.

(c) Capital gains and losses must be taxed (at full rates) on an overall basis, rather than on a realization basis.

The above conditions are consistent with those specified in an earlier work by Sandmo (1974) that analyzed the effects of corporate taxes on investment incentives.

The main aspects of nominal corporate income taxes discussed in economics and accounting literature are (a) the treatment of depreciation and allowances for tax purposes, and (b) the treatment of valuation of the inventory stock and the implied cost of materials employed in calculating the cost of goods sold.

Depreciation allowances based on historical costs tend to underestimate the real cost of capital services used by the firm. This has two effects:

(1) The accumulated depreciation fund is lower than replacement costs and will not therefore be sufficient to replace the old machines.

(2) The fact that costs of capital service are underestimated leads to over-estimation of the firm's real profits. As a result, the tax liability of firms increases in real terms without an increase in real economic profits. Therefore, after-tax profitability declines.

In inventory valuation, the cost of materials is calculated using either the first-in-first-out (FIFO) or the last-in-first-out (LIFO) method. If the FIFO method is used, the costs of materials, which are based on historical purchase prices, are underestimated and real profits are overstated. This, again, leads to an excessive tax on corporations in a period of inflation. If the LIFO method is used, costs of materials are evaluated in current (or last) prices and thus represent approximately the replacement value of the materials used. This aspect of accounting practices in the United States was discussed by Davidson and Weil (1976), Shoven and Bulow (1976), and Fabricant (1978) in reference to a proposal made by the Financial Accounting Standards Board. More recent discussions are presented by Feldstein and Summers (1978), Arak (1980), and Gonedes (1981).

A discussion of inventory valuation methods used in Scandinavia and several Western European industrial countries with regard to means of eliminating inflation from inventory accounting is presented in Strömberg (1977).

With regard to the effect of taxation and inflation on depreciation allowances, the use of book value rather than replacement value depreciation tends to reduce the real value of depreciation allowances compared with allowances in a stable economy. This leads some authors to suggest replacement-cost depreciation rather than historically based depreciation (see, for example, Davidson and Weil (1976)). Other authors, such as Landskroner and Levy (1979), have suggested and discussed methods of accelerated depreciation in which expenditures on assets are depreciated (and deducted from income before tax) over shorter periods. While both methods tend to increase the present value of depreciation allowances and reduce the tax burden on corporations, they differ in some ways. First, on a theoretical level, when replacement-cost depreciation is used, the present value of the depreciation allowance is not unaffected by inflation, since the discount factor of the depreciation stream also increases with inflation. As a result, the net present value of replacement-cost depreciation declines with inflation. On the other hand, accelerated depreciation may increase the present value of the depreciation allowance compared with noninflationary situations. As a result, government tax receipts from the business sector will decline in real terms.[4]

As a practical matter, accelerated depreciation is easier to apply, since calculation of replacement value is sometimes very difficult and may require some arbitrary assumptions. For example, how does one determine the component of price increase when the new machines are not only more expensive but also of better quality? Many governments use accelerated depreciation, and the U.S. Government has included such measures in the Economic Recovery Tax Act of 1981.

Two other aspects of the effects of taxation and inflation on taxation of corporate income are the deductibility of nominal interest expenses and the capital gains tax. While the taxation of nominal interest leads to excess taxation of lenders, it tends to benefit borrowers, who can deduct their full interest payments from their taxable income. This is particularly true when the interest rate is not fully adjusted according to the modified Fisher effect. For example, consider the case where interest is adjusted according to the classical Fisher effect, $i = r + \pi$, where r and i denote the real and nominal interest rates and π denotes the expected inflation rate, which is equal here to the actual inflation rate. The after-tax interest rate for borrowers will decline from $r(1 - t)$ to $i(1 - t) = r(1 - t) - \pi t$. The actual gain is much higher if the firm has long-term debts and the current inflation was not expected (so that the interest on the firm's loans does not reflect the expected inflation). As suggested by Feldstein and Summers (1978), firms in the United States have benefited significantly from their net debtor positions.

With regard to capital gains taxes, Feldstein and Summers (1978) argue that taxes paid by stockholders on capital gains and dividends, as well as taxes on interest payments by suppliers, should be considered part of a corporation's overall tax.

In a detailed calculation for the year 1977, Feldstein and Summers determined that while the direct corporate tax was 42.5 percent of corporate income taxation on dividends, taxation of interest income and capital appreciation raised the tax rate to 66.3 percent. The extra tax attributable to inflation was about 60 percent of the corporate tax for 1973–77. The results of the significant increase in the corporate tax burden owing to inflation are not consistent with the study by Gonedes (1981), who for 1947–74 found that the tax-effects hypothesis (p. 227) "that real rates of income tax will vary directly with the rate of inflation" is not supported by the data. He explains these surprising results for a nominal tax system by saying that (p. 258)

---

[4] It should be noted that the implicit (or explicit) assumption of this discussion is that the government does not want to use inflation as a method of increasing business (and household) taxes. This assumption is not always realistic.

"indirect indexation" was attained by alternative options, such as liberalization of depreciation rules. An additional reduction in taxes was attained by the increased use of debt-induced tax shelters.

In evaluating excess taxation of the corporate sector, one should consider several implications. First, excess taxation on corporations and preferential treatment of housing may have been important causes of the decline in the stock market and the decline in corporate investment in the 1970s.

Second, the induced reduction in profitability also reduced the demand for investment and the derived demand for loans by business firms. This reduction in corporate loan demand in real terms suggests that the real return to savers will decline with an increase in the rate of inflation and that the nominal interest rate will rise by less than is predicted by the modified Fisher effect. The reason will be a drop in the real rate induced by a negative shift on corporate loan demand that, in turn, is caused by the harmful effect of inflation on profits.

Finally, the excess taxes paid by corporations finance government expenditures and may be viewed as another form of "inflation tax" that is added to other taxes collected by the government to finance its operations. A reduction in excess taxation of corporations without a change in government budget expenditures leads to an increase in the budget deficit, a reduction in planned expenditures, or an increase in other taxes (e.g., an increase in the direct rate of personal or corporate income taxes).

A recent estimate by the Office of Tax Analysis in the U.S. Treasury, reported by Auerbach (1982), indicates that a proposal to correct corporate taxation by a method of accelerated depreciation (the Economic Recovery Tax Act of 1981) may lead, when it is enacted in 1986, to a loss of $55 billion in corporate taxes. If this is done, it will largely eliminate the corporate income tax as a source of government revenue. (For comparison, corporate taxes paid in 1980 were about $65 billion.)

References

Aaron, Henry, *Inflation and the Income Tax* (Washington: The Brookings Institution, 1976).

Arak, Marcelle, "The Effect of the Federal Individual Income Tax on Real After-Tax Incomes During Inflation," *Southern Economic Journal* (Chapel Hill, North Carolina), Vol. 42 (April 1976), pp. 720–23.

————, "Inflation and Stock Values: Is Our Tax Structure the Villain?" *Quarterly Review*, Federal Reserve Bank of New York, Vol. 5 (Winter 1980), pp. 3–13.

Auerbach, Alan J., *Taxes, Firm Financial Policy, and Cost of Capital: An Empirical Analysis*, Working Paper No. 955, National Bureau of Economic Research (Cambridge, Massachusetts, August 1982).

Ball, R.J., "Some Econometric Analysis of the Long-Term Rate of Interest in the United Kingdom, 1921–61," *Manchester School of Economics and Social Studies* (Manchester, England), Vol. 33 (January 1965), pp. 45–96.

Carlson, John A. (1977 a), "A Study of Price Forecasts," *Annals of Economic and Social Measurement* (New York), Vol. 6 (Winter 1977), pp. 27–56.

————, (1977 b), "Short-Term Interest Rates as Predictors of Inflation: Comment," *American Economic Review* (Nashville, Tennessee), Vol. 67 (June 1977), pp. 469–75.

Carr, Jack, and others, "Tax Effects, Price Expectations and the Nominal Rate of Interest," *Economic Inquiry* (Long Beach, California), Vol. 14 (June 1976), pp. 259–69.

Darby, Michael R., "The Financial and Tax Effects of Monetary Policy on Interest Rates," *Economic Inquiry* (Long Beach, California), Vol. 13 (June 1975), pp. 266–74.

Davidson, Sidney, and Roman Weil, "Inflation Accounting: Implications of the FASB Proposal," in Aaron (1976), pp. 81–120.

Fabricant, Solomon, "Accounting for Business Income under Inflation: Current Issues and Views in the United States," *Review of Income and Wealth* (New Haven, Connecticut), Series 24 (March 1978), pp. 1–24.

Fama, Eugene F., "Short-Term Interest Rates as Predictors of Inflation," *American Economic Review* (Nashville, Tennessee), Vol. 65 (June 1975), pp. 269–82.

————, "Stock Returns, Real Activity, Inflation and Money," *American Economic Review* (Nashville, Tennessee), Vol. 71 (September 1981), pp. 545–65.

Feldstein, Martin S., "Inflation, Income Taxes, and the Rate of Interest: A Theoretical Analysis," *American Economic Review* (Nashville, Tennessee), Vol. 66 (December 1976), pp. 809–20.

————, and Lawrence Summers, "Inflation Tax Rules and the Long-Term Interest Rate," *Brookings Papers on Economic Activity: 1* (1978), The Brookings Institution (Washington), pp. 61–99.

————, and Lawrence Summers, "Inflation and the Taxation of Capital Income in the Corporate Sector," *National Tax Journal* (Philadelphia), Vol. 32 (December 1979), pp. 445–70.

————, and Joel Slemrod, "Inflation and the Excess Taxation of Capital Gains on Corporate Stock," *National Tax Journal* (Philadelphia), Vol. 31 (June 1978), pp. 107–18.

————, and Joel Slemrod, "Personal Taxation, Portfolio Choice, and the Effect of the Corporation Income Tax," *Journal of Political Economy* (Chicago), Vol. 88 (October 1980), pp. 854–66.

————, Joel Slemrod, and Shlomo Yitzhaki, "The Effects of Taxation on the Selling of Corporate Stock and the Realization of Capital Gains," *Quarterly Journal of Economics* (Cambridge, Massachusetts), Vol. 94 (June 1980), pp. 777–91.

Fisher, Irving, *Appreciation and Interest* (1896; New York: A.M. Kelley, reprint, 1965).

————, *The Theory of Interest* (New York: Macmillan, 1930).

Friedman, Benjamin M., *Federal Reserve Policy, Interest Rate Volatility, and the U.S. Capital Raising Mechanism*, Working Paper No. 917, National Bureau of Economic Research (Cambridge, Massachusetts, June 1982).

Gandolfi, Arthur E., "Taxation and the 'Fisher Effect'," *Journal of Finance* (New York), Vol. 31 (December 1976), pp. 1375–86.

————, "Inflation, Taxation and Interest Rates," *Journal of Finance* (New York), Vol. 37 (June 1982), pp. 797–807.

Gibson, William E., "Price Expectations Effects on Interest Rates," *Journal of Finance* (New York), Vol. 25 (March 1970), pp. 19–34.

————, "Interest Rates and Inflationary Expectations: New Evidence," *American Economic Review* (Nashville, Tennessee), Vol. 62 (December 1972), pp. 854–65.

Gonedes, Nicholas J., "Evidence on the 'Tax Effects' of Inflation under Historical Cost Accounting Methods," *Journal of Business* (Chicago), Vol. 54 (April 1981), pp. 227–70.

Hendershott, Patric H., and Sheng Cheng Hu, "Inflation and Extraordinary Returns on Owner-Occupied Housing: Some Implications for Capital Allocation and Productivity Growth," *Journal of Macroeconomics* (Detroit, Michigan), Vol. 3 (Spring 1981), pp. 177–203.

Joines, Douglas H., "Estimates of Effective Marginal Tax Rates on Factor Incomes," *Journal of Business* (Chicago), Vol. 54 (April 1981), pp. 191–226.

Kama, Kunio, "The Determination of Interest Rates in Japan, 1967–1978," *Economic Review* (Tokyo), Vol. 32 (January 1981), pp. 21–33.

Karni, Edi, "Inflation and Real Interest Rate: A Long-Term Analysis," *Journal of Political Economy* (Chicago), Vol. 80 (1972), pp. 365–74.

Lahiri, Kajal, "Inflationary Expectations: Their Formation and Interest Rate Effects," *American Economic Review* (Nashville, Tennessee), Vol. 66 (March 1976), pp. 124–31.

Landskroner, Yoram, and Haim Levy, "Inflation, Depreciation and Optimal Production," *European Economic Review* (Amsterdam), Vol. 12 (December 1979), pp. 353–67.

Leiderman, Leonardo, "Interest Rates as Predictors of Inflation in a High-Inflation Semi-Industrialized Economy," *Journal of Finance* (New York), Vol. 34 (September 1979), pp. 1019–25.

Levi, Maurice D., "Taxation and 'Abnormal' International Capital Flows," *Journal of Political Economy* (Chicago), Vol. 85 (June 1977), pp. 635–46.

————, and John H. Makin, "Anticipated Inflation and Interest Rates: Further Interpretation of Findings on the Fisher Equation," *American Economic Review* (Nashville, Tennessee), Vol. 68 (December 1978), pp. 801–12.

————, and John H. Makin, "Fisher, Phillips, Friedman and the Measured Impact of Inflation on Interest," *Journal of Finance* (New York), Vol. 34 (March 1979), pp. 35–52.

————, and John H. Makin, "Fisher, Phillips, Friedman and the Measured Impact of Inflation on Interest: A Reply," *Journal of Finance* (New York), Vol. 36 (September 1981), pp. 963–69.

Lutz, Friedrich A., "Inflation and the Rate of Interest," *Quarterly Review*, Banca Nazionale del Lavoro (Rome), No. 109 (June 1974), pp. 99–117.

Macrae, C. Duncan, and Anthony M.J. Yezer, "The Personal Income Tax and Family Labor Supply," *Southern Economic Journal* (Chapel Hill, North Carolina), Vol. 43 (July 1976), pp. 783–92.

Makin, John H., "Anticipated Inflation and Interest Rates in an Open Economy," *Journal of Money, Credit and Banking* (Columbus, Ohio), Vol. 10 (August 1978), pp. 275–89.

————, "Effects of Inflation Control Programs on Expected Real Interest Rates," *Staff Papers*, International Monetary Fund (Washington), Vol. 29 (June 1982), pp. 204–32.

————, "Real Interest, Money Surprises, Anticipated Inflation and Fiscal Deficits," *Review of Economics and Statistics* (Cambridge, Massachusetts), Vol. 65 (August 1983), pp. 374–84.

Mandelker, Gershon, and Kishore Tandon, "The Effects of Inflation on Common Stock Returns: An International Comparison 1966–1979," paper presented at Financial Management Association Meetings at Cincinnati, Ohio (unpublished, October 1981).

Modigliani, Franco, and Richard Cohn, "Inflation, Rational Valuation and the Market," *Financial Analysts Journal* (New York), Vol. 35 (March/April 1979), pp. 24–44.

Mundell, Robert A., "Inflation and Real Interest," *Journal of Political Economy* (Chicago), Vol. 71 (June 1963), pp. 280–83.

Nelson, Charles R., and G. William Schwert, "Short-Term Interest Rates as Predictors of Inflation: On Testing the Hypothesis that the Real Rate of Interest Is Constant," *American Economic Review* (Nashville, Tennessee), Vol. 67 (June 1977), pp. 478–86.

Neumann, Manfred J.M., "Price Expectations and the Interest Rate In an Open Economy: Germany, 1960–72," *Journal of Money, Credit and Banking* (Columbus, Ohio), Vol. 9 (February 1977), pp. 206–27.

Nielsen, Niels Christian, "Inflation and Taxation," *Journal of Monetary Economics* (Amsterdam), Vol. 7 (March 1981), pp. 261–70.

Nowotny, Ewald, "Inflation and Taxation: Reviewing the Macroeconomic Issues," *Journal of Economic Literature* (Nashville, Tennessee), Vol. 18 (September 1980), pp. 1025–49.

Piper, A.G., "Reporting the Effects of Inflation in Company Accounts in the United Kingdom," *Quarterly Review of Economics and Business* (Urbana, Illinois), Vol. 19 (Spring 1979), pp. 45–56.

Roll, Richard, "Interest Rates on Monetary Assets and Commodity Price Index Changes," *Journal of Finance* (New York), Vol. 27 (May 1972), pp. 251–77.

Sandmo, Agnar, "Investment Incentives and Corporate Income Tax," *Journal of Political Economy* (Chicago), Vol. 82 (April 1974), pp. 287–302.

Sargent, Thomas J., "Anticipated Inflation and the Nominal Rate of Interest," *Quarterly Journal of Economics* (Cambridge, Massachusetts), Vol. 86 (May 1972), pp. 212–25.

————, "Interest Rates and Expected Inflation: A Selective Summary of Recent Research," *Explorations in Economic Research*, National Bureau of Economic Research (New York), Vol. 3 (Summer 1976), pp. 303–25.

Schoenfeld, Hanns-Martin W., "Inflation Accounting—Development of Theory and Practice in Continental Europe," *Quarterly Review of Economics and Business* (Urbana, Illinois), Vol. 19 (Spring 1979), pp. 57–74.

Shoven, John B., and Jeremy I. Bulow, "Inflation Accounting and Nonfinancial Corporate Profits: Financial Assets and Liabilities," *Brookings Papers on Economic Activity: 1* (1976), The Brookings Institution (Washington), pp. 15–57.

Siebke, Juergen, "Price Expectation and Interest Rates in the Federal Republic of Germany," in *Monetary Policy and Economic Activity in West Germany*, ed. by S.F. Frowen, A.S. Courakis, and M.H. Miller (New York: John Wiley, 1976), pp. 147–55.

Steuerle, Eugene, and Michael Hartzmark, "Individual Income Taxation, 1949–79," *National Tax Journal* (Philadelphia), Vol. 34 (June 1981), pp. 145–66.

Stiglitz, Joseph E., "Taxation, Corporate Financial Policy, and the Cost of Capital," *Journal of Public Economics* (Amsterdam), Vol. 2 (February 1973), pp. 1–34.

————, "On the Almost Neutrality of Inflation: Notes on Taxation and the Welfare Costs of Inflation," in *Development in an Inflationary World*, ed. by M. June Flanders and Assaf Razin (New York: Academic Press, 1981), pp. 419–57.

Strömberg, Dorothea, "How to Eliminate Inflation from Inventory Accounting: A Comparison of Stock Valuation in West European Industrial Countries," *Intertax* (Deventer, Netherlands), No. 8 (1977), pp. 287–99.

Summers, Lawrence H., "Taxation and Corporate Investment: A q-Theory Approach," *Brookings Papers on Economic Activity: 1* (1981), The Brookings Institution (Washington), pp. 67–127.

————, *The Non-Adjustment of Nominal Interest Rates: A Study of the Fisher Effect*, Research Paper No. 836, National Bureau of Economic Research (Cambridge, Massachusetts, January 1982).

Tanzi, Vito, "Inflation, Indexation and Interest Income Taxation," *Quarterly Review*, Banca Nazionale del Lavoro (Rome), No. 116 (March 1976), pp. 64–76.

————, "Inflation and the Incidence of Income Taxes on Interest Income: Some Results for the United States, 1972–74," *Staff Papers*, International Monetary Fund (Washington), Vol. 24 (July 1977), pp. 500–13.

————(1980 a), *Inflation and the Personal Income Tax* (Cambridge, England: Cambridge University Press, 1980).

————(1980 b), "Inflationary Expectations, Economic Activity, Taxes, and Interest Rates," *American Economic Review* (Nashville, Tennessee), Vol. 70 (March 1980), pp. 12-21.

————(1982 a), "Inflationary Expectations, Taxes, and the Demand for Money in the United States," *Staff Papers*, International Monetary Fund (Washington), Vol. 29 (June 1982), pp. 155–70.

————(1982 b), "Inflationary Expectations, Economic Activity, Taxes, and Interest Rates: Reply," *American Economic Review* (Nashville, Tennessee), Vol. 72 (September 1982), pp. 860–63.

————, and George Iden, "The Impact of Taxes on Wages in the United States: An Example of Supply-Side Economics?" (unpublished, International Monetary Fund, April 7, 1981).

Taylor, Herbert, "Fisher, Phillips, Friedman and the Measured Impact of Inflation on Interest: A Comment," *Journal of Finance* (New York), Vol. 36 (September 1981), pp. 955–62.

Thornton, Henry, "An Enquiry into the Nature and Effects of the Paper Credit of Great Britain" (London: J. Hatchard, 1802).

Tobin, James, "Money and Economic Growth," *Econometrica* (Evanston, Illinois), Vol. 33 (October 1965), pp. 671–84.

Vasarhelyi, Miklos A., and Edward F. Pearson, "Studies in Inflation Accounting: A Taxonomization Approach," *Quarterly Review of Economics and Business* (Urbana, Illinois), Vol. 19 (Spring 1979), pp. 9–27.

Walsh, Carl E., *Interest Rate Volatility and Monetary Policy*, Working Paper No. 915, National Bureau of Economic Research (Cambridge, Massachusetts, June 1982).

Yohe, William P., and Denis S. Karnosky, "Interest Rates and Price Level Changes, 1952–69," *Review*, Federal Reserve Bank of St. Louis (December 1969), pp. 19–36.

3

Recent Literature on the Impact of Taxation and Inflation on the International Financial Market

URI BEN-ZION

In addition to short-run capital flows arising from balance of trade disequilibria, international capital movements are generated by financial incentives created by interest rate differentials across countries. More specifically, if an individual in a given country can earn a higher return in a foreign country than he can obtain domestically, he will transfer funds to the foreign market in two stages. In the first, he will buy foreign currency; in the second, he will use that currency to buy foreign assets.

Portfolio equilibrium requires equalization of after-tax returns on alternative financial investments when all the alternatives are measured in the same (local) currency. This equilibrium condition is, in the absence of taxation, the base of the interest-rate-parity hypothesis. This proposition, and some of its recent empirical tests, serve as a starting point for this short survey.

The main body of literature on international financial market equilibrium has disregarded the taxation aspect. This paper's discussion of the effects of taxation and inflation on international capital movements will deal with the few papers that address themselves to this issue. The effects of taxation and the question of optimal tax policy toward foreign income has, however, been discussed to some extent in the context of multinational corporations, but since this issue is not directly related to the main focus of the present survey, it will not be discussed here.

I. INTEREST RATE PARITY

Consider a two-country world, consisting of Country A and Country B, and an "integrated" international financial market where investors in each country can buy securities and bonds in their own country as well as in the foreign country. The current one-period interest rates are denoted by i_A and i_B, respectively; S denotes the spot exchange rate, which is defined as the price of one unit of currency of Country B in terms of the currency of Country A; and FS denotes the future spot rate one period ahead. While i_A, i_B, and S are observed in period t, FS is an unknown in period t.

In a world with integrated capital markets, an individual in either country—say Country A—can invest in period t one unit of local currency and obtain a return equal to $1 + i_A$ in period $t+1$ by investing in a domestic bond, or he can obtain $(1 + i_B)(FS/S)$ by investing in foreign bonds. Under conditions of perfect information and certainty, where FS is known, the following equilibrium conditions should hold:

$$1 + i_A = (1 + i_B)(FS/S) \tag{1}$$

This, in a world of certainty, is known as the interest-rate-parity equation. But in a world of uncertainty, where FS is not known, the expected return on foreign investment may depend on the prediction of the future exchange rate (or the rate of depreciation or appreciation). Different investors may have different preferences (and choices) between bonds denominated in the currency of Country A and bonds denominated in the currency of Country B (hereinafter referred to as bonds of Country A and of Country B, respectively) according to their views of the future exchange rate FS and their attitudes toward risk.

With regard to risk, it is commonly assumed in the literature that in period $t+1$, investors in each country prefer to hold instruments denominated in domestic currency; therefore, an investment in foreign bonds is more risky because it involves some degree of exchange rate uncertainty.

One solution to reduce the risk of investment in foreign instruments (see Stein (1965) and references cited therein) is to hedge against the risk of fluctuations in the value of foreign currency by selling in the forward market the foreign exchange to be obtained in period $t+1$. In this case, the covered arbitrage version of the interest-rate-parity equation can be written as

$$1 + i_A = (1 + i_B)(F/S) \tag{2}$$

where F denotes the forward delivered exchange rate or the price at time t of the currency of Country B to be delivered at period $t+1$.

In the rest of the paper, equation (2) (rather than equation (1)) will be referred to as the interest-rate-parity equation.[1] Equations (1) and (2) can be written in terms of the interest differential as

$$(1+i_A)/(1+i_B) = F/S$$

or

$$(i_A - i_B)/(1 + i_B) = (FS - S)/S \qquad (1')$$

and

$$(i_A - i_B)/(1 + i_B) = (F - S)/S \qquad (2')$$

The intuitive explanation of this relationship is that if the interest rate in Country B is lower than the interest rate in Country A, then an investor will hold bonds of both countries only if he expects to be compensated by an appreciation of Country B's currency. If the interest rate in Country B, i_B, is rather small (or if the maturity of the bond is quite short), equations (1') and (2') can be approximated as

$$i_A - i_B = (FS - S)/S \qquad (1'')$$

$$i_A - i_B = (F - S)/S \qquad (2'')$$

Equation (1") states that the percentage increase in the exchange rate is equal to the interest rate differential, while equation (2") states that the forward exchange premium is equal to the interest rate differential. It should again be noted that under certainty, when both equations hold, the forward rate is equal to the future exchange rate.

Under uncertainty, assuming risk aversion and given the risk of unexpected exchange rate fluctuations, a trader in Country A will buy bonds in Country B (without covered arbitrage) only if the expected return there is above the expected return in Country A, or

$$(1+i_B)E_A(FS) > 1+i_A \qquad (3)$$

---

[1] Many empirical tests have been conducted in forward markets on the question whether the forward rates are good predictors of the future rate and whether the financial markets are efficient. Although there are some findings that forward rates can serve as predictors for future rates (e.g., Cornell (1977) and Callier (1981)), there are also indications that forward rates are affected by speculation (e.g., Kesselman (1971)). A survey of that literature is given by Levich (1979). More recent findings, derived using more elaborate statistical techniques, are presented by Hansen and Hodrick (1980); these findings raise doubts about the hypothesis that the forward rates are unbiased predictors of the future spot rates and suggest the existence of a risk premium in the forward market.

where $E_A(FS)$ denotes the expected future exchange rate for investors in Country A. Similarly, for investors in Country B to invest in bonds in Country A, assuming again the riskiness of foreign investment,

$$1 + i_B < (1 + i_A)[S/(E_B(FS))] \tag{4}$$

where $E_B(FS)$ denotes the exchange rate expected by investors in Country B.

A comparison of equations (3) and (4) suggests that investors in Country A and Country B will hold open positions, as a result of buying bonds, in both Countries A and B only if (a) they have different expectations with regard to the future exchange rate; (b) risk premiums are required to induce them to hold foreign bonds; or (c) there are other factors affecting portfolio decisions—for example, transaction costs, risks of political intervention (Aliber (1973)), default risk (Stoll (1968)), and differential taxes on domestic and foreign interest income and capital gains.

The literature contains many empirical tests of the validity of the hypothesis of covered interest rate parity. One of the earliest tests, performed by Stein (1965), considered the United States, the United Kingdom, and Canada. Frenkel and Levich (1977, 1981) formulated the interest-rate-parity equilibrium conditions in a world with transaction costs and concluded that the forward premium could deviate from the interest rate differential in a range that depends on the transaction costs. A relevant empirical question in testing interest rate parity is whether the observed deviation from the prediction of the theory can be explained by governments' intervention, which disturbs capital markets' response. A study by Dooley and Isard (1980) explains the deviation from interest rate parity by the United States and the Federal Republic of Germany that resulted from capital controls in the German market, while Otani and Tiwari (1981) calculate the deviation from interest rate parity in the Tokyo and London markets and explain it in terms of the control measures and moral "pressure" used by the Japanese Government.

II. TAXATION AND INTEREST RATE PARITY UNDER INFLATION

Most of the literature on interest rate parity, both empirical and theoretical, does not take into consideration the effect of taxes on international equilibrium. By ignoring taxes, the literature implicitly assumes that taxes have no effect on capital flows, or that taxes have the same proportional effect on both sides of the interest-rate-parity equation. In view of the tax rules in Western countries, neither of these implicit assumptions seems to be correct. A number of recent articles, which are discussed below, incorporate taxation issues in the context of interest-rate-parity formulation.

Levi (1977) considered the tax rules of Canada and the United States with regard to foreign-generated income, as well as the differential tax treatment of income and capital gains.

Starting from equation (2'), which yields interest rate parity without taxes [$i_A = i_B + (1+i_B)((F-S)/S)$], Levi considers the case where the tax rate on capital gains (from foreign exchange transactions) is lower than the tax rate on regular income. If $i_A > i_B$, the returns to residents of Country A from investing in foreign bonds will consist of regular income (i_B) and a capital gain ($F-S$), while the return on investment in the home country (i_A) will be fully taxed at the higher income tax rate. Therefore, if the equality before taxes holds (equation (2')), after taxes there will be an incentive for residents of Country A to move their funds to Country B. In order to obtain equilibrium, equality of after-tax returns between the local market A and the foreign market B should be established; this would require that equation (2') be changed to

$$i_A = i_B + [(1+i_B)((F-S)/S)] + \theta \qquad (5)$$

where θ can be viewed as denoting the excess pretax premium on local bonds, which reflects their less favorable tax treatment. (This premium is similar to the premium paid on taxable bonds, compared with nontaxable bonds.)

In the opposite case, when $i_A < i_B$, equality before taxes implies that the term $(F-S)/S$ in equation (2') is negative, which suggests that residents of Country A will not be able to take advantage of the lower capital gains tax by investing in the bonds of Country B. However, they may be able to generate a capital gain by borrowing in Country B and investing the proceeds in local bonds. In this case, although the investors pay higher interest in Country B on their loans (than in Country A), they will have a capital gain from the depreciation of the loan in local-currency terms. At the same time, it will be beneficial for tax reasons for an investor in Country B to borrow in Country A and invest domestically. Therefore capital flows will again be generated, even though equation (2') will hold. Levi also applies his analysis to the specific tax law in the United States that allows special treatment of long-term (on assets held more than six months) capital gains.

The main contribution made by Levi's analysis is the emphasis it places on the role of taxation and its importance as an explanation of observed deviations from pretax interest rate parity. Levi's study provides a rational explanation of international capital movements, like two-way capital flows, which would seem "abnormal" in the absence of tax factors.

In a related paper, Hartman (1979) has considered the effect of taxation on capital flows between two countries in an inflationary environment. He considers in particular the effect of different tax arrangements with respect to income generated domestically and abroad. In a world with no taxes, theory suggests the simultaneous existence of the Fisher effect, the interest rate parity, and purchasing power parity (see also Roll and Solnik (1979) and Ben-Zion and Weinblatt (1982)).

The introduction of taxes leads to the modified Fisher effect, which indicates that the interest rate in a country will increase by more than the rate of anticipated inflation—that is, $i_A = r_A + \pi_A/(1-t_A)$, where r_A denotes the real interest rate, π_A denotes the rate of anticipated inflation in Country A, and t_A denotes the income tax rate.[2] Consider now an investor from Country B who is subject to a rate of income tax t_B in his country, with nominal and real interest rates i_B and r_B, respectively.

Let us assume for simplicity that inflation in Country B is zero and that the real rates of interest are r_A and r_B. Here, the inflation in Country A will affect the equality between the real after-tax returns; this will tend to create capital flows, which are induced only by anticipated inflation and taxation, and will lead, according to Hartman, to real changes in capital intensities in the two countries.

Recently Tanzi and Blejer (1982) have developed a similar model in which local investors in a developing country hold foreign assets (bonds) as part of their portfolios and the interest rate adjusts to inflation according to the modified Fisher effect. Tanzi and Blejer assume, furthermore, that investors in Country B (the developing country) can avoid (at least de facto) paying taxes on interest income earned in Country A (the United States).

If originally, when there is no inflation, after-tax interest rates are equal,

$$(1-t_B)r_B = r_A \tag{6}$$

then, as a result of inflation in Country A, the return on investment

---

[2] See Darby (1975), Feldstein (1976), and Tanzi (1976).

in that country will increase, according to the modified Fisher effect, to $(r_A + \pi/1 - t_A)$, which will lead to capital flows from Country B to Country A.[3]

An important implication of the Tanzi-Blejer model is that inflation in the United States attracts capital flows from other countries, owing to the (de facto) preferential tax treatment of interest income of non-residents in the United States, and explains the recent appreciation of the U.S. dollar in terms of other currencies.

Ben-Zion and Weinblatt (1982) have further extended the ideas of differential tax treatment in a period of inflation that were presented in Hartman (1979), and Tanzi and Blejer (1982). They assume a tax treaty between countries, under which residents pay taxes only in their own country on the interest income earned abroad in their own currency.[4] Under the assumption of the two-country model presented above and of purchasing power parity, inflation in Country A will raise the real pretax return for a nonresident investing in Country A from r_A to $[r_A + (1 + \pi_A)(t_A/1 - t_A)]$, thereby inducing capital movements from Country B to Country A. This differential, in turn, arises because tax agreements and adjustments in the exchange rate, according to purchasing power party, make nonresidents, unlike residents, pay taxes only on the "real" interest rate in Country B derived from investment in Country A. At the same time, nonresidents benefit from the modified Fisher effect in Country A, which is based on taxation of nominal interest income in that country.

The interaction between the modified Fisher effect and purchasing power and interest rate parities was discussed in a recent paper by Howard and Johnson (1982). Assuming the existence of purchasing power parity, they show that the interest rate parity will cause a change in the real rate of interest, so that the modified Fisher effect will not hold. Alternatively, the modified Fisher effect may hold, but the real exchange rate will have to change. Furthermore, they show that the nonneutrality of inflation arises from the taxation of nominal inflation and that it would disappear if taxes were levied on real interest income.

An important result that follows from the above-mentioned literature is that the flow of capital and the relative exchange rate appreciation in the country with higher inflation (Country A) leads to an

---

[3] Under the purchasing-power-parity hypothesis, this result holds regardless of the rate of inflation in Country B.

[4] Although the Ben-Zion and Weinblatt model is similar in spirit to the one developed by Hartman, it emphasizes that international capital flows, mainly short-term financial flows, will not normally affect capital intensities in the two countries (which are a result of long-term investment capital flows).

increase in the volume of imports and reduction in employment in that country and may further aggravate inflation and unemployment.

III. CONCLUDING COMMENTS AND AGENDA FOR RESEARCH

Although a large body of literature has in recent years dealt with the effect of inflation on interest rates across countries, and the impact of these variables on exchange rates and capital flows, most of the literature on the latter has ignored the existence of taxation.

The works of Levi (1977), Hartman (1979), and Tanzi and Blejer (1982) have shown the crucial role played by taxation in the determination of capital mobility and the relevance of alternative assumptions regarding the tax treatment of foreign interest income. Using these approaches, it was shown by Ben-Zion and Weinblatt (1982) that tax considerations create a significant incentive for short-term capital flows and that these flows may change the real rate of interest or the path of the real exchange rate (Howard and Johnson (1982)), as well as affect other important variables.

Differences of opinion about the theoretical implications, the process of achieving market equilibrium, and—particularly—the empirical assessment of taxation's effects on the international capital market are far from being resolved. A clear conclusion that emerges from a reading of the existing literature is that the standard relationships upon which open-economy macroeconomic modeling is based—namely, the interest-rate-parity hypothesis, purchasing power parity, and the "open" Fisher effect—do not hold in their simple formulation in the presence of taxes; consequently, they should be modified to provide a more realistic framework for analyzing developments in the real world.

In terms of research needs, it is apparent that priority should be given to the development of a comprehensive framework that incorporates the effects of differential taxation, tax agreements, tax evasion, and other fiscal considerations into the determinants of capital flows and of equilibrium in the international capital market. Of equal importance is the evaluation of the empirical effects of these factors. The assessment of the magnitude of these effects is essential if one is to obtain a correct perspective of their importance and of their policy implications. A prerequisite, however, to such empirical evaluation is the collection of institutional and legal information on the tax treatment of international flows in different countries.

Two additional related topics that need review are (1) the evaluation of the potential importance of international tax policy in developing countries for the growth of their capital markets, and (2) the theoretical and empirical implications of tax considerations for optimal portfolio composition in an open economy.

It seems that research in this important area may significantly improve our understanding of the effects of the tax policy of one country on international markets and on real variables in other countries.

References

Aliber, Robert Z., "The Interest Rate Parity Theorem: A Reinterpretation," *Journal of Political Economy* (Chicago), Vol. 81 (November/December 1973), pp. 1451–59.

Ben-Zion, Uri, and J. Weinblatt, "Purchasing Power, Interest Rate Parities and the Modified Fisher Effect in the Presence of Tax Agreements" (unpublished, August 1982).

Callier, Philippe, "Speculation, Interest Arbitrage, and the Forward Foreign Exchange Rate of the Canadian Dollar: Updated Evidence," *Journal of Macroeconomics* (Detroit, Michigan), Vol. 3 (Spring 1981), pp. 293–99.

Cornell, Bradford, "Spot Rates, Forward Rates, and Exchange Market Efficiency," *Journal of Financial Economics* (Amsterdam), Vol. 5, No. 1 (1977), pp. 55–65.

Darby, Michael R., "The Financial and Tax Effects of Monetary Policy on Interest Rates," *Economic Inquiry* (Long Beach, California), Vol. 13 (June 1975), pp. 266–74.

Dooley, Michael P., and Peter Isard, "Capital Controls, Political Risk and Deviations from Interest Rate Parity," *Journal of Political Economy* (Chicago), Vol. 88 (April 1980), pp. 370–84.

Feldstein, Martin, "Inflation, Income Taxes and the Rate of Interest: A Theoretical Analysis," *American Economic Review* (Nashville, Tennessee), Vol. 66 (December 1976), pp. 809–20.

Frenkel, Jacob A., and Richard M. Levich, "Transaction Cost and Interest Arbitrage: Tranquil versus Turbulent Periods," *Journal of Political Economy* (Chicago), Vol. 85 (December 1977), pp. 1209–26.

_____, "Covered Interest Arbitrage in the 1970s," *Economics Letters* (Amsterdam), Vol. 8, No. 3 (1981), pp. 267–74.

Hansen, Lars P., and Robert J. Hodrick, "Formal Exchange Rates as Optimal Predictors of Future Spot Rates: An Econometric Analysis," *Journal of Political Economy* (Chicago), Vol. 88 (October 1980), pp. 829–53.

Hartman, David G., "Taxation and the Effects of Inflation on the Real Capital Stock in an Open Economy," *International Economic Review* (Osaka, Japan), Vol. 20 (June 1979), pp. 417–25.

Howard, David H., and Karen H. Johnson, "Interest Rates, Inflation, and Taxes: The Foreign Connection," *Economics Letters* (Amsterdam), Vol. 9, No. 2 (1982), pp. 181–84.

Kesselman, Jonathan, "The Role of Speculation in Forward Rate Determination: The Canadian Flexible Dollar 1953–1960," *Canadian Journal of Ecomomics* (Toronto), Vol. 4 (August 1971), pp. 279–98.

Levi, Maurice D., "Taxation and 'Abnormal' International Capital Flows," *Journal of Political Economy* (Chicago), Vol. 85 (June 1977), pp. 635–46.

Levich, Richard M., "The Efficiency of Markets for Foreign Exchange: A Review and Extension," in *International Financial Management: Theory and Application,* ed. by Donald R. Lessard (Boston, Massachusetts: Warren, Gorham & Lamont, 1979), pp. 243–76.

Otani, Ichiro, and Siddharth Tiwari, "Capital Controls and Interest Rate Parity: The Japanese Experience, 1978–81," *Staff Papers,* International Monetary Fund (Washington), Vol. 28 (December 1981), pp. 793–815.

Roll, Richard, and Bruno Solnik, "On Some Parity Conditions Encountered Frequently in International Economics," *Journal of Macroeconomics* (Detroit, Michigan), Vol. 1 (Summer 1979), pp. 267–83.

Stein, Jerome L., "International Short-Term Capital Movements," *American Economic Review* (Nashville, Tennessee), Vol. 55 (March 1965), pp. 40–66.

Stoll, Hans R., "An Empirical Study of the Forward Exchange Market Under Fixed and Flexible Exchange Rate Systems," *Canadian Journal of Economics* (Toronto), Vol. 1 (February 1968), pp. 55–78.

Tanzi, Vito, "Inflation, Indexation and Interest Income Taxation," *Quarterly Review,* Banca Nazionale del Lavoro (Rome), No. 116 (March 1976), pp. 64–76.

————, and Mario I. Blejer, "Inflation, Interest Rate Policy, and Currency Substitution in Developing Economies: A Discussion of Some Major Issues," *World Development* (Oxford, England), Vol. 10 (September 1982), pp. 781–89.

4

Level and Volatility of U.S. Interest Rates: Roles of Expected Inflation, Real Rates, and Taxes

JOHN H. MAKIN and VITO TANZI

This paper analyzes the major forces affecting the behavior of interest rates, placing particular emphasis on the unusually high levels and variability of rates in recent years. The approach is eclectic in the sense that strong prior views are not allowed to rule out consideration of any possible avenue of investigation that might help to explain unusual interest rate movements.

I. THEORETICAL BACKGROUND

As Irving Fisher theorized a long time ago, the market interest rate (hereinafter referred to as the interest rate) on a security maturing in t periods of time is approximately the sum of an expected real rate (hereinafter referred to as the real rate) and the level of inflation expected over t periods. A change in the level or the volatility of interest rates should thus arise from (a) a change in the level or the volatility of the real rate, (b) a change in the level or the volatility of expected inflation, or (c) a change in the impact that unit changes in either or both of these variables have on interest rates.

In fact, it has been difficult to explain fully the behavior of interest rates for two reasons. First, econometric models estimated for a particular sample period have tended to perform poorly outside of the sample period. Second, since both expected inflation and the real rate are unobservable variables, attribution of movements in interest rates to either of these components has depended crucially on the use of proxies to represent their behavior. The latter problem has been highlighted recently, when efforts to slow money growth while actual and expected fiscal deficits are growing have resulted in higher real

rates, slowdowns in economic activity, and currency appreciation. Furthermore, contrary to a considerable body of economic theory, it
appears that the real rate may be quite responsive over more than
the very short run (say, one quarter) to monetary and fiscal policy
actions and/or to fluctuations in economic activity.

The possible relationship between the configuration of monetary
and fiscal policy and the real rate has had a significant impact on
analysis of costs attributed to measures aimed at controlling inflation
(see Makin (1982 b)). Based on conventional macroeconomic theory,
it would be considered unusual to hear calls for tax increases or cuts
in government spending in the midst of a serious recession. Yet such
calls have been heard with increasing frequency since the onset of the
U.S. recession in the summer of 1981; and, indeed, in the summer
of 1982, there was a major tax increase in the United States. The
usual arguments for pump-priming measures aimed at ending recessions have become less convincing amid widespread concern that fiscal
deficits, both actual and projected, have been responsible for the high
real rates that have depressed U.S. expenditure on new plant and
equipment, housing, and durables. The possible "crowding-out" of
private investment by large government borrowing requirements to
finance large fiscal deficits is at the core of the ongoing debate over
the effects of a tight monetary and loose fiscal configuration of macroeconomic policy.

Another element to be considered in the investigation of interest
rate movements is the role played by taxes. Changes in actual or
perceived tax rates on interest income from financial instruments,
relative to tax rates on incomes from alternative assets, should affect
the relationship between nominal interest rates and real interest rates,
given the level of expected inflation. This means that when actual or
perceived marginal tax rates change, empirical models estimated over
a given sample period may break down outside of that period even
when the other variables needed to explain interest rates are identified
and accurately predicted.

Empirical investigations of interest rate behavior through the mid-
1970s by Tanzi (1980 a) and Levi and Makin (1978) suggest that
investors tended to adjust interest rates to insulate, to a large extent,
real rates from the effects of expected inflation but not of income
taxes. This "fiscal illusion" (Tanzi (1980 a)) may be expected to have
disappeared for several reasons. First, the high rates of inflation in
recent years would inevitably make the effect of taxes on real rates
obvious to most investors. These effects are far less obvious when
inflation is low. Second, these tax effects were discussed in several

well-known articles, such as those by Darby (1975), Feldstein (1976), and Tanzi (1976). Third, as inflation rates climbed, a combination of "bracket-creep" and higher interest rates tended to enlarge the absolute gap between before-tax and after-tax real interest incomes while simultaneously enhancing the attractiveness of returns on real assets that were subject only to low capital gains tax rates (and only upon realization) or to no tax at all, as is true for many collectibles and antiques (Tanzi (1982 a and 1982 b)). As expected inflation rose, expected after-tax real interest rates quickly became negative when allowance was made for taxation of nominal interest earnings.

Section II of this paper briefly describes a framework for proximate analysis of interest rate behavior. Section III considers in more detail the role of expected inflation. A theoretical framework for analysis of real rates is developed in Section IV. Section V presents results of some empirical tests. Section VI discusses remaining puzzles concerning behavior of interest rates. Section VII presents some concluding remarks and summarizes suggestions for future investigation.

II. PROXIMATE SOURCES OF INTEREST RATE MOVEMENTS

The Fisher equation describing an interest rate, i, in terms of a real rate, r, and expected inflation π is written as [1]

$$i_t = r_t + \pi_t \tag{1}$$

where the subscript t denotes time. When taxes are considered, the aim is to define as the investor's objective an after-tax real rate r^* written as

$$r_t^* = i_t(1-\tau) - \pi_t \tag{2}$$

where τ denotes the perceived marginal tax rate on nominal interest income. Transposing equation (2) to place i_t on the left-hand side, the result is

$$i_t = \left(\frac{1}{1-\tau}\right)\left[r_t^* + \pi_t\right] \tag{3}$$

---

[1] The interaction term $r_t\,\pi_t$ is ignored here, since it is relatively small for the United States.

Equation (3) summarizes the proximate determinants of the interest rate discussed earlier. Movements in i can be decomposed into movements in after-tax real returns, changes in expected inflation, and/or changes in tax rates that alter the impact on i of *given* changes in r^* or π. These three sources of movements in i, together with some modifications that arise from more detailed consideration of determinants of the after-tax real rate, will be explored in turn. It is, however, immediately evident from equation (3) that for a given level of expected inflation, the provisions of the U.S. Economic Recovery Tax Act of 1981 will elevate observed interest rates, since accelerated depreciation allowances should raise the expected after-tax real returns on investment projects. However, the impact of such a rise in r^* would be somewhat diminished by reduced marginal individual income tax rates, particularly in higher tax brackets, which would lower τ.

As for interest rate volatility, an expression for the variance of interest rates based on equation (3) is given by

$$\sigma_i^2 = [1/(1-\tau)]^2 \, \sigma_{r^*}^2 + [1/(1-\tau)]^2 \, \sigma_\pi^2$$
$$+ \, 2[1/(1-\tau)]^2 \, \rho_{r_\pi^*} \, \sigma_{r^*} \sigma_\pi \tag{4}$$

where σ_π^2 denotes the variance of anticipated inflation, $\sigma_{r^*}^2$ the variance of the after-tax real rate, and $\rho_{r_\pi^*}$ the coefficient of correlation between r^* and π. Notice that when taxes are ignored, as in equation (1), the variance of i is written as

$$\sigma_i^2 = \sigma_{r^*}^2 + \sigma_\pi^2 + 2\rho_{r_\pi^*}\sigma_{r^*}\sigma_\pi \tag{5}$$

The effects of considering tax rates are evident when equations (4) and (5) are compared. Ignoring the effects of possible correlation between r^* and π ($\rho_{r_\pi^*} = 0$ for now), the volatility of after-tax real rates unambiguously produces *more* volatility in i, since for any $\tau > 0$, $[1/(1-\tau)]^2 > 1$. (Given $\tau = 0.35$, $[1/(1-\tau)]^2 = 2.37$.) Given an average tax rate of 35 percent on interest income, a rise of 1 percent in the variance of the after-tax real rate raises the variance of i by 2.37 times the effect of a rise in the variance of the real rate when taxes are ignored, as in equation (5). Furthermore, the higher is τ, the greater will be the volatility of i, ceteris paribus. Of course, this argument assumes that there is no fiscal illusion, so that tax effects are fully recognized by investors.[2] Uncertainty over future tax policy

---

[2] Thus if it is true that in the past two to three years fiscal illusion has disappeared, equation (4) would go a long way toward explaining the greater volatility of interest rates in this period than in earlier periods.

can have a powerful impact on the observed volatility of i. Equation (4) suggests also that the effects of a rise in the variance of expected inflation on the observed variance of i will be magnified.

It will be seen in the detailed discussion of real rates that theoretical considerations (the Mundell-Tobin effect) suggest a negative correlation between expected inflation and the real rate ($\rho_{r\pi} < 0$). Strong evidence for this effect is found in Fama and Gibbons (1982) and Makin (1983). Therefore, the variance of i, with or without taxes, is reduced (though the variance is greater with taxes than without).[3]

Consideration of the proximate sources of interest rate movements suggests a number of avenues for an explanation of high and volatile interest rates. These include determinants of inflationary expectations, after-tax real rates, and possible effects of changes in actual or perceived marginal tax rates on financial assets and alternative assets.

III. BEHAVIOR OF EXPECTED INFLATION

Survey data on inflationary expectations provide a rich source of information on the outlook regarding the level and stability of the value of nominal contracts whose prices determine interest rates. As already discussed, expected inflation is a major determinant of interest rates. Since expectations about inflation are necessarily predictions, it is also relevant to consider the implications for interest rate behavior of the dispersion of such views about their mean value as well as of the symmetry of such dispersion above and below the mean. It is also useful to consider the variance and skewness of expected inflation.

The variance across expectations of inflation held by survey respondents may either be taken at face value as an index of the dispersion of views on the outlook for inflation or as a measure of uncertainty about inflation. The latter concept relates to the uncertainty attached to the single-valued forecast given by a respondent who is asked simply to describe his expectation regarding some future price

---

[3] The effect of a rise in σ_{r*}^2 on σ_i^2 (where, for convenience $\sigma_{r*}^2 \approx \sigma_\pi^2$) is given by

$$\partial\sigma_i^2/\partial\sigma_{r*}^2 = \frac{2[1 + 2\rho r_\pi^*]}{(1-\tau)^2}$$

when tax rates are considered and, ignoring taxes, by

$$\partial\sigma_i^2/\partial\sigma_{r*}^2 = 2(1 + \rho_{r\pi^*})$$

For $\tau = 0.35$ and $\rho_{r\pi^*} = -0.25$, the first of these equations equals 3.55 while the second equals 2.6.

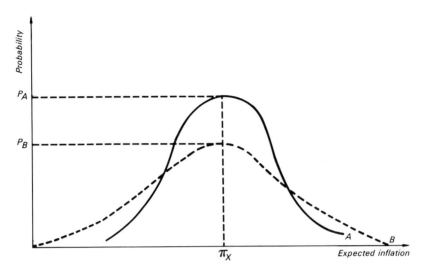

Figure 1. Normal Probability Distributions of Expected Future Prices

level relative to today's. An individual may give the same response, say π_x shown in Figure 1, at two points in time. However, distribution *A* in Figure 1 represents a forecast given with more certainty, and hence with a higher probability (P_A) attached to π_x than the forecast represented by distribution *B* (with probability P_B). It should be kept in mind that π_x is the most likely outcome for both distributions.

Uncertainty about inflation both across survey respondents and by individual investors may be linked as follows. If investors form their own expectations regarding inflation by sampling the outlook of forecasters, as does the Livingston survey of inflationary expectations,[4] they will be more uncertain as to the outlook for inflation when they discover an increase in the dispersion of outlooks across forecasters. Based on this reasoning, the variance of the Livingston survey of inflationary expectations is used as a measure of the uncertainty about inflation.

The sign of the impact of changes in inflation uncertainty on observable interest rates is not clear. It operates through an impact on the equilibrium after-tax real rate, which adjusts to equilibrate real savings and investment.[5] A rise in uncertainty about inflation will

---

[4] This survey is conducted by the *Philadelphia Inquirer* under the guidance of Joseph Livingston and compiled semiannually by the Federal Reserve Bank of Philadelphia.
[5] This discussion is drawn from Makin (1983).

cause risk-averse investors who are contracting to pay money to finance projects to reduce their investments because of the increased
uncertainty regarding the real value of contractual payments. Cukierman and Wachtel (1982) have shown that relative price uncertainty tends to increase with inflation uncertainty; such increased uncertainty will, in turn, reduce real investment, which, after all, represents
commitments to a given expected set of relative prices. Downward
pressure on the real investment schedule will, ceteris paribus, cause
the expected after-tax real rate to fall. At the same time, however, on
the other side of the market, risk-averse savers who are contracting
to receive dollars will, because of increased uncertainty regarding the
real value of contractual receipts, reduce the supply of funds at given
levels of income and of real balances. This will, ceteris paribus, cause
the expected after-tax real rate to rise. The net impact on the expected
after-tax real rate of the negative shift in real investment and real
savings schedules is uncertain. If the negative impact on investment
dominates, greater uncertainty about inflation depresses the equilibrium after-tax real rate and thereby the nominal rate. The reverse
holds true if the negative impact of uncertainty about inflation on
saving dominates. Results reported below, although statistically weak,
suggest that greater uncertainty about inflation tends to depress short-
term nominal interest rates, suggesting that the negative impact on
investment dominates the negative impact on savings.[6]

It is also possible that the asymmetry (skewness) of views about the
outlook for inflation may affect interest rates. Suppose that the probability distribution for a typical respondent X is as described by A in
Figure 2; in other words, the respondent considers π_x the most likely
outcome, but he also considers that outcomes that imply expectations

---

[6] Hartman and Makin (1982) employ a utility-maximizing framework in a two-period
model to develop an alternative rationale for the proposition that uncertainty about
inflation has a negative impact on the nominal rate. The approach yields a definition
of the after-tax real rate

$$r_t^* = i_t(1-\tau) - \pi_t + \sigma^2 \qquad (2')$$

which implies

$$i_t = \left(\frac{1}{1-\tau}\right)\Big[\lambda_0 + (1-\lambda_1)\pi_t - \lambda_2(m_t - {}_{t-1}m_t')$$
$$- (1+\lambda_3)\,\sigma_t^2 + \lambda_4 X_t - \theta\lambda_2\ time + V_t\Big] \qquad (10')$$

In equation (10′), the coefficient on σ_t^2 is negative even if λ_3 is negative and less than
unity in absolute value, with the impact of τ^2 on savings dominating its impact on
investment. In short, though the expectation of a negative impact of σ^2 on i is enhanced,
it may not be due to the impact on savings versus investment but rather to the alternative
definition of the after-tax real rate given by equation (2′).

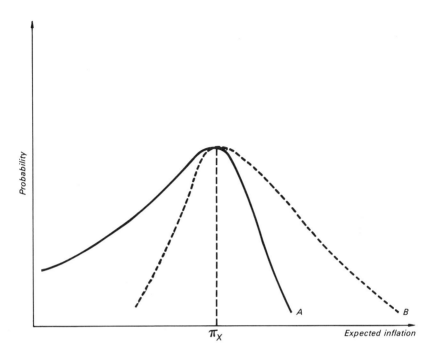

Figure 2. Asymmetrical Probability Distributions of Expected Future Prices

lower than π_x are more likely than outcomes implying expectations higher than π_x. Assume that, while the most likely outcome remains π_x, the shape of the probability distribution changes from A to B— that is, from negatively skewed to positively skewed, so that outcomes implying inflation higher than π_x become more likely than outcomes implying inflation lower than π_x. Although the reply that the respondent would give to the pollster would remain unchanged (and equal to π_x), his attitude as a lender or borrower would certainly change. As a lender, he would now expect to receive a higher rate of interest to compensate him for the higher risk. As a borrower, he would be willing to pay a higher rate. The net effect would be an increase in the market rate of interest. Therefore, given the average level and variance of expected inflation, the more positively skewed are such expectations, the higher is the rate of interest likely to be.[7]

Since 1981, two important considerations have been paramount in the minds of sophisticated investors. First, as the money supply was

[7] See also Fama (1976).

being expanded at a slower pace, the expectation was that the rate of inflation would fall. Second, as a growing fiscal deficit loomed large on the horizon, one significant probability was that the Federal Reserve Board would, at some point, reverse its policy in order to accommodate the fiscal deficit with monetary expansion. Under these circumstances, it seems safe to assume that, for many observers, while the point estimate of inflation (π_x in Figure 2) was falling, that fall was accompanied by a positive change in the skewness of the probability distribution describing expected inflation (such as the one represented by the change from A to B in Figure 2). As a consequence, a lower observed π might not be accompanied by as great a fall in the nominal rate of interest as might have been expected. Therefore, this effect would be reflected in a higher real rate. Unfortunately, we do not have data that would permit an empirical verification of this effect, so it will have to be left in the realm of theoretical speculation.[8]

While there is no information about the skewness of the probability distribution for *each* of the respondents in the Livingston survey sample, there is information about the variance across survey respondents on expected inflation. Table 1 reports the mean level and standard deviation of inflation forecasts from 1973 through the end of 1981 for the Livingston survey. The December 1981 forecast, of course, covers the first half of 1982. The steady rise of the mean until mid-1980 is consistent with steady upward pressure on the *level* of interest rates until that time. After that, and particularly during 1981, the 3.5 percent drop in the mean level of expected inflation clearly suggests that if real (after-tax) rates had remained constant, by December 1981 short-term interest rates should have been between 3.5 percent and 5.5 percent below what they were in December 1980. In fact, the rate on six-month treasury bills fell by about 2.5 percent over that period, implying that after-tax real rates rose considerably during 1981. Overall, the behavior of anticipated inflation suggests that, ceteris paribus, interest rates should have come down during 1981 by more than they actually did. Further, the rise in rates early in 1982 seems to be somewhat at variance with the slowing of actual inflation rates and the appearance of further survey data suggesting a drop in longer-term expected inflation.[9]

---

[8] Furthermore, the argument is likely to be more important for financial assets of longer maturity than for those of short maturity.

[9] During February 1982, Manufacturer's Hanover Trust reported a drop since late 1981 of about 2 percent in expected inflation over the coming five years, from the 9 percent range to the 7 percent range.

In the second half of 1982, rates on short-term treasury bills fell to levels broadly consistent with a tax-adjusted Fisher hypothesis.

Table 1. Means and Standard Deviation of Six-Month U.S. Consumer Price Index Forecasts

Month and Year	Mean	Standard Deviation Cross-section	Standard Deviation Over time
June 1973	4.00	1.31	
December 1973	5.17	2.10	
June 1974	7.12	2.38	1.34 (June 1973 to
December 1974	7.70	2.32	December 1975)
June 1975	5.64	2.12	
December 1975	5.84	1.38	
June 1976	5.30	1.30	
December 1976	5.23	1.81	
June 1977	5.92	1.36	0.66 (June 1976 to
December 1977	5.99	1.23	December 1978)
June 1978	6.40	1.57	
December 1978	6.97	1.75	
June 1979	8.31	2.35	
December 1979	10.14	2.37	
June 1980	10.67	2.57	1.46 (June 1979 to
December 1980	10.51	2.58	December 1981)
June 1981	8.86	2.83	
December 1981	6.96	2.21	

Source: Livingston survey data at annual rates.

Table 1 also suggests that the volatility of expected inflation *over time* has been considerably higher since mid-1979 than during the period of comparable length from mid-1976 through the end of 1978. The standard deviation of expected inflation rates during the later period was 1.46 percent, or more than twice the 0.66 percent during the earlier period. This rise may well have contributed to the rise in the volatility of interest rates since 1979. The rise in the volatility of expected inflation likely reflects the rise in the volatility of U.S. money growth rates since October 1979, when new operating procedures were adopted by the Federal Reserve Board.

It is also clear from Table 1 that cross-sectional uncertainty about expected inflation has risen steadily since 1977. This phenomenon, as discussed above, may be linked to a rise or fall in after-tax real rates.

IV. BEHAVIOR OF THE EXPECTED REAL INTEREST RATE

A strict version of the Fisherian relationship between interest rates and inflation assumes that the rate of interest rises pari passu with the rate of inflation. In other words, it assumes that the real rate of interest is constant. This version received a strong boost when a particularly influential study by Fama (1975) failed to reject the joint hypothesis of constancy of the real rate and rationality of inflation forecasts. A later study by Nelson and Schwert (1977) argued that Fama's test of that joint hypothesis was not sufficiently powerful. After applying more powerful tests, these authors concluded that the data permitted rejection of the constant real rate hypothesis. Mishkin (1981) argued that Fama's failure to reject constancy of the real rate might alternatively be viewed as an artifact of the sample period he employed (first quarter 1953 through second quarter 1973).

The recent behavior of interest rates is difficult to explain without recourse to the hypothesis that the real rate has fluctuated considerably. A relevant question then becomes how to explain movements in the real rate. Those movements have been substantial, particularly since 1979 (see Chart 1).

Studies by Levi and Makin (1978), Makin (1982 b), Mishkin (1981), Peek (1982), Tanzi (1980 a), and others have singled out many factors that may cause, at least in the short run, changes in the after-tax real rate of interest. Among these, the following deserve specific mention: (a) expected inflation itself; (b) the stage of the business cycle; (c) unanticipated changes in the fiscal deficit; (d) taxes; (e) unanticipated changes in the money supply; and (f) uncertainty about the level of inflation.

It has been speculated above on ways in which uncertainty about inflation might affect the after-tax real rate. And the role of taxes has already been discussed and the hypothesis has simultaneously been advanced that up to the mid-1970s there was too little tax effect because of a "fiscal illusion," which has progressively disappeared since then. This disappearance would, of course, be translated into an increase in the impact of changes in expected inflation on nominal interest rates.

Also operating through the measured impact of expected inflation on the nominal interest rate is the well-known Mundell-Tobin effect. Under the Mundell-Tobin effect, the real rate can be affected by changes in expected inflation. A rise in expected inflation causes a shift out of money balances and into real capital, thereby depressing the marginal product of capital and the equilibrium real rate. This is the Tobin effect. Mundell (1963) describes a similar phenomenon whereby a rise in anticipated inflation depresses equilibrium real cash balances, in turn increasing the steady-state level of flow savings owing to the real balance effect. Equilibrium is restored by means of a lower real interest rate, which increases the level of investment until it equals the higher level of savings. This effect, operating as it does on the steady-state rate of saving, is not expected to be subsequently reversed in the absence of a further change in the rate of expected inflation.

The impact of the Mundell-Tobin effect on the relationship between expected inflation and nominal rates of taxes can best be understood with the aid of a structural model that determines the equilibrium value of the after-tax real rate. This approach also helps to clarify the role of uncertainty about inflation, money surprises, and surprise fiscal deficits in determining observable nominal interest rates. The structural model presented here, which extends the model developed in Makin (1983), yields a reduced-form equation for the after-tax real rate. The resulting expression for the after-tax real rate can then be substituted into a Fisher equation describing the observable nominal rate in terms of the after-tax real rate and expected inflation.

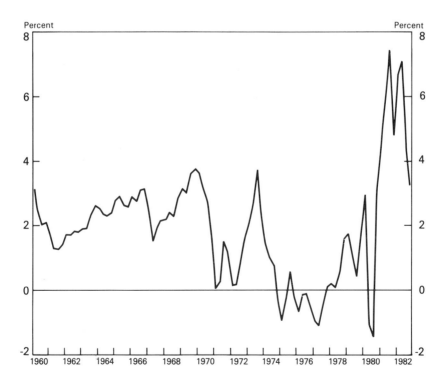

Chart 1. Expected Real Return on Three-Month U.S. Treasury Bills, 1960–82
(Quarterly averages less Livingston Survey estimates of expected inflation)

The structural equations are expressed in the familiar IS-LM format with some modifications, along with an expression for real income (output) in terms of a distributed lag on money surprises as derived by Blinder and Fischer (1981). The log of non-income-induced expenditure is written as

$$I_t = \alpha_0 - \alpha_1 r_t^* - \alpha_2 \sigma_t^2 + \alpha_3 X_t - \alpha_4 \pi_t \tag{6}$$
$$+ \alpha_5 GAP_t + e_{1_t} \quad (\alpha_i \geq 0 \text{ where } i = 1...5)$$

where

I_t = log of non-income-induced expenditure

r_t^* = expected after-tax real interest rate

σ_t^2 = a measure of inflation uncertainty

X_t = log of an exogenous expenditure shift

π_t = expected inflation

GAP_t = (actual real GNP − potential real GNP)/(potential real GNP)

e_{1_t} = an error term, normally distributed with zero mean (All error terms, e_i ($i=1,...,4$) take this form.)

Equation (6) describes non-income-induced expenditure. As such, it is negatively tied to the after-tax real rate and to uncertainty about inflation and is positively affected by any real exogenous shock to expenditure that is unrelated to other right-hand variables in equation (6). Expected inflation produces a negative impact on investment owing to the depressing impact on corporate profits arising from historical cost depreciation rules noted by Feldstein (1976) and Feldstein and Summers (1978).[10] *GAP* is a measure of capacity utilization, or the stage of the business cycle, first employed by Tanzi (1980 a). As *GAP* rises, so does pressure on existing capacity, signaling a need for more investment. In effect, *GAP* captures an accelerator effect on investment.

---

[10] The depressing impact on corporate profits of *actual* inflation may be offset by a reduction in the real value of corporate debt only to the extent that actual inflation is unanticipated. But expected inflation will not result in a lower value of corporate debt, since it will be reflected in a higher nominal interest rate demanded by lenders and paid by borrowers in the face of an anticipated depreciation of money against commodities. Expected inflation will, however, depress expected after-tax profits under existing depreciation rules.

The log of the sum of real saving, taxes, and imports is written as

$$Z_t = \gamma_0 + \gamma_1 y_t - \gamma_2(m_t - p_t) \\ - \gamma_3 \sigma_t^2 + e_2 \quad (\gamma_1, \gamma_2, \gamma_3 > 0) \tag{7}$$

where

Z_t = log of real saving

y_t = log of real income (output)

$(m_t - p_t)$ = log of real money balances

Equilibrium in the money sector is written as

$$(m_t - p_t) = \beta_0 + \beta_1 y_t - \beta_2(1-\tau)i_t + e_{3_t} \tag{8}$$

Equation (8) takes the after-tax nominal interest rate as the opportunity cost of holding money.

The supply side of the model represents real income (output) as

$$y_t = y_{n_t} + \sum_{i=0}^{n} \phi_i(m_i - {}_{i-1}m_i^e) + e_{4_t} \tag{9}$$

where

y_{n_t} = log of natural output, written as $\theta_0 + \theta_1$ time

$(m_i - {}_{i-1}m_i^e)$ = surprise money growth measured as the difference between the log of the current money supply and the log of the anticipated (as of $t-1$ for t) money supply.

Finally, the Fisher equation is written as equation (3)

$$i_t = \left(\frac{1}{1-\tau}\right)\left[r_t^* + \pi_t\right]$$

where

i_t = nominal interest rate
τ = marginal tax rate on interest income.

Equations (6) through (9) and equation (3) can now be used to solve for r_t^*. Setting equation (6) equal to equation (7), substituting from equation (8) for real balances and from equation (9) for real output, and substituting the resulting expression for r_t^* into equation (3) yield a reduced-form equation for the nominal interest rate in terms of a constant term, expected inflation, money surprises, uncertainty about inflation, exogenous demand disturbances, GAP, time, and an error term.[11]

$$i_t = \left(\frac{1}{1-\tau}\right)\left[\lambda_0 + (1-\lambda_1)\pi_t - \lambda_2 \sum_{i=0}^{n} \phi_i(m_i - {}_{i-1}m_i^e)\right.$$
$$\left. - \lambda_3\sigma_t^2 + \lambda_4 X_t + \lambda_5 GAP_t - \theta_1\lambda_2 \, time + V_t\right] \tag{10}$$

$$\lambda_0 = [(\alpha_0 - \gamma_0 + \gamma_2\beta_0 - \theta_0(\gamma_1 - \gamma_2\beta))/(\alpha_1 + (\alpha_1 + \alpha_2\beta_2)]$$

$$\lambda_1 = [(\alpha_4 + \gamma_2\beta_2)/(\alpha_1 + \gamma_2\beta_2)] \qquad (0 < \lambda_1 < 1)$$

$$\lambda_2 = [(\gamma_1 - \gamma_2\beta_1)/(\alpha_1 + \gamma_2\beta_2)] \qquad \lambda_2 > 0^{12}$$

$$\lambda_3 = [(\alpha_2 - \gamma_3)/(\alpha_1 + \gamma_2\beta_2)] \qquad \lambda_3 \gtrless 0$$

$$\lambda_4 = [\alpha_3/(\alpha_1 + \gamma_2\beta_2)] \qquad \lambda_4 > 0$$

$$\lambda_5 = [\alpha_5/(\alpha_1 + \gamma_2\beta_2)] \qquad \lambda_5 > 0$$

$$V_t = [(e_{1_t} - e_{2_t} + \gamma_2 e_{3_t} - \gamma_1 e_{4_t})/\alpha_1 + \gamma_2\beta_2)]$$

The coefficients on the interest rate equation (10) are functions of the underlying structural parameters defined in equations (3) and (6) through (9). It is useful to note that the measured impact upon nominal interest of each of the explanatory variables in equation (10) also depends upon the effective marginal tax rate, τ, on interest income. While the underlying structural parameters are unidentified (they cannot be measured based on empirical estimation of equation (10)), this framework is still useful for three reasons. First, it shows clearly

---

[11] It is assumed that money surprises are independent of the error term in equation (10).

[12] λ_2 is positive, since γ_1, the elasticity of real saving plus imports with respect to real income, is unity, given a constant ratio of savings plus taxes and imports to income, while β_1, the elasticity of demand for real balances with respect to real income, and λ_2, the (elasticity) real balance effect on saving plus imports, are both fractions.

why it may be that even with nonzero tax rates applied to interest income, the measured coefficient on expected inflation will be less than $[1/(1-\tau)]$ and may even be less than unity. Second, it clearly shows that the measured impact on interest rates of all explanatory variables is conditional on the tax rate, τ. Since that rate may vary over time, it suggests a reason for changes over time in the fit of many interest rate equations. Finally, the derivation of equation (10) makes clear the theoretical basis for a negative relationship between expected inflation and the expected after-tax real rate.[13]

The impact of expected inflation on the nominal interest rate reflects a combination of four factors: (1) the Fisher effect, whereby the nominal interest rate rises by the full amount of a rise in expected inflation; (2) the tax effect, whereby the nominal interest rate must rise by more than the rise in expected inflation to maintain a constant expected after-tax real return; (3) the Mundell-Tobin effect, captured in equations (7) and (8), whereby a rise in expected inflation decreases equilibrium real cash balances, in turn increasing the steady-state level of flow savings owing to the real balance effect, with equilibrium being restored by means of a lower after-tax real interest rate, which raises investment to the higher level of savings; and (4) the Feldstein-Summers effect, whereby a rise in anticipated inflation depresses expected after-tax profits and causes investment to fall. In sum, tax effects move the coefficient above unity, while the Mundell effect and the Feldstein-Summers effect both push it below unity. Typical parameter values for τ and λ_1 indicate an expected value of 0.75 for the coefficient describing the impact of expected inflation on the nominal interest rate.[14] Even though tax effects by themselves tend to push the coefficient above unity, the combined depressing impact of the Mundell effect and the Feldstein-Summers effect may result in a net impact below unity. The general equilibrium approach employed here resolves the apparent "mystery" regarding a less than unitary impact of expected inflation on interest rates when taxes are considered.

The hypothesized negative impact of money surprises on the real rate arises from their positive impact on real income, which, in turn, increases real saving and requires a decrease in the real rate to produce an equilibrating increase in real investment. This effect outweighs the simultaneous upward pressure on the real rate that results from excess demand for real balances associated with increased real income. (See

---

[13] This phenomenon may also arise in open economies where inventory behavior results in inertia of commodity prices. See Criswell (1983).

[14] Parameter values which make $\partial i / \partial \pi = 0.75$ are $\alpha_1 = 0.5$; $\alpha_4 = 0.2$; $\gamma_2 = 0.2$; $\beta_2 = 0.5$; $\tau = 0.33$.

footnote 14.) The effect of money surprises may be contemporaneous, or it may persist over a number of periods owing either to stickiness or, more rigorously, to attempts to restore desired inventory stocks. (See Blinder and Fischer (1981).)

It is important to distinguish between the real income impact of a money surprise described here and an expectations effect like that reported by Mishkin (1981). Mishkin reports a positive relationship between quarterly money surprises and *end-of-period* short-term interest rates. The result arises, in Mishkin's view, from a positive impact of a money surprise on expected inflation. In contrast, this study employs *period-average* short-term rates as a dependent variable in order to capture the real income impact under way during the quarter, before comparison of an actual with an anticipated money supply gives rise to an expectations effect. A fuller discussion of Mishkin's results and their relationship with the results obtained here is contained in Makin (1982 c). An alternative liquidity rationale for a negative relationship between money surprises and short-term rates is discussed in Makin (1982 b) and Khan (1980).

The impact of uncertainty about inflation on the equilibrium after-tax real rate is ambiguous, as was discussed earlier. The negative impact of uncertainty about inflation on real investment is measured by α_2 in equation (6). The negative impact on real saving of uncertainty about inflation is measured by γ_3 in equation (7). The ambiguous impact on the interest rate is given by λ_3 in equation (10).

The impact of exogenous shifts in aggregate demand on the after-tax real rate is unambiguously positive. If there is an exogenous upward shift in aggregate demand, the after-tax real rate must rise to "crowd out" private investment in order to restore commodity market equilibrium. The model represented by equations (6) through (10) makes it clear that tests of the possible impact of fiscal deficits on interest rates cannot be conducted by inserting a measure of the actual fiscal deficit directly into an interest rate equation. Since tax proceeds rise with income, the built-in portion of deficits is endogenous and typically countercyclical. Interest rates are typically procyclical; therefore, the coefficient on the actual deficit (measured as a positive number) term in the interest rate equation will be downwardly biased and possibly negative.[15]

Expected future deficits have been identified by some as a source of higher interest rates. However, such effects ought to be confined to long-term rates. Measurement of the impact of expected future

---

[15] This is confirmed by results reported in Section V. For a thorough discussion of government deficits and aggregate demand, see Feldstein (1982).

deficits on long-term rates is confounded by the cyclical biases just discussed, together with the fact that few actual time series on anything like a comprehensive measure of expected future deficits exist for years before 1980. Some analysts contend that the impact on interest rates of fiscal deficits arises only from their impact on longer-run inflationary expectations. Others suggest that the expected "crowding out" that large fiscal deficits imply for credit markets will raise real rates and thereby raise nominal rates. But for all of these longer-run concepts, measurement presents a serious difficulty.

One way to avoid these difficulties is to test the impact on interest rates of unanticipated movements in the fiscal deficit.[16] This approach purges the deficit of its systematic component, which—as noted above— tends to bias downward the deficit's measured impact on interest rates. Further, given period-average short-term rates as the dependent variable, it is possible, as with money surprises, to capture the impact on interest rates of higher-than-expected sales of government securities during the quarter. This impact should occur before the end of the quarter, when comparison of an actual with an anticipated fiscal deficit may give rise to an expectations effect. More specifically, a surprise increase in the deficit may cause market participants to expect higher money growth and, therefore, higher inflation. But if this expectations effect is already captured in the expected inflation term, the surprise deficit will appear to have no additional explanatory power. The use of a period-average interest rate as a dependent variable, as noted, avoids this problem of apparent redundancy of fiscal deficits in an interest rate equation. It is expected that a surprise deficit will raise the period-average interest rate.

Once a measure is obtained of the impact on interest rates of a surprise intraquarter rise in the fiscal deficit, expressed in terms of basis points per billion dollars per quarter, some idea of the cumulative effect over a year of a rise in predicted deficits can be obtained. The presumption is that if forecast fiscal deficits over a year rise by, say, $100 billion, the instant impact on interest rates is equivalent to the present discounted compound impact of $25 billion per quarter in fiscal deficit surprises over the coming year. Based on estimates to be reported below, a $100 billion rise in the estimated annual deficit distributed as a surprise of $25 billion per quarter over four quarters would raise three-month treasury bill rates by 40 basis points.

---

[16] Another way could be to use the full-employment budget surplus. This was tried in place of the unanticipated deficit, and the results are reported below. The full-employment budget surplus did not enter significantly into the estimated interest rate equation.

The *GAP* variable, as defined above, is positively related to the interest rate. A rise in *GAP* or pressure on capacity produces an accelerated effect on investment, which, ceteris paribus, requires a higher expected after-tax real rate to maintain equilibrium (Tanzi (1980 a)).

After consideration of all these factors, it is clear from equation (10) that regression of nominal interest on a constant, a surprise deficit, a money surprise, *GAP*, a measure of uncertainty about inflation, and expected inflation ought to (a) test the hypothesized positive impact on the after-tax real interest rate of an exogenous shock to aggregate demand (measured by an unanticipated deficit); (b) test the hypothesized negative impact of a money surprise on the after-tax real rate by checking to see if the coefficient on the surprise is significantly less than zero;[17] (c) test the hypothesized negative impact of expected inflation on after-tax real interest by checking to see if the coefficient on expected inflation is significantly below $[1/(1-\tau)]$; (d) measure the net impact of uncertainty about inflation on the after-tax real rate; and (e) test the impact of *GAP* on the after-tax real rate. Contemporaneous and lagged money surprises may depress the real interest rate insofar as they increase real output above its natural level.

V. SOME EMPIRICAL TESTS

Some empirical tests that attempt to incorporate several of the above hypotheses are reported below. These tests, however, will not be able to capture some of those hypotheses, such as the disappearance of fiscal illusion. As a prelude to those tests, it is, perhaps, useful to report some results of the simplest possible test for the Fisherian

---

[17] Besides Mishkin's (1982) expectations effect, some investigators—including Grossman (1981), Engel and Frankel (1982), and Roley (1982)—have found a short-run "policy expectations effect," whereby a positive difference between a consensus forecast and the announced *weekly* increase in the money supply causes short-run interest rates to *rise*. The result is seen to follow from an anticipated tightening of Federal Reserve policy in response to excessive money growth.

This finding, like Mishkin's, is not inconsistent with a finding that prior to operation of an expectations effect, when an actual money number materializes that can be compared with a forecast, an income or liquidity effect occasioned by money growth above its anticipated path will depress interest rates. The dependent variable in the "policy expectations effect" studies is the change in three-month treasury bill yields from 3:30 p.m. to 5:00 p.m. on Friday afternoon; this is done in order to isolate a pure expectations effect. Detection of an income or liquidity effect in these studies would require regressing the average interest rate from 5:00 p.m on Friday of the previous week to 3:30 p.m. on the current Friday on the *current* Friday's money surprise. A negative interest impact via an income or liquidity effect ought to lead the money surprise. These issues are discussed further in Makin (1982 c).

relationship, such as that reflected in an equation of the type $i_t = r_t + \beta\pi_t$, where all the symbols have the same meaning as above. The results obtained are of some interest.

(1) The worst period for a test of this simple Fisherian relationship insofar as proximity to one of the coefficients on expected inflation is concerned is between the late 1950s and the mid-1970s. For this period, the coefficient of expected inflation β is below 0.70.[18]

(2) If one keeps, say, 1958 as the initial period and extends the period beyond 1975 to 1981, β rises to well over 0.80.

(3) If one keeps the terminal year at 1981 but moves the initial year beyond 1958, the coefficient of π changes little up to the mid-1960s, but then it starts rising. For the period after 1970, the coefficient of π is significant and substantially exceeds unity, which is consistent with what one would expect from the partial equilibrium framework with taxes.

(4) The results are about the same whether one uses 3-month, 6-month, or 12-month treasury bills.

These findings obtained by estimating the basic Fisher equation suggest that either security markets do not fully reflect changes in anticipated inflation or else significant movements in the after-tax real rate have, in varying degrees over separate subperiods, distorted inferences drawn from estimating the basic Fisher equation.[19] In the light of the theory of interest rate behavior developed in Section IV, the latter possibility seems most likely.[20]

Results of estimating interest rate equations suggested by equation (10) in Section IV are presented in Table 2. Particular attention is given to implications of proper modeling of residuals made possible by the use of transfer function procedures discussed in Box and Jenkins (1970). An attempt is made to check for the possible atrophy since 1979 of fiscal illusion.

The fit of the equation for the full period (equation (2.1) in Table 2) is displayed in Chart 2. Actual and predicted values listed in Table 3 indicate that the model tracks interest rates well within the sample period. Use of the transfer function procedure implies that the good-

---

[18] This was a period of accelerating inflation.

[19] They may also indicate that it is not just the rate of inflation but also the *change* in that rate that may be significant. For example, the Mundell-Tobin effect may be tied to *accelerating* inflation rather than to the rate of inflation itself.

[20] Summers (1982) has argued, however, that nominal interest rates do not adjust by the full amount implied by the Fisher hypothesis as modified to allow for marginal tax rates on interest earnings. His results, based on both pre- and post-World War II data, arise from equations that employ actual inflation rates in place of expected inflation and that generally do not include variables to control for movements in the expected real rate.

Table 2. Interest Rate Equations: Various Time Periods[1]

Equation	Constant	Expected Inflation[2]	Money Surprise[3]	Surprise Deficit[4]	Inflation Uncertainty	GAP[5]	Sample Period[6]
				Full Period			
(2.1)	2.859 (13.84)	0.746 (6.46)	-0.044 (6.94)	0.004 (2.88)	-0.006 (0.04)	0.134 (4.01)	1960.I-1981.IV
				Subperiods			
(2.2)	3.001 (13.34)	0.661 (5.06)	-0.046 (6.91)	0.005 (2.41)	-0.055 (0.49)	0.150 (4.24)	1960.I-1975.IV
(2.3)	2.976 (15.58)	0.664 (6.37)	-0.046 (7.59)	0.004 (2.61)	-0.005 (0.41)	0.148 (4.81)	1960.I-1979.III
(2.4)	2.948 (15.46)	0.691 (6.64)	-0.046 (7.42)	-0.004 (2.82)	-0.029 (0.21)	0.146 (4.66)	1960.I-1980.IV

[1] The dependent variable in all equations is the three-month treasury bill rate. All equations are estimated as transfer functions. Residuals are modeled by an ARMA (1,1) model. (The t-statistics, which are shown in parentheses, are all above 5.0.) White noise test significance levels for the first 24 residuals are, respectively, 0.49, 0.21, 0.11, and 0.26 for equations (2.1) through (2.4).
[2] Anticipated inflation is based on Livingston survey data on six-month expected inflation. Interpolation is employed to obtain a quarterly series.
[3] Money surprises are measured as residuals from an ARMA (0,8) model of money (M_1) growth. For a full discussion of this procedure and of alternatives, see Makin (1983).
[4] Surprise deficits are measured as residuals from a univariate time-series model of the government finance deficit measured in billions of U.S. dollars at an annual rate (line 80 of the U.S. country pages in the Fund's monthly publication, International Financial Statistics).
[5] GAP is calculated from quarterly data on U.S. real gross national product capacity estimated by the U.S. Council of Economic Advisers and actual U.S. real gross national product.
[6] The time variable in equation (10) is captured by the noise model of residuals estimated simultaneously with the coefficients on explanatory variables in the interest rate equation employing the transfer function estimation procedure.

Table 3. Actual Versus Predicted Values of the Three-Month U.S. Treasury Bill Rate[1]

Year	Quarter	Actual	Predicted	Year	Quarter	Actual	Predicted
1960	I	3.87	. . .	1971	I	3.84	4.94
	II	2.99	3.06		II	4.24	3.65
	III	2.36	2.45		III	5.00	4.81
	IV	2.31	2.29		IV	4.23	5.07
1961	I	2.35	2.48	1972	I	3.44	3.65
	II	2.30	2.54		II	3.77	4.28
	III	2.30	2.43		III	4.22	3.75
	IV	2.46	2.63		IV	4.86	4.99
1962	I	2.72	2.71	1973	I	5.70	5.63
	II	2.71	2.92		II	6.60	5.70
	III	2.84	2.86		III	8.32	7.82
	IV	2.81	2.74		IV	7.50	8.31
1963	I	2.91	2.10	1974	I	7.62	7.26
	II	2.94	3.09		II	8.15	8.61
	III	3.29	2.97		III	8.19	7.84
	IV	3.50	3.40		IV	7.36	8.27
1964	I	3.53	3.63	1975	I	5.75	6.07
	II	3.48	3.56		II	5.39	5.36
	III	3.50	3.25		III	6.33	6.03
	IV	3.68	3.88		IV	5.63	6.77
1965	I	3.89	3.59	1976	I	4.92	4.85
	II	3.87	3.87		II	5.16	5.17
	III	3.86	3.95		III	5.15	5.68
	IV	4.16	4.18		IV	4.67	4.91
1966	I	4.60	4.48	1977	I	4.63	5.30
	II	4.58	4.68		II	4.84	5.06
	III	5.03	4.79		III	5.50	5.65
	IV	5.20	5.05		IV	6.11	5.85
1967	I	4.51	4.77	1978	I	6.39	6.78
	II	3.66	4.40		II	6.48	6.33
	III	4.29	3.57		III	7.31	7.27
	IV	4.74	5.04		IV	8.57	7.84
1968	I	5.04	5.13	1979	I	9.38	9.37
	II	5.51	5.03		II	9.38	9.11
	III	5.20	5.54		III	9.67	10.29
	IV	5.58	4.93		IV	11.84	9.95
1969	I	6.09	6.09	1980	I	13.35	12.71
	II	6.19	6.01		II	9.62	12.71
	III	7.01	6.30		III	9.15	6.91
	IV	7.35	6.96		IV	13.61	11.44
1970	I	7.21	6.66	1981	I	14.39	12.82
	II	6.67	6.94		II	14.91	12.75
	III	6.33	5.76		III	15.05	12.44
	IV	5.35	6.19		IV	11.75	12.44
				1982	I	12.81	8.35
					II	12.42	7.33
					III	9.32	6.32
					IV	7.91	5.22

[1] Predicted values based on equation (2.1) in Table 2.

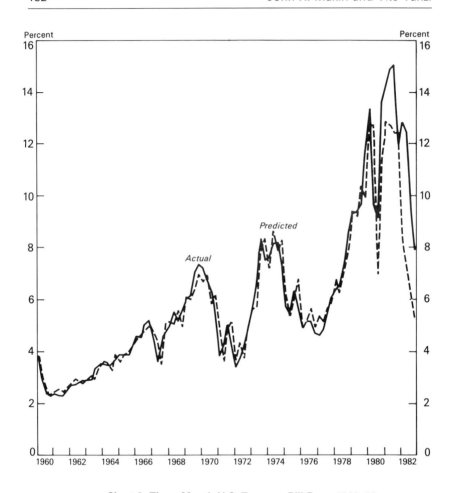

Chart 2. Three-Month U.S. Treasury Bill Rate, 1960–82

ness of fit reflects explanatory power both of the independent variables employed and of the past history of interest rates.[21]

Initial estimation of the equations just described resulted in het-
eroscedastic error terms. A Park-Glejser test strongly supported the
hypothesis that error variances grew over time. Therefore, in all results reported here, variables have been divided by the positively trended
series on expected inflation to adjust for heteroscedasticity.

---

[21] Estimation employing ordinary least squares with adjustment for serial correlation
of residuals yields nearly identical results. This is not surprising, since this procedure
is nearly equivalent to a transfer function with an (autoregressive) AR (1) noise model
and equations in Table 2 are estimated employing an (autoregressive moving average)
ARMA (1,1) model.

A number of conclusions emerge from Table 2. First, the coefficient on expected inflation is in all cases below unity. All of the subsample estimates of that coefficient lie within one standard error of the full-period result. Second, the money surprise variable produces the hypothesized negative impact on interest rates.[22] The *GAP* variable produces the hypothesized positive impact on interest rates in a manner consistent with results reported by Tanzi (1980 a).[23]

The impact on interest rates of an exogenous shock to aggregate demand, as measured by an unanticipated increase in the fiscal deficit, is of particular interest. The model presented in Section IV suggests a positive relationship that would represent the potential "crowding out" of private investment that has been widely discussed in connection with large projected U.S. deficits after passage of the Economic Recovery Tax Act of 1981. Of course, here it is suggested that only deficits differing from those projected subsequently to passage of that legislation will produce an impact on interest rates beyond that embodied in projections made at the time of its passage.

Results reported in Table 2 for all sample periods suggest that a surprise increase in the deficit at an annual rate of $10 billion during a quarter (an actual $2.5 billion surprise during the quarter) would raise the interest rate on three-month treasury bills by four basis points.[24] This effect may seem small, but it should be remembered that this is the impact on the short-term bill rate only. Deficit "surprises" of $20 billion to $40 billion a quarter have not been uncommon since 1981, and surprises of this magnitude imply annual rates of $80 billion to $160 billion, which, in turn, would raise the short-term rate by 32 to 64 basis points. The impact on longer-term rates could be larger.

Recall that discussion of the expected coefficient on expected inflation suggested that tax effects tend to push it above unity and that the Mundell-Tobin and Feldstein-Summers effects tend to push it

---

[22] Money surprises are measured as residuals from an ARMA (0,8) model of money (M_1) growth. For a full discussion of this procedure and of alternatives, see Makin (1983).

[23] The time variable in equation (10) is captured by the noise model of residuals estimated simultaneously with the coefficients on explanatory variables in the interest rate equation using the transfer function methodology.

[24] Estimation employing the actual deficit in place of the surprise deficit gives

$$i_t = 2.187 + 1.067\,\pi_t - 0.024\,(m_t - {}_{t-1}m_t^e) - 0.251\,\sigma_t^2 + 0.001\,def._t$$
$$\quad (15.57) \quad (7.25) \quad\quad (3.61) \quad\quad\quad (1.60) \quad\quad (1.1)$$

As noted earlier, the countercyclical deficit combined with the procyclical interest rates tends to bias downward the estimated coefficient on the deficit. The result also suggests an enhanced negative impact of inflation uncertainty σ_t^2 on the interest rate when *GAP* is excluded from the estimated equation (see below).

below unity. The reported results below unity are consistent with our hypothetical predicted value of 0.75 based on "reasonable" parameter values.

The significant negative impact on interest rates of the money surprise term is consistent with reported findings in a number of related studies. Levi and Makin (1978) report that output growth decreases interest rates, and Makin (1982 a) reports that surprise money growth increases output growth. Therefore, it is to be expected that both variables would be negatively correlated with interest rates. The findings are also consistent with the hypothesis that surprise money growth produces the liquidity effects discussed in Makin (1982 b) and Khan (1980).

Uncertainty about inflation was not significant in the presence of all of the other variables. This is, of course, theoretically possible, since uncertainty about inflation depresses both saving and investment schedules. Indeed, results reported here suggest that it is not possible to reject the hypothesis that the net impact on the equilibrium after-tax real rate of these shifts is zero.

This result differs from findings reported in Levi and Makin (1978) and Makin (1983) of a significant negative coefficient on uncertainty about inflation. The reason for the different finding reported here may be linked to the presence of the GAP variable, which was not included in the other studies. A rise in GAP produces a significant positive impact on the interest rate. At the same time, it is negatively correlated with the measure of uncertainty about inflation σ^2 ($\rho = -0.32$). The GAP variable is likely proxying for σ^2, with a rise in GAP associated with lower inflation uncertainty. No simple economic explanation for this association comes readily to mind, but it does reconcile results reported here with the finding reported elsewhere of a significant negative relationship between interest rates and inflation uncertainty. A rise in GAP may, in addition to its shift impact on investment, proxy for a drop in σ_2, which, in turn, is associated with higher interest rates.

Compared with the simple Fisher equation, results discussed at the beginning of this section and reported in Table 2 suggest that the impact of expected inflation on interest has been remarkably stable over a number of subperiods. It appears that the variability of that impact discovered in a number of investigations of the simple Fisher equation is due to time-varying bias on estimates drawn from equations that have omitted significant explanatory variables.

Table 4. Actual Versus Predicted U.S. Treasury Bill Rate and Velocity Growth Surprises, 1982

Quarter	Actual	Predicted	Actual Minus Predicted	Surprise Velocity Growth
I	12.81	8.35	4.46	−3.32
II	12.42	7.33	5.09	−0.12
III	9.32	6.32	3.00	−0.86
IV	7.91	5.22	2.69	−3.31

VI. REMAINING PUZZLES CONCERNING INTEREST RATES

Many aspects of interest rate behavior are still not well understood, particularly the behavior in recent years. Although the inflation and inflationary expectations fell sharply during 1982, both short-term and long-term rates remained high, particularly during the first half of that year. The inconsistency of this experience with what the present model would have predicted is clear from Table 4. Interest rates for 1982 were badly unpredicted by the model when the model parameters (estimated using data for 1960–81) were used jointly with actual values of exogenous variables for 1982.

One possible explanation for this result may be the very unusual behavior of monetary velocity during 1982. M_1 velocity grew at an average annual rate of 3.2 percent from 1950 to 1982, although growth rates usually fell somewhat during contractions. But the drop in actual velocity during 1982 was a remarkable 4.8 percent. Based on a quarterly time series of M_1 velocity behavior for 1960–81, growth of velocity during 1982 should have been about 2.95 percent. The unanticipated drop in annual velocity growth over the year was 7.75 percent, distributed over the quarters as shown in Table 3.

If, as some have suggested, including the Federal Reserve Board (see the testimony of Chairman Paul A. Volcker before the U.S. Senate Committee on Banking, Housing, and Urban Affairs on February 16, 1983[25]), the collapse in velocity growth during 1982 represented a large and unpredictable increase in money demand, then excess money demand may have been responsible for the very high interest rates during much of 1982. The drop in interest rates during the last half

---

[25] *Federal Reserve Bulletin* (Washington), Vol. 69 (March 1983), pp. 167–74.

of the year may have reflected some relief of that excess demand condition resulting from the rapid acceleration of money growth during that period. The annual growth rate of money (M_1) was 1.5 percent during the first half of 1982 and 15.1 percent during the second half.

It is tempting to attribute the persistence of high short-term interest rates during much of 1982, even in the face of lower expected inflation, to the unexpectedly sharp drop in velocity that occurred at the same time. However, coincidence does not necessarily imply causality, and it is reasonable to ask if a stable relationship has existed between unanticipated movements in velocity and interest rates over a longer period and in the presence of the other explanatory variables in equation (10). As a matter of fact, unexpected velocity growth has, contrary to expectations, a weak positive impact on interest rates when included as an explanatory variable in equations like those reported in Table 2, either for the 1960–81 or the 1960–82 sample period.[26] When interest rates are regressed on anticipated inflation together with velocity shocks, the velocity shocks again have a significant *positive* impact on nominal interest rates and the explanatory power is comparable to that of equations reported in Table 2.

The inconsistency between the negative association between velocity shocks and interest rates during 1982 and the positive association typical of the 1960–81 sample period can be explained as a manifestation of the identification problem first encountered by Henry Schultz in 1938. As Schultz discovered, where demand is highly volatile relative to supply, price and quantitative measures map out a positive relationship. During 1982, a positive shock to money demand dominated money supply shifts, and the sharp drop in velocity reflected an excess money demand shift which caused interest rates, controlled for the level of expected inflation, to rise. Alternatively, during most of the postwar period, including 1960–81, shocks to money supply have dominated shocks to money demand. As a result, a sharp drop in velocity usually reflects a positive shock to money supply, which, in turn, produces a simultaneous negative impact on interest rates while liquidity effects dominate expectation effects. The result, consistent with findings reported in Table 2 on the effects of unexpected money growth, is a dominant positive association between velocity shocks and interest rates during much of the postwar period.

In short, most of the shocks to monetary equilibrium which have caused short-term rates to move above or below levels implied by

---

[26] Unexpected velocity growth was employed in place of surprise growth of the money supply, since velocity growth is defined as GNP growth less money supply growth and therefore is likely to be highly correlated with money growth.

changes in expected inflation, at least during the 1960–81 sample period, have been supply shocks. In contrast, 1982 was characterized by dominance of a (positive) demand shock. Such a demand shock prevented short-term interest rates from falling by as much as expected inflation. Once the situation was alleviated, short-term rates fell roughly by as much as expected inflation. The expected real rate on three-month treasury bills fell from 7.09 percent during the second quarter of 1982 to 3.25 percent during the fourth quarter of 1982.

VII. CONCLUDING REMARKS

This paper has attempted to demonstrate a need to expand the simple Fisherian view whereby changes in interest rates are explained largely by changes in expected inflation. The need for this expansion became particularly evident during the early 1980s. Our measure of expected inflation dropped from 10.5 percent per annum during the fourth quarter of 1980 to 7.6 percent per annum during the third quarter of 1981. Over the same period, average yields on three-month treasury bills *rose* from 13.6 percent to 15.1 percent. Some explanation for this apparent discrepancy in terms of the results reported here may be useful.

The failure of interest rates to display a sustained drop during 1981, as the expected rate of inflation fell steadily, resulted from a combination of forces. During the first quarter of 1981, some downward pressure was exerted on interest rates, but a sustained fall was prevented by a rise in economic activity. Our measure of excess capacity (minus *GAP*) fell from 5.5 percent during the fourth quarter of 1980 to 4.3 percent during the first quarter of 1981. Our estimates suggest that this change alone would add about 25 basis points to short-term rates.

Rates remained high during the second quarter of 1981 owing, among other things, to a shift to unexpectedly tight money. (See Makin (1982 b) for a fuller discussion.) This shift, by itself, raised short-term rates by about 24 basis points, according to our estimates. Unexpectedly tight money persisted into the third quarter of 1981, during which passage of the Economic Recovery Tax Act of 1981 also added to the upward pressure on rates. Short-term rates were 2.61 percentage points above the level predicted by our interest rate equation for the third quarter of 1981, suggesting that some exogenous shock pushed up rates. This was the largest positive residual during the 20 years covered by our sample, and it seems to be attributable to fundamental changes in the outlook for the cyclical pattern of deficits attributable to passage of the Economic Recovery Tax Act of 1981. (This factor is discussed further below.)

In the fourth quarter of 1981, there was a sharp fall in short-term rates. This fall was attributable to, among other things, (a) a large increase in excess capacity (29 basis points); (b) a large positive surprise in money growth (36 basis points); (c) a surprise surplus during that quarter (16 basis points); and (d) a drop in inflationary expectations (48 basis points). The actual fall of 330 basis points was greater than the 129 basis points indicated here, but the discrepancy is considerably reduced by accounting for the effects of variables other than expected inflation. In practice, our noise model, or the past history of the three-month treasury bill rate itself, accounts for all but 69 basis points of the remaining actual fall in rates.

During December 1981 and January 1982, there was a sharp acceleration of money growth accompanied by a rise in interest rates. This would be contrary to our prediction if part of the sharp increase had come as a surprise. It must be remembered, however, that the sharp increase coincided with the first appearance of reports of sharply higher projections of U.S. fiscal deficits totaling $338.7 billion for fiscal years 1982 through 1984. These projections, which were revised upward even further during 1982, suggest another reason for persistently high interest rates during the first half of 1982. If these figures materialize, they may well break the traditional countercyclical pattern historically followed by U.S. fiscal deficits. If the U.S. economy expands during 1982–84, a rise in fiscal deficits will coincide with attempts by the private sector to increase borrowing.

Traditionally, in the expansionary phase of the cycle, there has been a drop in fiscal deficits. The perception of a change in the cyclical pattern of deficits has kept interest rates high since the end of 1981, whereas normally the dramatic drop in inflation and expectations about future inflation would have lowered rates. Viewed in this way, it may be that the surprise increase in money growth during December 1981 and January 1982, in fact, reduced the upward pressure on rates caused by the likelihood of procyclical U.S. fiscal deficits coupled with the then prevailing expectation that the U.S. economy would recover during the second quarter of 1982.[27]

Finally, it is possible that an atrophy of fiscal illusion resulting in a rise in perceived tax rates employed to calculate real after-tax returns has tended to increase observed pretax market rates. Such a rise in

---

[27] A sharp drop in interest rates did materialize by August 1982, when it became clear that recovery of the U.S. economy was to be delayed and when monetary policy began to become more accommodative.

perceived tax rates would magnify the impact on observed pretax interest rates of rises in expected after-tax real rates.

The high volatility of interest rates since 1979 is explained fairly straightforwardly by the sharp rise in the volatility of expected inflation (the variance of π rose from 0.44 during June 1976–December 1978 to 2.13 during June 1979–December 1981) and by the likely increase in volatility of expected after-tax real rates resulting from increased uncertainty about the cyclical pattern of U.S. fiscal deficits and from pressures created by adherence to monetary targets. The increased variance of expected inflation likely reflects, in part, the increased volatility of money growth since 1979. This is disquieting in view of the Federal Reserve System's stated goal of reducing volatility of money growth under its new operating procedures, but its impact on uncertainty about the outlook for inflation was quite predictable. Persistent success in targeting aggregates ought to reduce sharply the volatility of expected inflation. The net result will be more stable nominal rates, even given some higher level of real rate volatility.

Overall interest rates have remained high since 1980, although progress in lowering expected inflation would normally have brought reductions, because a number of forces have acted to raise after-tax real rates since that time. Interest rates have been highly volatile in response to the increased uncertainty about the outlook for inflation and for expected real rates.

These findings suggest a need for further investigation in a number of areas. Can effects of tax policy on interest rates be considered separately from the effects of other variables? Analysis by Peek (1981) suggests that this may be possible. How significant a factor is the perceived structural change in the cyclical behavior of U.S. fiscal deficits in pushing up real rates? Is there evidence that fiscal illusion has moderated and, if so, by how much? Might it be expected to reappear given a sharp reduction in expected inflation? If higher real rates persist owing to "crowding out" associated with persistently enlarged fiscal deficits, what will be the effects on private savings, on international capital flows, and on private investment? What are the implications of increased uncertainty about expected inflation? Finally, and perhaps most important, what are the implications for the world economy of the unusual behavior exhibited by U.S. interest rates since 1979? More specific questions include possible effects on observed and real exchange rates, effects on worldwide economic growth and capital formation, and implications for the form of the international monetary system.

References

Alamouti, Kaveh (1980), "An Analysis of the International Relationship Among Real Rates of Return" (unpublished, London Business School, Institute of Finance and Accounting, January 1980).

Blinder, Alan S., and Stanley Fischer, "Inventories, Rational Expectations and the Business Cycle," *Journal of Monetary Economics* (Amsterdam), Vol. 8 (November 1981), pp. 277–304.

Box, George E.P., and Gwilym Jenkins, *Time Series Analysis, Forecasting and Control* (San Francisco: Holden-Day, 1970).

Criswell, Andrew R., "Inventories, Price Inertia and Exchange Rate Dynamics" (mimeographed, University of Notre Dame, Department of Finance, March 1983).

Cukierman, Alex, and Paul Wachtel, "Relative Price Variability and Non-uniform Inflationary Expectations," *Journal of Political Economy* (Chicago), Vol. 90 (February 1982), pp. 146–57.

Darby, Michael R., "The Financial and Tax Effects of Monetary Policy on Interest Rates," *Economic Inquiry* (Long Beach, California), Vol. 13 (June 1975), pp. 266–74.

Engel, C., and J. Frankel, "Why Money Announcements Move Interest Rates: An Answer from the Foreign Exchange Market" (mimeographed, University of California at Berkeley, Institute of Business and Economic Research, February 1982).

Fama, Eugene F., "Short-Term Interest Rates as Predictors of Inflation," *American Economic Review* (Nashville, Tennessee), Vol. 65 (June 1975), pp. 269–82.

———, "Inflation Uncertainty and Expected Returns on Treasury Bills," *Journal of Political Economy* (Chicago), Vol. 84 (June 1976), pp. 427–48.

———, and Michael Gibbons, "Inflation, Real Returns and Capital Investment," *Journal of Monetary Economics* (Amsterdam), Vol. 9 (May 1982), pp. 297–323.

Feldstein, Martin, "Inflation, Income Taxes, and the Rate of Interest: A Theoretical Analysis," *American Economic Review* (Nashville, Tennessee), Vol. 66 (December 1976), pp. 809–20.

———, "Government Deficits and Aggregate Demand," *Journal of Monetary Economics* (Amsterdam), Vol. 9 (January 1982), pp. 1–20.

_____, and Lawrence Summers, "Inflation, Tax Rules and the Long-Term Interest Rate," *Brookings Papers on Economic Activity: 1* (1978), The Brookings Institution (Washington), pp. 61–99.

Fisher, Irving, *The Theory of Interest* (New York: Macmillan, 1930).

Grossman, Jacob, "The 'Rationality' of Money Supply Expectations and the Short-Run Response of Interest Rates to Monetary Surprises," *Journal of Money, Credit and Banking* (Columbus, Ohio), Vol. 13 (November 1981), pp. 409–24.

Hartman, Richard, and John H. Makin, *Inflation Uncertainty and Interest Rates*, Working Paper No. 906, National Bureau of Economic Research (Cambridge, Massachussetts, June 1982).

Khan, Mohsin S., "Monetary Shocks and the Dynamics of Inflation," *Staff Papers*, International Monetary Fund (Washington), Vol. 27 (June 1980), pp. 250–84.

Levi, Maurice D., and John H. Makin, "Anticipated Inflation and Interest Rates: Further Interpretation of Findings on the Fisher Equation," *American Economic Review* (Nashville, Tennessee), Vol. 68 (December 1978), pp. 801–12.

_____, "Fisher, Phillips, Friedman and the Measured Impact of Inflation on Interest," *Journal of Finance* (New York), Vol. 34 (March 1979), pp. 35–52.

Makin, John H. (1982 a), "Anticipated Money, Inflation Uncertainty and Real Economic Activity," *Review of Economics and Statistics* (Amsterdam), Vol. 64 (February 1982), pp. 126–34.

_____(1982 b), "Effects of Inflation Control Programs on Expected Real Interest Rates," *Staff Papers*, International Monetary Fund, (Washington), Vol. 29 (June 1982), pp. 204–32.

_____(1982 c), "Money Surprises and Short-Term Interest Rates: Reconciling Contradictory Findings" (unpublished, University of Washington, (Seattle, Washington) August 1982).

_____, "Real Interest, Money Surprises, Anticipated Inflation and Fiscal Deficits," *Review of Economics and Statistics* (Amsterdam), Vol. 55 (August 1983), pp. 374–84.

Mishkin, Frederic S., "The Real Interest Rate: An Empirical Investigation," in *The Costs and Consequences of Inflation*, ed. by Karl Brunner and Allan H. Meltzer, Carnegie-Rochester Conference Series on Public Policy, Vol. 15 (Amsterdam: North-Holland, 1981), pp. 151–200.

_____, "Monetary Policy and Short-Term Interest Rates: An Efficient Markets-Rational Expectations Approach," *Journal of Finance* (New York), Vol. 37 (March l982), pp. 63–72.

Mundell, Robert A., "Inflation and Real Interest," *Journal of Political Economy* (Chicago), Vol. 71 (June 1963), pp. 280–83.

Nelson, Charles R., and G. William Schwert, "On Testing the Hypothesis that the Real Rate of Interest Is Constant," *American Economic Review* (Nashville, Tennessee), Vol. 67 (June 1977), pp. 478–86.

Peek, Joe, "Interest Rates, Income Taxes, and Anticipated Inflation," *American Economic Review* (Nashville, Tennessee), Vol. 72 (December 1982), pp. 980–91.

Roley, V. Vance, "The Response of Short-Term Interest Rates to Weekly Money Announcements" (unpublished, Federal Reserve Bank of Kansas City, April 1982).

Schultz, Henry, *The Theory and Measurement of Demand* (Chicago: University of Chicago Press, 1938).

Summers, Lawrence H., *The Non-Adjustment of Nominal Interest Rates: A Study of the Fisher Effect*, National Bureau of Economic Research, Working Paper No. 836 (Cambridge, Massachusetts, January 1982).

Tanzi, Vito, "Inflation, Indexation and Interest Income Taxation," *Quarterly Review*, Banca Nazionale del Lavoro (Rome), No. 116 (March 1976), pp. 64–76.

———(1980 a), "Inflationary Expectations, Economic Activity, Taxes, and Interest Rates," *American Economic Review* (Nashville, Tennessee), Vol. 70 (March 1980), pp. 12–21.

———(1980 b), *Inflation and the Personal Income Tax* (Cambridge, England: Cambridge University Press, 1980).

———(1982 a), "Inflationary Expectations, Economic Activity, Taxes, and Interest Rates: Reply," *American Economic Review* (Nashville, Tennessee), Vol. 72 (September 1982), pp. 860–63.

———(1982 b), "Inflationary Expectations, Taxes, and the Demand for Money in the United States," *Staff Papers*, International Monetary Fund, (Washington), Vol. 29 (June 1982), pp. 155–70.

5

Inflation and the Incidence of Income Taxes on Interest Income in the United States, 1972–81

VITO TANZI

Inflation affects individuals and income classes in their roles as consumers, taxpayers, wage earners, savers, asset holders, lenders, borrowers, etc. Because of this multiplicity of influences, it is difficult, and perhaps impossible, to assess the *total* economic impact of inflation. For this reason, empirical studies have been limited to analyzing the impact of inflation on individuals or income classes specifically as consumers, savers, or wage earners. This partial approach, however, does not answer the question of whether the *total* impact of inflation is beneficial to individuals in particular income classes, but it provides information that can be useful for policy purposes. This paper, therefore, follows this partial approach and analyzes the impact of inflation on individuals in connection with the tax treatment of interest paid or received in the United States.

I. THEORETICAL BACKGROUND

When a country enters an inflationary period, the nominal rate of interest charged on loans must be increased if the lender's real interest income and the borrower's real cost of funds are to remain unchanged. More specifically, in a world without income taxes, an increase in the market interest rate equal to the rate of inflation would be sufficient to keep the real rate of return on loans (and their real cost to borrowers) at the preinflation level. However, income taxes complicate these simple conclusions. When interest income is subject to income taxes and interest payments are deductible expenses, the increase in the nominal rate has to be somewhat greater. During an

143

inflationary period,[1] the nominal or market rate of interest would have to be r^* where

$$r^* = r + \frac{\alpha}{1 - t} \tag{1}$$

In this equation r^* can be called the required interest rate; r is the interest rate that would prevail in the absence of inflation; α is the rate of inflation over the relevant period (assumed to be one year); and t is the rate at which the interest income of the individual is taxed. If this required rate of interest is established, the lender who receives it will be as well off or as badly off, depending on who he is, as in the noninflationary situation, provided that he does not suffer from money illusion.[2] Equally, the borrower who pays the required rate r^* will also be no better off nor worse off.

If income taxes with proportional rates are levied, the t in equation (1) will be fixed, so that the required rate r^* will be the same for every taxpayer regardless of his income. Consequently, if such a rate is established, the real positions of lenders and borrowers will not change except in relation to loans that were contracted in the preinflationary era and that covered several years. However, in most countries income taxes are levied with progressive, rather than proportional, rates. This means that taxpayers at different income levels are taxed at different rates. It follows that equation (1) has to be rewritten as

$$r^*_i = r + \frac{\alpha}{1 - t_i} \tag{2}$$

where the i refers to a particular individual or income class. As t_i depends on the income level, the required interest rate is no longer the same for all individuals. Consequently, no market rate could ever adjust to leave *all* lenders and borrowers in the same situation that existed before inflation.

---

[1] See Vito Tanzi, "Inflation, Indexation, and Interest Income Taxation," *Quarterly Review*, Banca Nazionale del Lavoro (Rome), No. 116 (March 1976), pp. 64–76; Michael R. Darby, "The Financial and Tax Effects of Monetary Policy on Interest Rates," *Economic Inquiry* (Long Beach, California), Vol. 13 (June 1975), pp. 266–740; Martin Feldstein, "Inflation, Income Taxes, and the Rate of Interest: A Theoretical Analysis," *American Economic Review* (Nashville, Tennessee), Vol. 66 (December 1976), pp. 809–20.

[2] If the individual suffers from money illusion, his subjective evaluation of the situation may cause him to lose his objectivity and he may feel better or worse off than he actually is. Also, it must be reiterated that these statements concern the individual only in relation to his lending and borrowing activities. Inflation obviously affects him in other ways, so that the *total* effect of inflation may be either beneficial or damaging to him.

If the market rate of interest should adjust fully for the rate of inflation and for, say, an *average* tax rate, it would be too high for some taxpayers and too low for others, depending on the income tax rate to which they were subject. More specifically, the higher the income of individuals (the higher their marginal tax rate), the higher needs to be the rate of interest that they have to receive *as lenders*— or that they have to pay *as borrowers*—in order for them to remain in the preinflationary real situation.[3] However, ignoring risk and other factors that may influence individual loans, the interest rates that become established in the market are uniform for all taxpayers, so that some taxpayers are bound to gain (or lose) more than others.

In this paper, an attempt is made to obtain some general empirical estimates for individual taxpayers of gains and losses by income classes associated with the recent inflation (and the taxation of interest income) in the United States. The analysis is conducted in relation to the income classes for individual taxpayers shown in various issues of *Statistics of Income: Individual Income Tax Returns* (hereinafter referred to as *Statistics of Income*), a publication of the U.S. Internal Revenue Service. Thus, enterprises are ignored. The data to be analyzed pertain to the 1972–81 period. These were years when the rate of inflation increased sharply; therefore, they are particularly suitable for the kind of analysis pursued in the paper. The United States is used as an important and convenient example; however, the theory and the procedure are as applicable to other countries as they are to the United States.

The period analyzed is divided into two subperiods, 1972–74 and 1977–81. The reason for this is simply that the analysis is concerned with the effects of accelerating inflation on the incidence of income taxes on interest income. Inflation accelerated sharply over the 1972–74 period, but the sharp recession that followed brought about equally sharp declines in prices. However, this respite from inflation was of a short duration. The 1977–81 period was again a period of high and accelerating inflation, at least until 1980.

II. DETERMINATION OF REQUIRED RATES FOR THE UNITED STATES, 1972–74 and 1977–81

The consumer price index rose by 3.3 percent in 1972, by 6.2 percent in 1973, and by 11.0 percent in 1974. *If interest income had not*

---

[3] Throughout this paper, it is assumed that interest paid is a deductible expense in relation to the determination of taxable income.

been taxed, the percentage changes—which correspond to the α in the two equations above—would have produced a rate of interest that would have left the lenders with *zero* real interest income. In other words, if the rate of interest had been exactly equal to the rate of inflation, the interest received by a lender would have been just sufficient to compensate him for the inflation-induced losses in the real value of the financial assets that he had loaned. Similarly, the interest that a borrower would have had to pay would have just balanced (for him) the decline in the real value of his liability. However, *interest income was taxed*, and the tax rates therefore varied, ceteris paribus, with the taxpayer's level of income. Furthermore, interest payments were deducted as costs from gross income in the determination of taxable income. Thus, the value of these deductions (in terms of the reduction in tax liability) was closely and directly related to the income of the taxpayer.

Table 1 shows the effective average tax rates for 1972, 1973, and 1974—that is, the ratio of tax liabilities to adjusted gross income[4]— for the 24 income classes reported in the *Statistics of Income*. These average tax rates ranged from very low figures for low incomes to about 50 percent for very high incomes. When these rates are combined with the rate of inflation for each year in the expression

$$\frac{\alpha}{1 - t_i}, \text{ where } i = 1, \ldots, 24$$

for particular income classes, it is seen what rate of interest each class should have received if the result would be *zero* real interest income. Anything above these rates, which are shown in Table 2, would have left lenders with positive real interest income and anything below them would have left lenders with negative real interest income. Mutatis mutandis, borrowers who, given their income level, paid the rates indicated in Table 2 would have been paying a zero real interest rate on the borrowed capital. If they had paid more, they would have incurred positive real costs of borrowing, while they would have received net subsidies if they had paid less.

The t_i rates used in these calculations are the effective average tax rates—that is, the ratio of tax payments to adjusted gross income for each income class. An alternative would be to use the ratio of tax

---

[4] Adjusted gross income is defined as gross income from all sources that is subject to tax and is adjusted to reflect allowances for business expenses.

Table 1. Ratios of Tax Payments to Adjusted Gross Income, 1972–74[1]

Adjusted Gross Income	1972	1973	1974
(In thousands of U.S. dollars)		*(In percent)*	
Under 1	1.8	1.8	4.5
1–2	3.5	4.1	3.3
2–3	2.6	2.6	2.5
3–4	4.9	5.1	5.1
4–5	6.4	6.6	6.7
5–6	7.5	7.5	7.8
6–7	8.3	8.4	8.6
7–8	8.9	9.2	9.3
8–9	9.4	9.8	10.0
9–10	9.6	10.0	10.3
10–11	10.1	10.4	10.6
11–12	10.3	10.5	10.7
12–13	10.6	10.9	11.1
13–14	11.0	11.2	11.4
14–15	11.4	11.5	11.7
15–20	12.5	12.6	12.7
20–25	14.4	14.3	14.5
25–30	16.0	16.0	15.9
30–50	19.1	19.0	18.9
50–100	26.8	26.4	26.5
100–200	34.6	34.4	34.9
200–500	40.8	40.6	41.5
500–1,000	45.4	45.7	45.6
Above 1,000	45.7	46.8	49.2

Source: U.S. Internal Revenue Service, *Statistics of Income–1972: Individual Income Tax Returns* (Washington, 1974).

[1] These ratios are called effective average tax rates ($t_i = T_i/AGI_i$).

payments to taxable income;[5] still another would be to use the statutory *marginal* tax rates at which the incomes of given classes are taxed. These two alternatives would have substantially increased the values of t_i, thus leading to much higher $\dfrac{\alpha}{1 - t_i}$ ratios. These two alternatives could be defended on the assumption that interest income is a marginal income, so that it is taxed at the marginal rate to which an individual is subject; this is true because most exemptions and deductions apply to other income sources (wages, salaries, etc.). There is some validity to this argument, especially in inflationary situations

---

[5] Taxable income is defined as adjusted gross income minus personal deductions and personal exemptions.

Table 2. Interest Rates Required to Provide Lenders with Zero Real Interest Income, 1972–74[1]

Adjusted Gross Income	1972	1973	1974
(In thousands of U.S. dollars)		*(In percent)*	
Under 1	3.36	6.31	11.52
1–2	4.42	6.47	11.38
2–3	3.39	6.37	11.28
3–4	3.47	6.53	11.59
4–5	3.53	6.64	11.79
5–6	3.57	6.70	11.93
6–7	3.60	6.77	12.04
7–8	3.62	6.83	12.13
8–9	3.64	6.83	12.22
9–10	3.65	6.89	12.26
10–11	3.67	6.92	12.30
11–12	3.68	6.93	12.32
12–13	3.69	6.96	12.37
13–14	3.71	6.98	12.42
14–15	3.73	7.01	12.46
15–20	3.77	7.09	12.60
20–25	3.86	7.23	12.87
25–30	3.93	7.38	13.08
30–50	4.08	7.65	13.56
50–100	4.51	8.42	14.97
100–200	5.05	9.45	16.90
200–500	5.57	10.44	18.80
500–1,000	6.04	11.61	20.22
Above 1,000	6.08	11.65	21.65

Sources: Table 1 and (for the rates of inflation) U.S. Council of Economic Advisers, *Economic Report of the President* (Washington, 1976).

[1] The percentages in the table are obtained from the expression $\alpha/1 - t_i$. The rate of inflation α was 3.3 percent in 1972, 6.2 percent in 1973, and 11.0 percent in 1974.

when nominal interest income is likely to increase by a far greater percentage than wage and salary income;[6] thus, the higher marginal income is likely to be taxed at higher-than-average rates. After deliberating over these alternatives, the author decided to select the more conservative one. Therefore, the effective average tax rates were used in this analysis.

[6] Furthermore, it can be argued that lending comes mainly from saving, which is a residual. This line of argument relies on the assumption that it is the marginal, and not the average, rate that is more important in determining whether individuals save or lend.

Table 3. Ratios of Tax Payments to Adjusted Gross Income, 1977–81

Adjusted Gross Income	1977	1978	1979	1980	1981
(In thousands of U.S. dollars)			*(In percent)*		
2–4	2.23	2.06	1.79	2.13	2.33
4–6	5.12	5.23	4.78	4.71	4.71
6–8	6.84	6.99	7.08	7.13	7.09
8–10	8.08	8.33	8.05	8.04	7.90
10–12	9.17	9.56	9.43	9.44	9.42
12–14	10.41	10.54	10.26	10.51	10.60
14–16	11.11	11.45	11.09	11.29	11.44
16–18	11.85	12.09	11.81	12.18	12.13
18–20	12.51	12.71	12.27	12.68	12.87
20–25	13.65	13.64	13.16	13.47	13.78
25–30	15.34	15.35	14.53	14.70	14.83
30–50	18.53	18.38	17.43	17.55	17.63
50–100	26.53	26.03	24.90	24.58	23.89
100–200	35.18	34.71	33.69	33.58	32.27
200–500	42.01	41.51	40.89	40.29	38.64
Above 500	49.23	47.46	48.11	46.55	43.11

Source: U.S. Internal Revenue Service, *Statistics of Income: Individual Income Tax Returns* (Washington, several years).

Tables 3 and 4 provide the same information for 1977–81 as Tables 1 and 2 provide for 1972–74. It should be noted that the breakdown in adjusted gross income is slightly different in the two sets of tables, so that the two sets could not be combined into one table.

III. TAX INCIDENCE IN THE UNITED STATES

The 1972–74 period

In 1972, the $\frac{\alpha}{1 - t_i}$ ratio (calculated as described above) ranged from 3.4 percent for taxpayers with an adjusted gross income less than \$1,000 to 6.1 percent for those with an adjusted gross income above \$1 million. In 1973, the $\frac{\alpha}{1 - t_i}$ ratio ranged from 6.3 percent to 11.7 percent; in 1974, it ranged from 11.5 percent to 21.7 percent. It follows that, in order to have received a zero real income from a loan, a taxpayer in the lowest income class should have received a rate of interest of 3.4 percent in 1972, 6.3 percent in 1973, and 11.5 percent in 1974. A taxpayer in the highest income class should have received rates of 6.1 percent in 1972, 11.7 percent in 1973, and 21.7

Table 4. Interest Rates Required to Provide Lenders with Zero Real Interest Income, 1977–81[1]

Adjusted Gross Income	1977	1978	1979	1980	1981
(In thousands of U.S. dollars)			*(In percent)*		
2–4	6.65	7.86	11.51	13.79	10.65
4–6	6.85	8.13	11.87	14.17	10.91
6–8	6.98	8.28	12.16	14.54	11.19
8–10	7.07	8.40	12.29	14.68	11.29
10–12	7.16	8.51	12.48	14.91	11.48
12–14	7.26	8.61	12.59	15.09	11.63
14–16	7.31	8.70	12.71	15.22	11.74
16–18	7.37	8.76	12.81	15.37	11.84
18–20	7.43	8.82	12.88	15.46	11.94
20–25	7.53	8.92	13.01	15.60	12.06
25–30	7.68	9.10	13.22	15.83	12.21
30–50	7.98	9.43	13.69	16.37	12.63
50–100	8.85	10.41	15.05	17.90	13.66
100–200	10.03	11.79	17.04	20.33	15.35
200–500	11.21	13.16	19.12	22.61	16.95
Above 500	12.80	14.65	21.78	25.26	18.28

Source: Table 3 and (for the rate of inflation), U.S. Council of Economic Advisers, *Economic Report of the President* (Washington, 1982).

[1] The percentages in the table are obtained from the expression $\alpha/1 - t_i$. The rate of inflation α was 6.5 percent in 1977, 7.7 percent in 1978, 11.3 percent in 1979, 13.5 percent in 1980, and 10.4 percent in 1981.

percent in 1974. These are also the rates that would have left the borrowers with zero net interest costs.[7]

How do these estimated rates relate to actual rates? This is not an easy question to answer, as there is not just one rate but rather a whole spectrum of rates. Table 5 shows bond yields and interest rates on selected financial assets for 1972–81. In 1972, the rates shown ranged from 4 percent to over 7 percent; in 1973, they ranged from 5 percent to 8 percent; and in 1974, they ranged from 6 percent to about 10 percent. Relating these rates to those required for a zero real interest income (i.e., those in Table 2), it can be seen that, while in 1972 most taxpayers would have received positive interest incomes on new loans, in 1973 this became difficult for taxpayers with a high adjusted gross income, especially for those with an income of about $50,000, and in 1974 this became very difficult (and perhaps impossible) for practically everyone. In 1974, the rate of interest should have ranged from more than 11 percent for low-income groups to more than 21 percent

[7] For corporations that are taxed at approximately 50 percent, the $\frac{\alpha}{1 - t_i}$ ratio would have been 6.6 percent in 1972, 12.4 percent in 1973, and 22.0 percent in 1974.

Table 5. Interest Rates and Bond Yields, 1977–81

(In percent per annum)

| Year | U.S. Government Security | | | Corporate Bond (Moody's Aaa) | High-Grade Municipal Bonds (Standard and Poor's) | Prime Commercial Paper of Four to Six Months Maturity |
	Three-month treasury bills[1]	Three-year issues[2]	Ten-year bonds[2]			
1972	4.071	5.85	5.63	7.21	5.27	4.69
1973	7.041	6.92	6.30	7.44	5.18	8.15
1974	7.886	7.81	6.99	8.57	6.09	9.87
1977	5.265	6.69	7.42	8.02	5.56	5.61
1978	7.221	8.29	8.41	8.73	5.90	7.99
1979	10.041	9.72	9.44	9.63	6.39	10.91
1980	11.506	11.55	11.46	11.94	8.51	12.29
1981	14.077	14.44	13.91	14.17	11.23	14.76

Source: U.S. Council of Economic Advisers, *Economic Report of the President* (Washington, several years).

[1] Rate on new issues within period; bank-discount basis.
[2] Yields on the more actively traded issues adjusted to constant maturities by the U.S. Treasury.

for very-high-income groups (and for corporations), in order to leave them with a positive interest income. As, by 1974, interest rates were generally far below these levels, the income tax had obviously become a capital tax for all lenders, and particularly for those with a high income.[8]

The conclusions reached in the preceding paragraph relate to *lenders*, and the reverse is true for borrowers. Consequently, while in 1972 most of the borrowers paying the prevailing rates of interest had positive real costs of borrowing (as the interest rates that they paid exceeded the required rates shown in Table 2), by 1974 most borrowers were receiving (*as borrowers*) net capital *subsidies*.[9]

The 1977–81 period

Tables 4 and 5 provide the information needed for carrying out the same analysis as above for the 1977–81 period. Table 4 estimates the range of required rates for various income classes. In 1979 and 1980 those rates are shown to be particularly high. For example, taxpayers with an income above $100,000 needed to receive interest

---

[8] The rates shown in Table 5 relate to new loans. Lenders (or borrowers) of money in earlier years were probably receiving (or paying) somewhat lower rates.

[9] To the extent that the corporate sector is a net borrower, it must also have gained from the tax treatment of interest income between 1972 and 1974.

rates of over 20 percent to obtain a zero real rate. The comparison of these two tables shows clearly that the lenders that bought taxable financial instruments ended up with negative real rates and, if they were in high-income brackets, with sharply negative real rates. These high-income groups could reduce the "capital taxes" by buying tax-free bonds, but they could not escape these taxes completely. The situation dramatized by Tables 4 and 5 implies that the combination of inflation and high taxes on nominal income was to a large extent determining the allocation of savings in the market. In other words, it was causing an inevitable fragmentation of the financial market.

Taxpayers may be lenders, borrowers, or both. Within each income class, borrowers or lenders may predominate. Therefore, whether an income class gains or loses from the tax treatment of the lending and borrowing activities of its members in an inflationary situation depends on the net balance between borrowing and lending. As lenders, individuals receive interest payments from individual borrowers, banks and other financial intermediaries, corporations, and federal, state, and local governments, as well as from foreign sources. As borrowers, individuals pay interest to individual lenders, banks and other financial intermediaries, corporations, and, to a much lesser extent, to governments and foreign lenders. To the extent that these flows (i.e., interest paid or received by individuals) are reported and are taxable, they are reflected in data from the U.S. Internal Revenue Service, used in the calculation of Tables 6 and 7. Before considering these tables, a few comments should be made about the U.S. Internal Revenue Service's interest statistics.

In Tables 6 and 7, *interest received* refers to the taxable portion of interest received on bonds, debentures, notes, mortgages, personal loans, bank deposits, and savings accounts.[10] It is important to note that these figures exclude the interest on tax-exempt state and local government obligations, as this income does not have to be reported on U.S. tax returns.[11] The figures also exclude interest received by individuals who do not file tax returns. Interest paid, on the other hand, includes interest paid on personal debts, mortgages, bank loans, and installment purchases of real or personal property. It does not, however, include interest paid or money borrowed to buy tax-exempt

---

[10] U.S. Internal Revenue Service, *Statistics of Income, 1972: Individual Income Tax Returns* (Washington, 1974), p. 277.

[11] In 1974, interest paid by state and local governments amounted to $9.4 billion. About half of this was received by banks. See *Survey of Current Business* (U.S. Department of Commerce, Washington), Vol. 56 (January 1976), Table 17, p. 44, and U.S. Advisory Commission on Intergovernmental Relations, *Understanding the Market for State and Local Debt* (Washington, 1976).

Table 6. Net Differences Between Interest Received and Paid by Amount of Adjusted Gross Income, 1972–74

Adjusted Gross Income	1972	1973	1974
(In thousands of U.S. dollars)	*(In millions of U.S. dollars)*		
Under 1	147.3	143.4	192.8
1–2	497.3	476.9	483.7
2–3	836.5	983.8	918.1
3–4	1,102.1	1,210.6	1,399.0
4–5	995.2	1,081.8	1,523.0
5–6	911.5	951.0	1,348.2
6–7	675.9	737.3	1,161.9
7–8	285.1	540.5	732.9
8–9	− 36.9	121.6	440.7
9–10	− 357.0	− 56.1	496.7
10–11	− 269.2	− 203.0	− 49.3
11–12	− 596.7	− 425.5	− 261.3
12–13	− 662.8	− 570.5	− 294.4
13–14	− 632.8	− 488.2	− 610.8
14–15	− 701.0	− 771.7	− 614.8
15–20	− 2,603.7	− 3,373.3	− 3,777.4
20–25	− 901.1	− 1,645.7	− 2,122.8
25–30	− 90.7	− 249.3	− 606.2
30–50	525.1	544.9	597.1
50–100	453.1	543.9	1,106.9
100–200	186.8	258.0	513.5
200–500	68.8	94.5	204.8
500–1,000	13.5	32.6	51.2
Above 1,000	10.9	24.0	32.3
Total interest received	6,709.1	7,744.8	11,202.8
Total interest paid	− 6,851.9	− 7,783.3	− 8,337.0
Net balance	− 142.8	− 38.5	2,865.8

Source: Same as Table 1.

securities, single premium life insurance, and endowment contracts. Furthermore, interest relating to income from businesses, royalties, and rents is deducted directly from the specific income so that it is not reflected in the data.

Tables 6 and 7 lead to some interesting conclusions. First, consider total interest received and paid. The two tables indicate that, while in 1972 and 1973 these two totals were very close, they started diverging by considerable amounts in 1974. In that year total interest received exceeded total interest paid by almost $3 billion. In 1977 this was still

**Table 7. Net Differences Between Interest Received and Paid by
Amount of Adjusted Gross Income, 1977–81**

Adjusted Gross Income	1977	1978	1979	1980	1981
(In thousands of U.S. dollars)		*(In millions of U.S. dollars)*			
Under 2	129.0	242.9	204.9	317.0	692.5
2–4	313.3	291.9	360.9	564.3	723.4
4–6	1,802.3	1,920.3	1,974.6	2.087.2	2,446.2
6–8	2,650.1	2,972.1	2,949.0	3,293.3	3,855.4
8–10	2,800.7	2,768.6	3,251.2	3,884.6	4,786.5
10–12	1,919.5	2,114.3	2,575.9	3,483.3	4,919.2
12–14	1,066.9	1,599.8	1,772.3	2,921.4	4,125.2
14–16	433.4	298.2	542.9	2,064.3	3,176.4
16–18	−507.4	−415.8	200.2	1,308.3	2,421.1
18–20	−1,240.1	−1,217.7	−827.0	259.0	1,928.6
20–25	−3,758.2	−5,049.3	−4,569.4	−2,113.5	1,043.2
25–30	−2,451.8	−4,203.0	−5,240.0	−4,184.4	−2,683.5
30–50	−2,232.4	−5.087.6	−8,503.6	−9,660.7	−6,374.3
50–100	720.0	86.5	372.3	1,785.8	3,323.8
100–200	457.2	375.5	509.5	1,389.8	2,593.4
200–500	234.0	259.8	455.0	868.2	1,570.6
Above 500	112.3	131.7	381.7	647.3	1,021.1
Total interest received	48,250.3	54,943.8	67,481.9	95,173.0	131,905.5
Total interest paid	−45,801.4	−57,855.3	−71,071.7	−86,257.9	−102,339.6
Net balance	2,448.9	−2,911.5	−3,589.8	8,915.1	29,565.9

Source: Same as Table 3.

true although the difference had been reduced to about $2.5 billion. In 1978 and 1979 interest paid came to exceed interest received by $3 billion to $3.6 billion. However, in 1980 and 1981 interest received came to exceed interest paid by very large amounts—$8.9 billion in 1980 and $29.6 billion in 1981.

Tables 6 and 7 also show, for each class and for each of the years under consideration, the net difference between the total interest income received by that class and the total interest deductions claimed by that class. This net difference indicates whether the class as a whole was a net lender or a net borrower. In 1972, all the classes with an adjusted gross income of less than $8,000 or more than $30,000 were net lenders, while those with an adjusted gross income greater than $8,000 but less than $30,000 were net borrowers. In 1973, the net borrowers were those with an adjusted gross income of more than

$9,000 but less than $30,000; all others were net lenders. In 1974, the net borrowers were those with an adjusted gross income of more than $10,000 but less than $30,000; all others were net lenders. In the 1977–81 period, fewer and fewer income classes were net borrowers. By 1981 only the income classes between $25,000 and $50,000 were net borrowers.

For these classes, interest deductions related to home ownership must have been particularly significant. As a consequence of the tax treatment of interest income and interest deductions, these groups received substantial capital subsidies. The interest payments that they made were far less than what would have been required to leave them with a zero real cost of borrowing. In both their lending and borrowing activities, they clearly gained from inflation. On the other hand, the other classes—the lower-income and higher-income classes— were subject to substantial capital taxes. For the very-high-income classes, these capital taxes may have exceeded 10 percent of the principal and they were very significant for the low-income classes as well. For this group, the interest income received was far below what would have been required to compensate an individual for the inflation-induced erosion of a loan.[12]

IV. NET BALANCE VIS-À-VIS THE U.S. GOVERNMENT

The preceding section has dealt with gains and losses among income classes related to the tax treatment of interest income during an inflationary situation. This section considers some gains or losses accruing to the U.S. Government as a consequence of the tax treatment of interest income and deductions. The Government gains from the taxation of interest income but loses from the deductions allowed for interest payments.[13] The question is whether, on balance, the Government was a gainer or a loser over the 1972–81 period.

The method followed is a simple one. The net positions of the income classes vis-à-vis interest income (the figures in Tables 6 and 7) were multiplied by the average tax rates (shown in Table 1). If the net position of a class was that of a creditor (i.e., if interest received exceeded interest paid), then the multiplication of the net income by the effective average tax rate gave a net positive tax payment. How-

---

[12] These conclusions apply to classes as a whole. Within each class some taxpayers are net debtors and some are net creditors. Therefore, the above conclusions do not necessarily apply to each individual.

[13] As the tax rates vary for the incomes of the various classes, whether the U.S. Government gains or loses depends to a large extent on where the interest income and the interest deductions accrue.

Table 8. Net Balance Vis-à-vis the U.S. Government, 1972–74

Adjusted Gross Income	1972	1973	1974
(In thousands of U.S. dollars)	*(In millions of U.S. dollars)*		
Under 1	2.6	2.6	8.7
1–2	17.4	19.6	16.0
2–3	21.7	25.6	23.0
3–4	54.0	61.7	71.3
4–5	63.7	71.4	102.0
5–6	68.4	71.3	105.1
6–7	56.1	61.9	99.9
7–8	25.4	49.7	68.2
8–9	−3.5	11.9	44.1
9–10	−34.3	−5.6	51.2
10–11	−27.2	−21.1	−5.2
11–12	−61.5	−44.7	−28.0
12–13	−70.3	−62.2	−32.7
13–14	−69.6	−54.7	−69.6
14–15	−79.9	−88.7	−71.9
15–20	−325.5	−425.0	−479.7
20–25	−129.8	−235.3	−307.8
25–30	−14.5	−39.9	−96.4
30–50	100.3	103.5	112.8
50–100	121.4	143.6	293.3
100–200	64.6	88.8	179.2
200–500	28.1	38.4	85.0
500–1,000	6.1	14.9	23.3
Above 1,000	5.0	11.2	15.9
Net balance	−181.4	−201.1	207.7

Source: Same as Table 1.

ever, if the net position was that of a debtor (interest paid exceeded interest received), the multiplication of the average tax rate by the net deduction gave an estimate of the taxes lost by the Government. The results are shown in Tables 8 and 9.

In 1972, the value of the interest deductions in terms of tax reductions amounted to $816.2 million, while the value of the tax payments was $634.8 million. As a consequence, the net loss in tax revenue to the Government associated with the tax treatment of interest income was $181.4 million. In 1973, the tax reduction associated with net deductions was $977.2 million while the value of tax payments was $776.1 million, so that the net loss to the Government in terms of forgone tax revenue was $201.1 million. In 1974, however, there was a drastic change in the net balance. In fact, while the value of the

Table 9. Net Balance Vis-à-vis the U.S. Government, 1977–81

Adjusted Gross Income	1977	1978	1979	1980	1981
(In thousands of U.S. dollars)		*(In millions of U.S. dollars)*			
Under 2	− 18.20	− 45.67	− 44.19	− 78.19	− 123.97
2–4	7.00	6.01	6.47	12.04	16.89
4–6	92.19	100.47	94.29	98.29	115.27
6–8	181.22	207.71	208.91	234.72	273.48
8–10	226.35	230.71	261.66	312.47	378.18
10–12	176.06	202.22	242.95	328.73	463.60
12–14	111.06	168.65	181.85	306.97	437.27
14–16	48.16	34.14	60.18	233.10	363.44
16–18	− 60.12	− 50.28	23.64	159.30	293.57
18–20	− 155.17	− 154.71	− 101.51	32.84	248.21
20–25	− 512.88	− 688.81	− 601.48	− 284.72	143.80
25–30	− 376.03	− 645.32	− 761.43	− 614.96	− 398.04
30–50	− 413.59	− 935.18	− 1,482.52	− 1,695.92	− 1,123.81
50–100	191.02	22.52	92.70	439.03	794.05
100–200	160.82	130.34	171.64	466.74	836.85
200–500	98.31	107.84	186.07	349.80	606.85
Above 500	55.28	62.50	183.63	301.31	440.15
Net balance	− 188.5	− 1,246.9	− 1,277.1	601.6	3,765.8

Source: Tables 1, 4, and 7.

deductions rose to $1,091.3 million, that of tax payments also rose to $1,299.0 million; the Government became a net gainer by $207.7 million. Between 1973 and 1974, there was a net change of about $400 million in the position of the taxpayers vis-à-vis the Government. Consequently, the Government was definitely a gainer from inflation in this context.[14] The slowdown in the rate of inflation that characterized the period following 1974 again changed the net balance. In 1977–79 the Government was a net loser from this slowdown in the inflation rate, but the rapid acceleration of prices in 1980 and 1981 again changed the net balance. By 1981 the Government was gaining about $3.8 billion a year.

V. CONCLUDING REMARKS

Inflation benefits or harms individuals in many ways, some of which are obvious while others are much less so. It is not easy to determine

---

[14] It should again be emphasized that these are very partial conclusions. They relate strictly to the tax treatment of interest income.

whether, on balance, an individual or an income class gains or loses. This paper deals with just one way in which inflation affects income classes. It attempts to show to what extent income classes have gained or lost because of the tax treatment of interest income and interest payments during the inflationary period of 1972–81. The main beneficiaries are seen to be the middle-income classes, which are more likely to have substantial deductions related to their home mortgages. It is also shown that, with respect to the tax treatment of interest income, the U.S. Government was a net gainer from accelerating inflation. Thus, the tax treatment of interest income per se resulted in a redistribution of income in favor of the middle-income classes and the Government. It needs to be emphasized that the results obtained relate to income classes rather than to individuals. Within each class, some individuals gained or lost more than others.

The redistributional effects emphasized in this paper would be removed, or at least reduced in intensity, if the part of interest income that was taxed and the part of interest payments that was deducted as a cost were equal to the real rate of interest. This alternative appears to be an attractive theoretical recommendation, which has received support from some authors. However, the practical and administrative implications of such a policy have not yet been given the attention that they deserve. Until these practical implications are defined, the theoretical recommendation should be kept in abeyance.

6

Inflationary Expectations, Taxes, and the Demand for Money in the United States

VITO TANZI

In his excellent article on the demand for money, Goldfeld cites Harry Johnson to the effect that the lack of "American evidence that the expected rate of change of prices enters the demand for money . . . [was] something of a puzzle" (Goldfeld (1973), p. 608). Goldfeld describes his own empirical results as a "mixed bag" (ibid., p. 613) and concludes that "even at the theoretical level," the question of "whether inflationary expectations have an independent role to play in the demand-for-money function" is controversial (ibid., p. 607). Studies dealing with developing economies, however, have generally found that inflationary expectations possess more explanatory power than institutionally rigid nominal interest rates in basic money demand functions. Furthermore, some recent studies for the United States have used both inflationary expectations and the rate of interest in the demand-for-money equation, but these studies have not provided sufficient theoretical justification for doing so.

This paper deals with the role of inflationary expectations from a theoretical and empirical point of view. It contains four sections. Section I presents a theoretical justification for introducing inflationary expectations as an independent variable in the demand-for-money function. The argument is based on the necessity of explicitly taking into account the effect of taxation on the rate of return, an effect that has been ignored in previous studies. Section II presents some simple empirical tests.[1] Section III outlines an alternative model to be sub-

---

[1] This study is based on the established literature in order to provide a better test of its principal innovations. Areas of disagreement and current research on the demand for money have been well surveyed by Laidler (1980, pp. 140–48).

jected to testing and presents the new empirical results. Section IV
draws some conclusions.

I. THEORY

Assume that an economy is growing at a steady pace and that the
price level is not expected to change. For such an economy, it is widely
agreed that the demand for money, m, can be represented by the
function

$$m = f(r, y) \tag{1}$$

where r and y denote, respectively the rate of interest and the level
of income. As the price level is constant, r and y, as well as m, represent
both nominal and real values. In this case, the rate of interest reflects
fully the opportunity cost of holding money.

Next, assume that, while the economy is still growing at a steady
pace, the price level is no longer stable but is increasing (and is expected to continue increasing) at an annual rate π. Does this require
a modification of equation (1)? Or, should π be included among the
independent variables that affect m? The basic arguments against this
inclusion would seem to be: (1) the Fisherian hypothesis about the
behavior of nominal interest rates during inflationary situations; and
(2) the Keynesian assumption that money as an asset is substituted
only for financial assets ("bonds") and not for real assets.

If R is the nominal rate of interest and r is the real rate of interest,
Fisher's hypothesis states that

$$R_t = r_t + b\pi_t$$

or, in a stricter version,

$$R_t = r + \pi_t \tag{2}$$

which implies that r is constant and that changes in π are fully reflected
in R. When the strict version of the Fisherian hypothesis holds, the
nominal rate of interest incorporates fully the expected rate of inflation. Furthermore, if interest income is assumed not to be taxed, an
individual who lends money at a nominal rate R receives a real return
equal to the real rate r, which, under the assumed conditions, is always
positive and constant.[2] This implies that R always exceeds π by the

---

[2] However, the real rate may, in fact, not be constant (see Tanzi (1980)).

amount of the real rate. Therefore, investment of money balances in financial assets that pay a nominal return equal to R will be preferred over investment in assets that are expected to pay an implicit nominal return equal to π. The latter can be called consumption goods and also include durables and non-income-yielding real assets, such as works of art and jewelry. In such a situation, the real rate of return on equity, at the margin, tends to be equal to the expected real rate of interest ($r = R - \pi$); consequently, there is no bias toward the preference for real over financial assets. The demand for money is limited to the amount needed for current transactions; temporary excesses over that amount lead to the purchase of interest-bearing financial assets (bonds) or income-yielding real assets (equity) rather than to increases in the holdings of "consumption goods." The reason for this is that the purchase of such assets is associated with an opportunity cost equal to the expected real rate of interest. Furthermore, if one still follows the traditional Keynesian assumption, even the substitution between money and income-yielding real assets (equity) would not take place, so that only financial assets would be purchased.

The next step toward realism requires that the existence of income taxes be recognized.[3] In today's real world, an individual who buys a financial asset bearing an interest rate equal to R does not retain the total interest income derived from the asset but only the amount remaining after income taxes are paid. Assuming that this individual's marginal tax rate, expressed as a fraction, is T, his after-tax interest rate would be reduced to R^T where

$$R^T = R (1 - T) \tag{3}$$

If the Fisherian relationship is still assumed to hold, equation (3) may be rewritten as

$$R^T = r (1 - T) + \pi (1 - T) \tag{4}$$

Obviously, the higher T is, the lower R^T will be when compared with R.

Consider the rate of return to the individual, ceteris paribus, if, instead of buying a financial asset, he buys, first, an equity and, second, consumption goods. As unrealized capital gains are not taxed, if this individual buys an equity whose nominal value is expected to increase at the rate of π and to pay an income (in the form of dividends, rent, etc.) equal to r, he expects to receive a net-of-tax *nominal* rate of return

---

[3] The role that income taxes may play in the demand for money has been largely ignored (see Tanzi (1979)).

equal to $\pi + r(1 - T)$. However, should the capital gain be realized, or should the investor take into account the tax liability that he will face in the future when he sells the asset, the actual rate of return would be considerably less than that shown above, especially since the total *nominal* increase in the value of the asset would be taxable. On the other hand, should he buy consumption goods, whose value is assumed to increase at the rate of inflation, he receives the full nominal rate of return equal to π, as the nominal increase in the value of the goods is not taxable.[4]

In summary, assuming that the Fisherian relationship holds, when (as in the United States) there is inflation and nominal incomes are taxed, the opportunity cost of holding money, measured in terms of forgone nominal yield, is[5] $[\pi (1 - T) + r (1 - T)]$ for financial assets, $[\pi + r (1 - T)]$ for equities *with unrealized capital gains*; and π for consumption goods.

As the rate of inflation rises, the relative importance of r in determining nominal income falls. Furthermore, the importance of r is also reduced by the tax because the higher T is, the lower $r(1 - T)$ is. In recent years the U.S. income tax has been progressive, with a marginal rate reaching 70 percent. This means that, once π became positive and significant, the expected net-of-tax return on financial assets soon fell below the return on the holding of consumption goods that (ignoring storage and other costs) is assumed to be equal to the rate of inflation. Thus, for many individuals (and at times for most),

$$\pi (1 - T) + r (1 - T) = R^T < \pi.$$

A vivid numerical illustration of this point is provided in Table 1. The table assumes that the strict version of the Fisherian hypothesis holds and that the real rate of interest is constant and equal to 2. Therefore, in the absence of taxes, the nominal rate R would be equal to the rate of inflation plus 2.

As the average tax rate on interest income in the United States has been estimated at between 0.30 and 0.40 during the 1970s,[6] the most

---

[4] Furthermore, even if these goods are eventually sold and some capital gain is realized, the sale does not generally create any tax liability. This is not true if the goods are held by corporations.

[5] It is assumed that equities and consumption goods are affected by the same rate of inflation π. If one were to assume differential rates, some modifications would need to be made in the analysis.

[6] Calculated by the author from data in U.S. Internal Revenue Service, *Statistics of Income: Individual Income Tax Returns* (Washington, annual issues). The data are available up to 1978. The average tax rate was probably higher after 1978 until the 1982 tax cut.

Table 1. Effect of Taxes on Yields

(In percent)

T	r	π_1	π_2	π_3	$R_1(1-T)$	$R_2(1-T)$	$R_3(1-T)$
0.00	2	5	10	20	7.0	12.0	22.0
0.10	2	5	10	20	6.3	10.8	19.8
0.30	2	5	10	20	4.9	8.4	15.4
0.40	2	5	10	20	4.2	7.2	13.2
0.50	2	5	10	20	3.5	6.0	11.0
0.70	2	5	10	20	2.1	3.6	6.6

Column group headers: "Assumed Inflation Rates" spans π_1, π_2, π_3; "After-Tax Rates of Interest" spans $R_1(1-T)$, $R_2(1-T)$, $R_3(1-T)$.

significant row in the table may be the one corresponding to $T = 0.40$. This row indicates that, even at an inflation rate of 5 percent, individuals subject to a marginal tax rate of 0.40 receive a measurably higher return from holding consumption goods than from purchasing financial assets paying 7 percent interest. When inflation reaches higher levels or when the tax rate is higher, the differentials become great indeed. For example, an individual with a marginal tax rate of 50 percent (not an unusually high rate) would receive a net-of-tax rate of return of only 6 percent when the rate of inflation is 10 percent and of only 11 percent when the rate of inflation is 20 percent. As a consequence, for many individuals the direct substitution of consumption goods for money becomes far more attractive than the substitution of financial assets for money. But this implies that, in the determination of the demand-for-money function, inflationary expectations become increasingly more important than nominal rates of interest and cannot, therefore, be ignored as determinants of that demand.

In conclusion, there seems to be ample theoretical justification for rewriting the demand for money function as

$$m_t = f(R_t, \pi_t, y_t) \tag{5}$$

with the understanding that, under inflationary conditions, y and π are important variables with well-specified signs (positive for y and negative for π) while the importance of R is no longer obvious. This conclusion implies that the omission of π from the equation introduces an upward bias in the coefficient of R. Therefore, that coefficient should fall when π is added.

The previous discussion is based on the assumption that the basic Fisherian hypothesis, stated as equation (2), holds. If (as was the case through much of the period studied in this paper) institutional reasons (such as usury laws) or inertia prevent the nominal rate of interest from increasing by as much as it is assumed to have increased under the Fisherian hypothesis, then the relative importance of π (as compared with R) in the demand-for-money equation would rise.[7] The greater the constraints on R, the greater is the significance of π.

This paper concentrates on the demand for money rather than on the choice between financial and real assets, but the analysis is also relevant to that choice. When the expected inflation rate is rising, individuals not only move out of money and into real goods, but they also move out of financial assets and into real goods. They do this for the reasons set forth above. Thus, because of these moves, bond prices fall while real asset prices (especially those of assets in limited or inelastic supplies) rise. In time, a new equilibrium is established, with less real money and higher nominal interest rates. On the other hand, a fall in the expected rate of inflation not only leads to an increase in the demand for money but also to a shift away from real goods and into financial assets. In this case, the higher demand for bonds increases bond prices and thus forces down the rate of interest. In a more complete analysis than that given here, it would be necessary to take these shifts into account.

II. PRELIMINARY TESTS

In order to test for the effects of inflationary expectations on the demand for money, a measure of those expectations is needed. One measure is provided by the Livingston series, as reworked by Carlson (1977). This series of "observed" inflationary expectations is used in this paper. It provides a direct measure over six-month periods. However, an observed price expectations variable may contain various types of errors that make it differ from the true, unobservable price expectations variable. Therefore, several alternative price expectations variables have been derived by the combined use of "observed" data and actual (known) price changes. These derived series—which incorporate expectation hypotheses suggested by Turnovsky and Frenkel—are also used and are referred to as extrapolative, adaptive, Frenkel, and distributed.[8] The period covered in the tests is June 1964–December 1978, using semiannual observations and taking 1964 as the initial year because there was little inflation before that period. December 1978 is the latest period for which the data were available when this paper was written.

---

[7] See Friedman (1980) for a discussion of institutional and market factors behind less-than-complete Fisherian adjustment.

[8] For details, see Tanzi (1980) and Lahiri (1976).

Preliminary tests involved the estimation of the following equations:

$$\ln m = a_0 + a_1 R + a_2 \ln y + a_3 \ln m_{-1} \tag{6}$$

$$\ln m = b_0 + b_1 \pi + b_2 \ln y + b_3 \ln m_{-1} \tag{7}$$

$$\ln m = c_0 + c_1 R + c_2 \pi + c_3 \ln y + c_4 \ln m_{-1} \tag{8}$$

where m and y are money (M_1) and income in 1972 prices, R is the rate of interest on six-month treasury bills, and π is the measure of inflationary expectations. The estimations are made in logarithmic form for m and y.

Table 2 shows the results. The first column identifies the series used for the inflationary expectation: "observed" refers to the direct use of the Livingston-Carlson series, while the four other entries in the first column refer to the series derived by the combination of that series with actual data of price level changes specified by various expectation hypotheses.

Table 2. Demand-for-Money Equations, 1964–78

Inflationary Expectation Used	Constant	R	π	$\ln y$	$\ln m_{-1}$	$\bar{R}^2$	H
(6) Observed	−0.4002 (0.47)	−0.5417 (1.95)		+0.0284 (0.73)	+0.8960 (6.08)**	0.844	0.860
(7a) Observed	−0.2549 (0.69)		−1.250 (5.44)**	+0.1412 (4.37)**	+0.8740 (14.37)**	0.901	0.144
(7b) Distributed	−0.1205 (0.35)		−1.1791 (5.62)**	+0.1273 (4.36)**	+0.8668 (14.52)**	0.904	0.533
(7c) Adaptive	−0.0029 (0.008)		−1.0406 (5.49)**	+0.1130 (4.09)**	+0.8627 (14.27)**	0.902	0.479
(7d) Extrapolative	−0.0752 (0.21)		−1.1838 (4.95)**	+0.1313 (3.93)**	+0.8258 (12.89)**	0.890	0.758
(7e) Frenkel	−0.3205 (0.85)		−1.2951 (5.43)**	+0.1508 (4.44)**	+0.8742 (14.35)**	0.900	−0.132
(8a) Observed	−0.4571 (1.14)	−0.2392 (1.21)	−1.1331 (4.58)**	+0.1369 (4.25)**	+0.9184 (13.03)**	0.902	0.026
(8b) Distributed	−0.4206 (1.10)	−0.3055 (1.67)	−1.0681 (5.01)**	+0.1271 (4.50)**	+0.9245 (13.75)**	0.911	0.567
(8c) Adaptive	−0.3570 (0.94)	−0.3387 (1.87)	−0.9425 (5.01)**	+0.1155 (4.38)**	+0.9273 (13.81)**	0.911	0.475
(8d) Extrapolative	−0.3577 (0.91)	−0.3940 (2.13)*	−1.0718 (4.66)**	+0.1344 (4.29)**	+0.9045 (12.85)**	0.904	0.554
(8e) Frenkel	−0.4866 (1.19)	−0.2117 (1.05)	−1.1798 (4.50)**	+0.1451 (4.23)**	+0.9133 (12.82)**	0.901	−0.179

Note: One asterisk indicates significance at the 5 percent level; two asterisks indicate significance at the 1 percent level; numbers in parentheses are t-values. A first-order Cochrane-Orcutt correction is employed in equation (6). The values of the H-statistic are within the acceptable range.

The results for the short-run demand for money may be summarized briefly:

(1) The comparison of equation (6) with equations (7a) through (7e) indicates that equations with inflationary expectations in place of the rate of interest have greater explanatory power. The $\overline{R}^2$ is raised substantially when the rate of interest (R) is replaced by the variable measuring inflationary expectations (π). Furthermore the t-values for π are sharply higher than those for R.

(2) There is little difference among the five series of inflationary expectations. The directly observed series performs about as well as the other derived series.

(3) Little is gained in terms of explanatory power when, as in equations (8a) through (8e), the rate of interest and inflationary expectations are jointly used in the same equations. However, in these equations the t-values for the inflationary expectations variables remain highly significant while those for the rate of interest are, for the most part, not significant. Furthermore, the coefficient of R falls sharply when π is added.

(4) The coefficients for the lagged dependent variable are somewhat higher when the equations contain the rate of interest than when they do not. This implies a long adjustment lag.

III. ALTERNATIVE MODEL

In Section I a theoretical argument is made for the inclusion of inflationary expectations among the arguments of the demand for money. Therefore, as indicated in equation (5), it is concluded that the demand for money should be written as

$$m_t = f(R_t, \pi_t, y_t) \tag{5}$$

The results in Table 2 indicate, however, that, empirically, very little is gained by putting both π and R in the same equation. The $\overline{R}^2$s are scarcely affected. Furthermore, the use of both R and π in the equation raises the problem of multicollinearity because $R_t = f(\pi_t)$. Elsewhere (Tanzi (1980)) it has been shown that

$$R_t = r_t + \pi_t + f(y_t - \bar{y}_t) \tag{9}$$

where r is the real rate of interest, π and R have the same meaning as they had above, and y_t and $\bar{y}_t$ represent, respectively, real actual and potential incomes. This equation indicates that, in the absence of changes in economic activity ($y_t = \bar{y}_t$) and expected inflation ($\pi = 0$), the nominal rate of interest would equal the real rate and would be constant. If $\pi_t > 0$ and $y_t = \bar{y}_t$, then the nominal rate of interest will

Table 3. Interest Rate Equations, 1964–78

(Equation (9))

Inflationary Expectation Used	Constant	π_t	ln G		
Observed	+0.0275	+0.8480	+0.3280	$\bar{R}^2 = 0.714$	
	(3.77)**	(5.12)**	(3.01)**	D-W = 1.640	
Distributed	+0.0286	+0.8265	+0.3609	$\bar{R}^2 = 0.653$	
	(3.91)**	(4.64)**	(3.01)**	D-W = 1.717	
Adaptive	+0.0323	+0.7252	+0.3256	$\bar{R}^2 = 0.603$	
	(4.91)**	(4.63)**	(2.76)*	D-W = 1.786	
Extrapolative	+0.0278	+0.8540	+0.3873	$\bar{R}^2 = 0.624$	
	(3.26)**	(4.10)**	(2.89)**	D-W = 1.725	
Frenkel	+0.0272	+0.8433	+0.3215	$\bar{R}^2 = 0.718$	
	(3.72)**	(5.18)**	(2.98)**	D-W = 1.642	

Note: One asterisk indicates significance at the 5 percent level; two asterisks indicate significance at the 1 percent level; numbers in parentheses are *t*-values. A first-order Cochrane-Orcutt correction is employed.

increase pari passu with the rate of inflation. If $y_t \neq \bar{y}_t$, then the real rate is affected because, empirically, it appears that the coefficient of π_t is close to unity (see Tanzi (1980)). The empirical relationship between the rate of interest and its determinants is shown in Table 3.[9]

Let us call the difference between y_t and $\bar{y}_t$ the gap and define it by G_t. Then

$$y_t = G_t + \bar{y}_t \tag{10}$$

Combining equations (5), (9), and (10), the demand-for-money equation may be restated as

$$m_t = f(\pi_t, G_t, \bar{y}_t) \tag{11}$$

Equation (11) states that the demand for money is a function of (1) potential income, (2) a measure of the difference between actual and potential income, and (3) inflationary expectations. The substitution of potential income for actual income is particularly significant because it introduces a true scale variable undistorted by cyclical fluctuations.[10] Therefore, the elasticity of the demand for money with respect to income can be estimated in a more meaningful way. Obviously, in the absence of cyclical fluctuations, the gap would disappear in such a way that the elasticity with respect to actual income would

---

[9] Note that, in order to avoid difficulties with the logarithm of a negative number, a ratio specification of the gap is employed in the empirical analysis.

[10] This approach is consistent with that of studies using permanent income as an explanatory variable. See Laidler (1977, pp. 140–48).

become identical to that with respect to potential income. Also, if inflationary expectations are reduced to zero when the gap is also zero, the relevant opportunity cost for holding money would be the real rate of interest. In this case, the real rate of interest would be constant; therefore, it would no longer play a role in the determination of *changes* in the demand for money. These would then depend exclusively on changes in a scale variable—namely, income.

Let us restate the model to be tested. From equation (5), let

$$\ln m_t^* = \alpha_0 + \alpha_1 \ln y_t + \alpha_2 R_t + \alpha_3 \pi_t + \varepsilon_t \tag{12}$$

where

$m_t^* =$ long-run demand for real money balance
$y_t \quad =$ real (actual) income
$R_t \quad =$ nominal interest rate
$\pi_t \quad =$ expected rate of inflation
$\varepsilon_t \quad =$ error term
$\alpha_1 > 0 \quad \alpha_2, \alpha_3 < 0$

From equation (9),

$$R_t = \beta_0 + \beta_1 \pi_t + \beta_2 \ln G_t + u_t \tag{13}$$

where $\beta_1 > 0$, $\beta_2, > 0$, and $u_t =$ error term

$$\ln G_t = \ln y_t - \ln \bar{y}_t \tag{14}$$

Combining equations (13) and (14) with (12),

$$\ln m_t^* = \gamma_0 + \gamma_1 \ln G_t + \gamma_2 \ln \bar{y}_t + \gamma_3 \pi_t + w_t \tag{15}$$

where

$\gamma_0 = \alpha_0 + \alpha_2 \beta_0$
$\gamma_1 = \alpha_1 + \alpha_2 \beta_2$
$\gamma_2 = \alpha_1$
$\gamma_3 = \alpha_2 \beta_1 + \alpha_3$
$w_t = \alpha_2 u_t + \varepsilon_t$

Let us assume that

$$\ln m_t - \ln m_{t-1} = \theta(\ln m_t^* - \ln m_{t-1}) \tag{16}$$

where θ, which is $0 < \theta < 1$, is a coefficient of proportionality that measures the speed at which the demand for money adjusts to its long-term desired level, m_t^*. Then, after due substitutions,

$$\theta \ln m_t^* = \theta \gamma_0 + \theta \gamma_1 \ln G_t + \theta \gamma_2 \ln \bar{y}_t + \theta \gamma_3 \pi_t + \theta w_t$$

Therefore, the short-run equation for the demand for money can be written as

$$\ln m_t = \phi_0 + \phi_1 \ln m_{t-1} + \phi_2 \ln G_t \qquad (17)$$
$$+ \phi_3 \ln \bar{y}_t + \phi_4 \pi_t + v_t$$

where

$\phi_0 = \theta(\alpha_0 + \alpha_2\beta_0)$
$\phi_1 = (1 - \theta)$
$\phi_2 = \theta(\alpha_1 + \alpha_2\beta_2)$
$\phi_3 = \theta(\alpha_1)$
$\phi_4 = \theta(\alpha_2\beta_1 + \alpha_3)$

Table 4 shows the regression equations corresponding to equation (17). These new equations, which correspond to the short-run demand for money obtained by using the alternative model suggested in this paper, are clearly superior to those obtained by using the traditional model with actual income and interest rate variables (see equation (6) in Table 2). Furthermore, in terms of explanatory power, these equations are comparable to those in Table 2 that use the inflationary expectation variable instead of the interest rate variable (see equations (7a) through (7e) in Table 2).

Table 4 has been estimated from a model that is conceptually different from the traditional one. In this model, (1) the interest rate has been replaced by its determinants, (2) inflationary expectation has been entered as a separate variable, and (3) a form of permanent income (potential income) has replaced actual income. This model

Table 4. New Demand-for-Money Equations, 1964–78
(Equation (17))

Inflationary Expectation Used	Constant	$\ln m_{t-1}$	$\ln G$	$\ln \bar{y}$	π	$\bar{R}^2$	H
Observed	−0.0743	+0.8572	+0.2390	+0.1275	−1.0284		
	(0.18)	(12.74)**	(2.30)*	(4.22)**	(3.84)**	0.905	0.196
Distributed	−0.0589	+0.8610	+0.1944	+0.1225	−1.0598		
	(0.15)	(13.10)**	(1.84)	(4.40)**	(4.08)**	0.909	0.437
Adaptive	+0.0180	+0.8588	+0.1719	+0.1128	−0.9694		
	(0.05)	(12.97)**	(1.57)	(4.26)**	(3.99)**	0.907	0.492
Extrapolative	+0.0502	+0.8316	+0.1693	+0.1301	−1.1272		
	(0.12)	(12.17)**	(1.41)	(3.84)**	(3.40)**	0.896	0.647
Frenkel	−0.1004	+0.8549	+0.2562	+0.1331	−1.0382		
	(0.23)	(12.74)**	(2.50)*	(4.23)**	(3.84)**	0.905	−0.057

Note: One asterisk indicates significance at the 5 percent level; two asterisks indicate significance at the 1 percent level; numbers in parentheses are *t*-values. The values of the *H*-statistic are within the acceptable range.

allows a separation of the effects associated with a true scale variable (potential income) from those associated with cyclical fluctuations. The explanatory power of the model is quite substantial. Of particular relevance is its clear indication that the variable measuring inflationary expectations plays a dominant role in the determination of the demand for money.

IV. CONCLUDING REMARKS

After experiencing several years of inflation, everyone should by now be aware that relationships that hold under stable conditions may not hold in an inflationary environment. However, in spite of this awareness, the pervasive influence of taxes on the selection of assets and the interaction of taxes with inflationary expectations in bringing about a fragmentation of the financial market are not yet fully understood. This paper has attempted to show how the desired asset composition of economic agents—and consequently, the demand for money—has been affected by taxes and by inflation. It has shown that, in this environment, given the nature of the U.S. tax system, inflationary expectations have come to play a far more powerful role than interest rates.

The inclusion of inflationary expectations among the determinants of the demand for money can no longer be considered controversial. In this sense, it can be said that the influences on the U.S. demand for money are no longer very different from those in other countries, including the developing countries. This conclusion vitiates the rule of thumb, attributed to Modigliani and supported by Dornbusch and Fischer in their macroeconomic textbook, as to how "to decide whether the nominal interest rate or the expected rate of inflation should be included as determining the demand for money." The rule of thumb is stated by Dornbusch and Fischer (1981, pp. 244–45): "If the nominal interest rate exceeds the expected rate of inflation, the nominal interest rate should be thought of as the cost of holding money. If the expected inflation rate exceeds the nominal interest rate, think of the expected inflation rate as the cost of holding money." When income taxes exist, even if the nominal interest rate exceeds inflationary expectations, the opportunity cost of money may often be better reflected by inflationary expectations than by the nominal return.

References

Carlson, John A. "A Study of Price Forecasts," *Annals of Economic and Social Measurement* (New York), Vol. 6 (Winter 1977), pp. 27–52.

Dornbusch, Rudiger, and Stanley Fischer, *Macroeconomics*, (New York: McGraw-Hill, 2nd ed., 1981).

Friedman, Benjamin M., "Price Inflation, Portfolio Choice, and Nominal Interest Rates," *American Economic Review* (Nashville, Tennessee), Vol. 70 (March 1980), pp. 32–48.

Goldfeld, Stephen M., "The Demand for Money Revisited," *Brookings Papers on Economic Activity*: III (1973), The Brookings Institution (Washington), pp. 577–638.

Lahiri, Kajal, "Inflationary Expectations: Their Formation and Interest Rate Effects," *American Economic Review* (Nashville, Tennessee), Vol. 66 (March 1976), pp. 124–31.

Laidler, David E. W., *The Demand for Money: Theories and Evidence* (New York: Harper and Row, 2nd ed., 1977).

———, "The Demand for Money in the United States—Yet Again," in *On the State of Macro-economics*, ed. by Karl Brunner and Allan H. Meltzer, Carnegie-Rochester Conference Series on Public Policy, Vol. 12 (Amsterdam: North-Holland, 1980), pp. 219–71.

Tanzi, Vito, "Income Taxes and the Demand for Money: A Quantitative Analysis," *Quarterly Review*, Banca Nazionale del Lavoro (Rome), Vol. 32 (March 1979), pp. 55–72.

———, "Inflationary Expectations, Economic Activity, Taxes, and Interest Rates," *American Economic Review* (Nashville, Tennessee), Vol. 70 (March 1980), pp. 12–21.

7

Inflation, Taxation, and the Rate of Interest in Eight Industrial Countries, 1961–82

MENACHEM KATZ

High interest rates in recent years have given new importance to the theories of interest rate determination and to the relationship between inflation and interest rates. Questions have arisen as to the impact of differential tax treatment of interest income and expense in various countries on the real rate of interest. This paper analyzes the relationship between interest rates and inflation, as well as the effects of taxation on this relationship, for a sample of eight industrial countries during the period 1961–82.

I. BACKGROUND OF THE STUDY

The classical theories of the determination of interest rates—Ricardo's theory of value, Wicksell and the Austrian school's natural rate, and the Fisherian theory on the interaction between time preference of individuals and the marginal productivity of capital—dealt with the determination of *real* interest rates. With the introduction of money into the analysis, the loanable funds (Fisher) approach and the liquidity preference (Keynes) or portfolio approach were developed. Periods of inflation made it necessary to recognize the distinction between the nominal rate of interest and the real rate of interest.

The Fisher effect, which had first been introduced by Thornton (1802) and subsequently formalized by Fisher (1896; 1930), suggests that as individuals anticipate higher rates of inflation they expect nominal rates of interest to reflect this increase.[1] However, Fisher (1930, p. 43) observed "... when prices are rising, the rate of interest

---

[1] See Chapter 2 (paper by Ben-Zion) for a survey of the literature on the Fisher effect.

172

tends to be high but not so high as it should be to compensate for the rise; and when prices are falling, the rate of interest tends to be low, but not so low as it should be to compensate for the fall." Employing a loanable funds framework, Fisher expected the anticipated inflation coefficient to be unity. When he observed a smaller coefficient, he noted that the erratic behavior of real interest rates is evidently a trick played on the money market by "money illusion" and he argued further that it was also due to "the instability of money."

Analysis of the effect of a change in anticipated inflation on the real rate of interest was introduced by Mundell (1963) and Tobin (1965). Mundell demonstrated that a rise in anticipated inflation would result in a decrease in the real rate of interest, the rationale being that such a rise depresses the real balance of equilibrium, thus causing an increase in saving to compensate for it. Equilibrium is restored by means of a lower real interest rate, which raises the level of investment to make it equal to the higher level of savings. Tobin introduced a portfolio effect. He noted that a rise in anticipated inflation causes a shift away from money balances into real capital, thereby depressing the marginal product of capital and the equilibrium of the real rate of interest. Thus, according to Mundell, the Fisher equation,

$$i = r + \pi^e \tag{1}$$

where i is the nominal rate of interest, r is the real rate of interest, and π^e is the anticipated rate of inflation, would imply that $dr/d\pi^e < 0$ and $di/d\pi^e < 1$ and not $di/d\pi^e = 1$, as Fisher would have expected.

More recently, economists have realized that the relationship between changes in anticipated inflation and interest rates should be adjusted for the tax effect. This concept of tax effect was developed independently by Darby (1975), Tanzi (1976), and Feldstein (1976), who noted that if the pretax Fisher effect—e.g., the coefficient of π^e (equation (1))—was unity, then the tax-adjusted Fisher effect should be $(1/1-\tau)$, where τ is the effective tax rate applied to interest income. As $1 > \tau > 0$, then $1/1-\tau > 1$ and the Fisher effect combined with the tax effect would result in a coefficient greater than unity. If a capital gains tax (θ) is introduced, the modified Fisher effect and the tax effect would be $\dfrac{1-\theta}{1-\tau}$, which could still be greater than unity but less than $1/1-\tau$ because τ is normally greater than θ.

As the Fisher equation reflects only partial equilibrium, a number of attempts have been made to develop more comprehensive models that incorporate macroeconomic effects as well as tax effects. Levi and Makin (1978) constructed a macroeconomic model wherein $di/d\pi^e$

was derived and was shown to depend on income, liquidity, and employment effects as well as on the taxes on interest income and capital gains. A more detailed model was constructed by Summers (1982), while Nielsen (1981) developed a general-equilibrium framework based on microeconomic optimizing behavior by both households and firms. Although he incorporated the personal income tax, the corporate income tax, and the capital gains tax into the model, his conclusions were similar to those derived earlier: that the nominal interest rate would increase by more than the pure Fisher effect but by less than would be required to keep constant the real after-tax rate of return.

Empirical studies on the relationship between interest rates and inflation with or without taxes have mainly focused on the United States rather than on other countries. This paper analyzes the various responses of interest rates to changes in expected and actual inflation rates in specific countries which have different rates of inflation and different tax treatments of interest income or capital gains. It also studies the changes in response coefficients over time as the world economy has moved from low to high rates of inflation and the effects, if any, of changes in the instruments of monetary policy on these response coefficients.

The present study is divided into three phases. In the first phase, tests are carried out on the relationship between (1) short-term and long-term interest rates, and (2) actual and expected inflation. The second phase deals with the impact of the acceleration in the inflation rate that occurred in the 1970s and the response of interest rates to inflation; it also examines the possible effects of the October 1979 change in the conduct of monetary policy on this relationship. In the third phase, the impact of taxation on the response of interest rates to inflation is studied.

The paper introduces to the literature on the Fisher effect a new technique developed by Frankel (1982) to derive a time series of expected inflation from the term structure of interest rate. The results show that the Fisher effect, based on expected inflation, was generally not significantly different from unity; the response coefficient of interest rates to actual inflation was significantly less than unity for all eight countries during the twenty-year period 1961–81. The results also indicate that the acceleration of inflation during the 1970s was accompanied by increases in these response coefficients; a slight increase was also observed following the October 1979 change in the U.S. conduct of monetary policy. The Fisher effect, adjusted for taxes on interest income and capital gains, was found to be broadly consistent with the estimated response coefficients of nominal interest rates to expected inflation.

In interpreting these results, it should be noted that in most of the sample countries interest rates have been an instrument of monetary policy. It should also be pointed out that some of the countries have employed credit rationing, while other countries have had a liberal approach to capital flows, or there has been offshore banking, which tended to "exogenize" interest rates. Thus, the response of interest rates to inflation would reflect the adjustment of interest rates by the monetary authorities to inflation in countries that have pursued monetary or interest rate controls and to external factors in countries that have pursued policies of free capital flows.

II. STRUCTURE OF THE STUDY

In studying the Fisher effect, it should be recognized that the Fisher equation relating interest rates to expected inflation is an ex post identity while ex ante it is nothing but a partial equilibrium. It is not a theory of interest rate determination in the strict sense and does not include all the variables that determine interest rates. A major theoretical issue, recognized in the literature, is the treatment of the effect of expected inflation on the expected real interest rate. In addition, methodological obstacles encountered in an empirical study of the Fisher effect are (1) the determination or measurement of expected inflation and (2) the measurement of the interaction between the expected real rate and expected inflation. The first obstacle was bypassed in a number of studies on the United States and the United Kingdom through use of the Livingston series on expected inflation or through use of actual inflation or distributed lags thereof. As for the second obstacle, attempts have been made to use proxy variables, such as capacity utilization, for this measurement, but these have raised additional methodological problems.

The present study uses a number of formulations for inflation, including actual inflation, distributed lags of present and past inflation, inflationary expectations formed by distributed lags of past inflation and monetary growth, and inflationary expectations derived from the term structure of interest rates based on the new Frankel technique.

With respect to the effect of expected inflation on the real interest rate, a number of tests are conducted in which the computed ex post real interest rate is subtracted from the nominal rate of interest so that the nominal rate of interest *less* the ex post real rate is regressed on actual or expected inflation rates. This is designed, in part, to take into account the effect of expected inflation on the real interest rate.

Inflation and the interest rate

As a first approximation, the actual rate of inflation is used for two reasons. First, actual inflation represents a form of rational expectations, with perfect foresight (Summers (1982, pp. 52–57)), and second, its use in testing would indicate the extent of an ex post response of interest to inflation. Thus, the estimated equation is

$$i_t = \beta_0 + \beta_1 \pi_t + u_t \tag{2}$$

where i_t is the short-term interest rate, and π_t the rate of inflation. When quarterly data, adjusted for serial correlation in the error term are used for the period 1961–81, the estimated coefficient of π_t is significant with a probability of 98 percent for seven of the eight countries—the exception being the United Kingdom (Table 1). Among the other seven countries, β_1 is significantly less than unity. The highest coefficients were found for the United States (0.671) and France (0.637), while Italy, Canada, and the Federal Republic of Germany

Table 1. Eight Industrial Countries: Regression of Short-Term Interest Rates on Inflation, 1961–81[1]

$$i_t = \beta_0 + \beta_1 \pi_t + u_t$$

Country	β_0	β_1	$\bar{R}^2$	D-W
Canada	4.373 (2.922)	0.491 (3.055)	0.923	1.718[b]
France	2.854 (3.595)	0.637 (6.854)	0.919	1.823[b]
Germany, Fed. Rep.	4.824 (3.237)	0.482 (2.485)	0.846	1.470[a]
Italy[2]	5.104 (2.281)	0.533 (4.444)	0.900	1.922[b]
Japan	5.799 (7.669)	0.228 (4.257)	0.835	1.355[a]
Netherlands	6.667 (8.765)	0.147 (2.790)	0.861	1.687[b]
United Kingdom	8.559 (4.833)	0.061 (0.818)	0.899	1.899[b]
United States	2.303 (3.499)	0.671 (7.248)	0.914	1.786[b]

[1] Inflation is defined as $\pi_t = [(P_t/P_{t-4}) - 1] \cdot 100$. Superscripts a and b represent one-lag and two-lag autoregressive error terms, respectively, adjusted by the Cochrane-Orcutt procedure; t-values are in parentheses.

[2] Data on short-term interest rates are available only from the first quarter of 1971 to the fourth quarter of 1981.

recorded coefficients of about one half; Japan and the Netherlands were well below these figures, with 0.228 and 0.147, respectively.

As $di/d\pi < 1$, the intercept cannot be regarded as the real interest rate. Table 5 (in the Appendix) summarizes average short-term interest rates, average rates of inflation, and average ex post real rates of interest for the twenty-year period 1961–81 and for the ten-year subperiods 1961–70 and 1971–81. With the exception of the United Kingdom, which had negative real interest rates for the period as a whole, all other countries, on average, experienced positive real interest rates. For the breakdown of the period into two subperiods, the more than doubling of average inflation rates was accompanied by a decline in average real interest rates for all countries. These computations, however, are in no way analytical proof of the Mundell-Tobin effect, but it is interesting to observe that, along with the rise in inflation rates, ex post real interest rates tend to be lower.

Thus, a second test is designed to establish the "true" coefficient of response of interest to inflation by superimposing the ex post average real interest rate on the regression as the intercept, β_0. The estimated equation is

$$i_t - \bar{r} = \beta_1 \pi_t + u_t \tag{3}$$

where $\bar{r}$ is the average real interest rate for the period 1961–81, defined as $\bar{r} = \bar{i} - \bar{\pi}$, and where $\bar{i}$ and $\bar{\pi}$ are average interest and inflation rates, respectively. The motivation behind this formulation is that β_1 reflects the response of the interest rate to changes in expected inflation most accurately when the intercept β_0 is equal to the real rate of interest. Also, by computing the average ex post real rate, account is being taken of the fact that $dr/d\pi^e \neq 0$. Thus, the results of the estimation, which are summarized in Table 2, are theoretically more defensible than the results of the previous test. These results show that, for the period as a whole, the response coefficients are the highest for France (0.888) and the United States (0.876), in the range of 0.5 for the Federal Republic of Germany, Italy, and Canada, and 0.213 for the Netherlands; Japan and the United Kingdom did not record significant coefficients.

To assess the cumulative effect of inflation on interest rates, two alternative schemes of distributed lags were employed, both using the Almon lag technique, with polynomials of the third degree corrected for autocorrelation. In the first scheme,

$$i_t = \alpha + \sum_{i=0}^{8} \beta_i \pi_{t-i} + u_t \tag{4}$$

Table 2. Eight Industrial Countries: Response of Short-Term Interest Rates to Inflation, 1961–81[1]

$$i_t - \bar{r} = \beta_1 \pi_t + u_t$$

Country	Period	$\bar{r}$	β_1	$\bar{R}^2$	D-W
Canada	1961–81	1.035	0.425 (2.450)	0.921	1.669[b]
	1961–70	1.993	0.936 (11.005)	0.888	1.881[a]
	1971–81	0.165	0.879 (6.221)	0.885	1.756[b]
France	1961–81	0.260	0.888 (15.660)	0.910	1.303[b]
	1961–70	1.315	0.417 (2.129)	0.938	1.427[a]
	1971–81	−0.699	0.973 (25.407)	0.866	1.796[b]
Germany, Fed. Rep.	1961–81	2.273	0.548 (3.051)	0.843	1.516[a]
	1961–70	2.425	0.170 (0.870)	0.745	2.024[a]
	1971–81	2.135	1.050 (6.910)	0.884	1.930[b]
Italy	1971–81	−2.220	0.505 (4.425)	0.893	1.895[b]
Japan	1961–81	0.134	−0.009 (−0.048)	0.591	1.933[a]
	1961–70	0.871	0.073 (1.113)	0.915	1.983[a]
	1971–81	−0.538	0.818 (3.106)	0.409	1.979[b]
Netherlands	1961–81	0.527	0.213 (3.837)	0.822	1.404[a]
	1961–70	2.473	0.039 (0.365)	0.664	1.501[a]
	1971–81	−1.242	0.283 (4.565)	0.888	1.524[a]
United Kingdom	1961–81	−1.102	0.062 (0.913)	0.893	1.383[a]
	1961–70	1.645	0.087 (0.786)	0.815	1.583[a]
	1971–81	−3.599	0.061 (0.651)	0.809	1.346[a]
United States	1961–81	0.439	0.867 (12.280)	0.908	1.785[b]
	1961–70	1.586	0.683 (5.481)	0.941	1.697[b]
	1971–81	−0.603	0.968 (14.384)	0.868	1.831[b]

[1] See Table 1, footnote 1.

Short-term interest rates are regressed on present and past inflation rates, with eight quarterly lags. In the second scheme,

$$i_t = \alpha + \sum_{i=1}^{8} \beta_i \pi_{t-i} + u_t \tag{5}$$

Short-term rates are regressed on the past eight quarterly lags. The formulation of equation (4) is a form of rational expectations, with actual inflation at time t, π_t representing expected inflation at time t, and π_{t-i} representing instrumental variables. Equation (5), on the other hand, represents an adaptive-distributive scheme of inflationary expectations. As could be expected, the results for $\Sigma\beta_i$ in the rational scheme are somewhat higher than those in the adaptive-distributive one, but the sums of the coefficients are less than unity (not recorded) in both.

As noted above, a major difficulty in estimation is that of the formulation of price expectations. Papers by Lahiri (1976), Tanzi (1980), and others have introduced a number of schemes or hypotheses on the formation of expectations. These include distributive, adaptive, and extrapolative schemes, which were then used along with the Livingston series of price expectations to generate a modified price expectations series. This last was in turn used to test the Fisher effect. In the absence of a Livingston series for countries other than the United States and the United Kingdom, variations of the above schemes, some of which have been recorded earlier, are used in the present study. All schemes were estimated by using ordinary least squares, with the possible deficiency that error terms were correlated with the explanatory variables, thus resulting in inconsistent estimates. In the following test, a two-stage least-squares estimation is carried out:

$$\pi_t = \alpha + \sum_{i=1}^{n} \delta_i \pi_{t-i} + \sum_{j=1}^{m} \gamma_j \mu_{t-j} + \varepsilon_t \tag{6}$$

$$i_t = \beta_0 + \beta_1 \pi_t + u_t \tag{6'}$$

where distributed lags of past inflation and money growth, μ, are employed as instrumental variables—both distributed lags of the Almon type with polynomials of the third degree corrected for autocorrelation (Carlino (1982)). The results, which are summarized in the Appendix, Table 6, are not as robust as those derived above by using simpler techniques. Another method, using the Fama approach of short-term interest rates as predictors of inflation, did not yield any significant results (not recorded).

A new technique for extracting a measure of expected inflation from the term structure of interest rates that was developed by Frankel (1982) is applied as described below. Proxies used as measures of expected inflation include either actual present or lagged values of inflation or survey data. The actual values of inflation do not incorporate all the pieces of information that enter into the formation of expectations, while survey data, such as the Livingston series, have been shown to contain deficiencies.

The Frankel method is based on the premise that long-term interest rates reflect expected future short-term rates and that long-term rates reflect the expected inflation rate more fully than do short-term rates. It is thus assumed that there exists a commonly held expectation (π^e) as to what the long-run inflation rate is and that, in the absence of future disturbances, the real rate of interest will converge to a constant in the long run. The gap is expected to be closed at a rate δ

$$di_t/dt = -\delta(i_t - \pi_0^e - \bar{r}) \tag{7}$$

where i_t is the short-term interest rate; π_0^e is the long-run inflation rate expected at time 0; and $\bar{r}$ is the long-run real interest rate.

The speed of adjustment is measured in the following way:

$$(i_t^{\tau 2} - i_t^{\tau 1}) = \alpha + \beta(i_{t-1}^{\tau 2} - i_{t-1}^{\tau 1}) + u_t \tag{8}$$

where $i_t^{\tau 2}$ is the interest rate on $\tau 2$ (long-term) maturity bonds issued at time t, $i_t^{\tau 1}$ is the interest rate on $\tau 1$ (short-term) maturity bonds issued at time t, and $\delta = -12 \log \beta$. Upon estimation of the above regression, β can be used to compute the weights of the linear combination of $i^{\tau 2}$ and $i^{\tau 1}$ so that

$$\pi_t^e + \bar{r} = \frac{W_{\tau 1}\, i_t^{\tau 2} - W_{\tau 2}\, i_t^{\tau 1}}{W_{\tau 1} - W_{\tau 2}} \tag{9}$$

and

$$W_{\tau 1} = -\frac{1 - \beta^{\tau 1}}{\tau 1 \log \beta}$$

and

$$W_{\tau 2} = -\frac{1 - \beta^{\tau 2}}{\tau 2 \log \beta}$$

Thus, from equation (9) a time series of expected inflation (plus a constant term) can be obtained.

The above technique is used for the estimation of a time series of expected inflation for six industrial countries, based on Eurocurrency

Table 3. Eight Industrial Countries: Response of Short-Term Interest Rates to Expected Inflation, September 1973–July 1982[1]

$$i_t - \bar{r} = \beta\pi_t^e + u_t$$

Country	β	$\bar{R}^2$	D-W	$\bar{r}$
Canada	0.991 (0.026)	0.969	1.530	0.908
France	1.022 (0.034)	0.754	2.042	1.252
Germany, Fed. Rep.	0.991 (0.036)	0.927	1.933	1.715
Italy	1.030 (0.025)	0.779	1.970	1.019
Japan[2]	1.162 (0.097)	0.905	2.432	−0.279
Netherlands	0.984 (0.040)	0.881	1.802	0.953
United Kingdom	0.997 (0.021)	0.814	2.120	−1.927
United States	0.993 (0.032)	0.961	2.028	1.027

[1] The variable π^e is derived by the Frankel procedure from the term structure of interest rates. One-lag autoregressive error term is adjusted by the Cochrane-Orcutt procedure; estimated standard errors are in parentheses.
[2] November 1975–March 1982.

deposit rates for 1 month and 12 months. The results of the estimation of equation (8) are presented in the Appendix, Table 7, while the estimated coefficients are used to generate $\pi_t^e + \bar{r}$, as shown in equation (9). It is assumed that 1-month and 12-month Eurocurrency deposit rates belong to the same risk class; otherwise, $\pi_t^e + \bar{r}$ will contain some risk factor.[2]

Once a time series of expected inflation had been obtained, two tests on the impact of inflationary expectations were conducted: in the first, short-term interest rates were regressed on expected inflation; and in the second, short-term rates *minus* the ex post real rate were regressed on expected inflation. The results of the first test (Appendix, Table 8) indicate β coefficients significantly greater than unity for all six countries, ranging from about 1.15 for the Federal Republic of Germany and the United States through 1.2 for the United Kingdom and the Netherlands and 1.48 for France and Japan. The results of the second test (Table 3) show coefficients of response to

---

[2] Ideally, rates for short-term and long-term government bonds of fixed maturities would be used, but these could not be obtained for all countries in the sample.

inflation not significantly different from unity for seven countries—
all but Japan, which recorded a coefficient of 1.16.

It should be mentioned here that a number of tests were conducted
on the relationships between inflation and long-term interest rates.
In the first test, long-term interest rates were regressed on actual
inflation, resulting in low coefficients of 0.10–0.25 for Canada, France,
the Netherlands, the United States, and Italy and insignificant coefficients for the Federal Republic of Germany, Japan, and the United
Kingdom (Appendix, Table 9). In the second test, long-term interest
rates were regressed on expected inflation as derived by the Frankel
method. The results indicate a high response coefficient (0.93), but
less than unity, for the interest rate of expected inflation for the
United States and 0.58 for France, while for all other countries in the
sample the response coefficient fell within the range 0.11–0.18 (Appendix, Table 10.)

Changes over time in the Fisher effect

Tests were made to measure changes in the Fisher effect following
the acceleration of inflation, as inflation rates were higher in the 1970s
than in the 1960s. The study also examined possible changes in the
Fisher effect following the October 1979 change in technique of monetary policy in the United States, which resulted in increased variability
of interest rates.[3]

In the first test, the twenty-year period 1961–81 was divided into
two subperiods—1961–70 and 1971–81. The main objective of this
test was to observe whether, during periods of higher inflation, interest rates responded more fully to inflation, that is, whether the β
was higher during the 1970s. The result (Appendix, Table 11) tends
to indicate that the coefficient of response was higher in the 1970s (it
is possible, however, that π was a better measure of π^e in the 1970s).
With the exception of the United Kingdom (which had insignificant
coefficients during both decades) and Canada (which had a significant
coefficient in the 1960s and insignificant coefficients in the 1970s),
all other countries recorded noticeably higher β's during the second
subperiod. The most significant changes occurred in the Federal Republic of Germany, where β rose from 0.176 to 1.303, and in France,
where it rose from 0.15 to 0.788; in the United States, the increase
was more modest—from 0.622 to 0.808.

In the above test, there is a possibility that changes in the intercept
might have affected the outcome. Although the intercept declined in

---

[3] See Chapter 4 (paper by Makin and Tanzi).

most countries during the second subperiod, the likelihood that intercept variability might somewhat obscure the outcome suggests a test in which changes in the intercept would not affect the response coefficients. To deal with this potential problem, a third test was constructed in which the intercept is held constant for the two subperiods so that the change in $di/d\pi$ will fully reflect the change in the response of interest rates to inflation. Thus, equation (10) is estimated (Appendix, Table 12).

$$i_t = \beta_0 + \beta_1\pi_{t1}D + \beta_2\pi_{t2}(1-D) + u_t \qquad (10)$$

where D is a dummy; $D = 1$ for $t1 = 1961-70$ and $D = 0$ for $t2 = 1971-81$. This test is designed to answer the question of whether β_2 is higher than β_1, given the fact that inflation was higher during the second period. The results indicate a general increase in response, as β_2 exceeds β_1 for France, the Federal Republic of Germany, the Netherlands, and Canada, which had insignificant coefficients in the previous test; the United States records a decline with $\beta_1 = 0.772$ and $\beta_2 = 0.680$ (a difference slightly less than one standard error of the coefficients). Japan and the United Kingdom recorded insignificant coefficients during both subperiods. The results of this test seem to reinforce those of the previous test in indicating that, as a result of higher rates of inflation, the response of interest rates to inflation tends to be higher.

As inflation rates accelerated during the 1970s, there was a decline in the ex post average real interest rate for the eight countries in the sample (Chart 1). Moreover, during 1971–81, negative average real interest rates were experienced in France, Italy, Japan, the Netherlands, the United Kingdom, and the United States, while the Federal Republic of Germany's average real interest rate was 2.135 and Canada's was marginally positive (Appendix, Table 5).

In applying different ex post real interest rates for the two subperiods for all countries, a comparison between the 1960s and 1970s shows that the response coefficient is significantly higher during the latter period for France, the Federal Republic of Germany, Japan, the Netherlands, and the United States; no significant change is recorded for Canada, whereas for the United Kingdom, the coefficient is not significant (Table 2). It is interesting to note that during the period 1971–81, β_1 for the Federal Republic of Germany is slightly greater than unity and for France and the United States not significantly different from unity.

In October 1979, the U.S. Federal Reserve Board changed its instrument of monetary policy from a combination of interest rates and money growth targets to one that set monetary growth targets. Changes

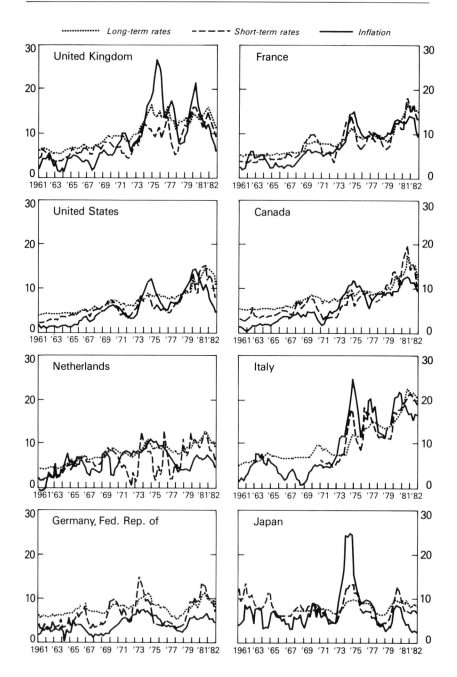

Chart 1. Eight Industrial Countries: Inflation and Interest Rates, 1961–82

(In percent)

in a similar direction occurred in the United Kingdom and in Japan, although in a considerably less pronounced manner. As a result, short-term interest rates have become more market determined while fluc-tuations of rates have become more pronounced. The analysis here tests whether these changes in the technique of monetary policy have affected the degree of response of interest rates to inflation.

Two tests similar to the ones above were conducted, using monthly data. The first is as follows:

$$i_t = \beta_0 + \beta_1 \pi_{1t} D + \beta_2 \pi_{2t} (1 - D) + u_t \tag{11}$$

where $D = 1$ for the period $t1 = $ January 1971–September 1979 and $D = 0$ for the period $t2 = $ October 1979–March 1982. The results of the estimation (Appendix, Table 13) indicate an increase in the response of interest rates to inflation in four of the eight countries in the sample: France, the Federal Republic of Germany, Italy, and the United States. Only the United States, however, recorded a sig-nificant increase (β_2 being greater than β_1 by one standard deviation of the mean coefficient). The second test for the period October 1979–March 1982, using monthly data, where $\bar{r}$ is the average ex post real interest rate for the period, resulted in response coefficients that are not significantly different from unity for five of the countries: Canada, France, the Federal Republic of Germany, Japan, and the United States (Appendix, Table 14). These results indicate somewhat higher coefficients than those obtained for the full period 1971–81 using quarterly data.

Impact of taxation on the Fisher effect

It is essential at this point to estimate the impact of taxation on the response of interest rates to inflation. The incorporation of tax con-sideration into the Fisher effect was done independently by Darby (1975), and Tanzi (1976); assuming that borrowers and lenders are concerned with the real after-tax interest, the formulation of the Fisher equation was modified to

$$i = r + \pi/(1 - \tau) \tag{12}$$

where τ is the effective personal tax rate applied to interest income. Feldstein (1976) and later Gandolfi (1982), in two different analytical frameworks, introduced the corporate sector as a borrower and inves-tor in the capital market, whose effective capital gains tax rate (θ) resulted in a further modification of the Fisher equation

$$i = r + \left(\frac{1 - \theta}{1 - \tau}\right) \pi \tag{13}$$

The expression derived by Levi and Makin (1978) from their macroeconomic framework was

$$\frac{di}{d\pi^e} = \frac{1}{(1-\tau)/(1-\theta) + L} \tag{14}$$

where L is a term incorporating liquidity, income, and employment effects. Computing the magnitude of $di/d\pi^e$ for the United States (assuming that $\tau = 0.5$), they found a range of $0.750-1.285$, depending on the paremeters in L. Neilsen's (1981) general-equilibrium model based on micro-optimization behavior of households and firms included (in addition to personal income tax and capital gains tax) company income tax, τ_1. Neilsen derived an expression for $di/d\pi$ that was shown as a range, depending on the relative magnitudes of all three tax rates

$$\frac{1-\theta}{1-\tau_1} < \frac{di}{d\pi} < \frac{1}{1-\tau} \tag{15}$$

The tax treatment of interest income and interest expense for the household sector, on the one hand, and corporate taxation on the other hand, varies quite substantially from country to country.[4] Preferential tax treatment of interest income of the household sector differs from country to country. It is most generous in Japan, where interest income of the equivalent of US\$56,000 per taxpayer is tax exempt; it is estimated that average tax payments on interest income during the 1970s were about 7 percent. Interest income is incorporated into total individual income and treated as part of global income in Canada, the Federal Republic of Germany, the United Kingdom, and the United States, while France, Italy, and Japan permit the nominal withholding taxes on interest income to become final taxes.

Deductibility of interest payments is most liberal in the Netherlands and in the United States, because it extends to general consumer credit and mortgages. Steuerle (1982) suggests that only 30 percent of income from capital in the United States is subject to individual income taxation; he estimated that about 80 percent of the assets held by individuals has been in forms for which there has been a tax preference arising from capital gains tax rates, exclusions, or some other means of nontaxation of some or all of the income from the assets. Interest payments on home mortgages are also deductible in Canada, France, and the United Kingdom, while in the Federal Republic of

---

[4] See Modi (1983) for a survey of the tax treatment of investment income and expense in industrial countries.

Germany and Japan, less generous schemes apply. In the Federal Republic of Germany, there are taxes on the imputed income of owner-occupied housing. Although many industrial countries tax long-term capital gains of individuals, either under a separate tax (e.g., the United Kingdom) or under the regular income tax after exempting a certain proportion of the gains (e.g., Canada and the United States), most industrial countries apply lower tax rates on long-term capital gains than on ordinary income. With respect to corporate taxation, double taxation exists in the United States at shareholder levels. In the Federal Republic of Germany, shareholders receive full credit for the tax paid by the corporation on dividends distributed; in other countries, there are partial imputations.

Acknowledging the difficulties in quantifying effective tax rates on interest income, company income tax, and capital gains tax for the countries in the sample, the author presents in the Appendix, Table 15, an estimate of average effective rates of interest income of individuals and corporations during the subperiod 1971–81. Tax rates on interest income of individuals for Canada, the Federal Republic of Germany, the Netherlands, the United Kingdom, and the United States represent the percentage ratio of tax paid to taxed income of "representative" taxpayers (defined as individuals whose assessable income constitutes about one third of the total taxed income in the highest-income brackets). For France and Italy, the rates are final withholding tax rates; for Japan, the rate represents the average ratio of interest income tax to interest income.[5] With respect to capital gains tax rates, owing to difficulties in obtaining effective rates, statutory rates have been chosen; as effective capital gains tax rates would be somewhat lower, the computed $(1 - \theta)/(1 - \tau)$ could be somewhat biased downward.

On the basis of these tax rate computations, the Fisher effect adjusted to the tax on interest income alone shows coefficients ranging from 1.075 for Japan and 1.299 for the United States to about 1.5 for France and the Federal Republic of Germany (Table 4). If both the individual interest income tax and the capital gains tax are taken into account, the tax-adjusted Fisher effect is less than unity for all but France (1.124) and Italy (1.072); it ranges between 0.847 for the Netherlands and 0.964 for the Federal Republic of Germany. However, since the capital gains tax rates used are the statutory rates, these tax-adjusted Fisher effects would be somewhat higher. If these are compared with the β's obtained for expected inflation, the two sets

---

[5] For a discussion on the use of average rates versus marginal rates, see Tanzi (1982).

Table 4. Eight Industrial Countries: Impact of Taxation on Adjustment of Interest Rates to Inflation, 1971–81

Country	$\dfrac{1}{1-\tau}$	$\dfrac{1-\theta}{1-\tau_1}$	$\dfrac{1-\theta}{1-\tau}$	β(of π^e)	β(of π)
Canada	1.176	1.069	0.906	0.991	0.879
France	1.493	1.136	1.120	1.022	0.973
Germany, Fed. Rep.	1.515	1.067	0.970	0.991	1.050
Italy	1.429	1.000	1.072	1.030	0.505
Japan	1.075	0.988	0.860	1.162	0.818
Netherlands	1.299	—	—	0.984	0.283
United Kingdom	1.316	0.795	0.921	0.997	0.061
United States	1.299	1.061	0.909	0.993	0.968

Source: Tax rates are based on those of Table 15 in the Appendix. β(of π) and β(of π^e) are regression coefficients of Tables 2 and 3, respectively.

tend to be fairly consistent for France, the Federal Republic of Germany, the Netherlands, the United Kingdom, and the United States. For Japan, the tax ratio is less than unity while the response coefficient is significantly greater than unity. If the response coefficient of interest rates to actual inflation in Japan is compared with the tax ratio, the two will be similar in order of magnitude—0.818 and 0.857, respectively.

The application of the Neilsen range shows that only in the United Kingdom $di/d\pi^e$ was between $1/1-\tau$ and $(1-\theta)/(1-\tau_1)$; in all the other countries, both $di/d\pi$ and $di/d\pi^e$ were smaller than the lower bound of the range.

In sum, when only personal interest income tax is used, the Fisher effect is expected to be greater than unity. Empirical results that tend to support a response coefficient of interest rates to expected inflation of greater than unity were obtained when a regression of the type $i_t = \beta_0 + \beta_1\pi_t^e + u_t$ was used without correcting for the effects of expected inflation on the real rate of interest. When both types of tax (interest income tax and capital gains tax) are taken into consideration, the tax-adjusted Fisher effect can be greater or less than unity. In fact, it was found to be greater than unity for France and Italy and less than unity for all other countries. These tax-adjusted coefficients for the Fisher effect were found to be consistent with the estimated response coefficients of nominal interest rates to expected inflation for France, the Federal Republic of Germany, the Netherlands, the United Kingdom, and the United States; they were found to be consistent with β's of actual inflation for Canada, the Federal Republic of Germany, Japan, and the United States.

III. CONCLUSION

The results of the tests conducted in the present analysis can be summarized in three parts:

1. The response coefficient of nominal short-term interest rates to expected inflation, derived from the term structure of interest rates and based on a new technique that had been developed by Frankel (1982), was significantly greater than unity in Japan (1.16) but not significantly different from unity for all other countries. The same test, without adjusting for real interest rates, resulted in response coefficients significantly greater than unity for all sample countries— about 1.15 for the United States and the Federal Republic of Germany, about 1.20 for the Netherlands and the United Kingdom, and about 1.50 for France and Japan.

The results indicate that the response of nominal short-term interest rates to actual inflation for the period 1961–81 was significantly less than unity for all eight countries. France and the United States recorded coefficients of about 0.90, the Federal Republic of Germany, Italy, and Canada about 0.45–0.55, and the Netherlands 0.21, while Japan and the United Kingdom had insignificant coefficients.

As for long-term interest rates, the response coefficient to expected inflation was high for the United States (0.93) and France (0.58) and in the range of 0.10–0.20 for the Federal Republic of Germany, Japan, the Netherlands, and the United Kingdom. The response coefficient of long-term interest rates to actual inflation was found to be 0.10–0.25 for Canada, France, Italy, the Netherlands, and the United States, and insignificant for the Federal Republic of Germany, Japan, and the United Kingdom.

2. The acceleration of inflation from the 1960s to the 1970s was generally accompanied by increases in the response coefficient of short-term interest rates to inflation. The change of instruments of monetary policy that occurred in October 1979 in the United States was accompanied by some increase in the Fisher coefficient to actual inflation, especially in the United States, Canada, and the Federal Republic of Germany.

3. The Fisher effect, adjusted for the interest income tax and the capital gains tax, can be greater or less than unity; it was found to be greater than unity for France and Italy and less than unity for all the other countries in the sample. These tax-adjusted Fisher effects were

found to be consistent with the estimated response coefficients of nominal interest rates to expected inflation for France, the Federal Republic of Germany, the Netherlands, the United Kingdom, and the United States; they were found to be consistent with the response coefficient of short-term interest rates to actual inflation for Canada, the Federal Republic of Germany, Japan, and the United States.

In interpreting these results, it should be noted that monetary policies of most countries have used interest rates as a major instrument, while in other countries free capital flows or the existence of offshore banking tended to make the determination of interest rates exogenous. Consequently, the response of interest rates to actual or expected inflation could reflect adjustments by the monetary authorities to inflation, on the one hand, or adjustments stemming from external factors, on the other hand.

Appendix

Table 5. Eight Industrial Countries: Mean Inflation and Short-Term Nominal and Real Interest Rates, 1961–81[1]

Country	Period	$\bar{i}$	$\bar{\pi}$	$\bar{r}$
Canada	1961–81	6.768	5.733	1.035
	1961–70	4.724	2.731	1.993
	1971–81	8.626	8.461	0.165
France	1961–81	7.422	7.162	0.260
	1961–70	5.354	4.039	1.315
	1971–81	9.302	10.001	−0.699
Germany, Fed. Rep.	1961–81	6.216	3.943	2.273
	1961–70	5.012	2.587	2.425
	1971–81	7.310	5.175	2.135
Italy	1961–81	. . .	9.377	—
	1961–70	. . .	—	—
	1971–81	12.081	14.301	−2.220
Japan	1961–81	5.878	5.744	0.134
	1961–70	4.913	4.042	0.871
	1971–81	6.754	7.292	−0.538
Netherlands	1961–81	7.863	7.336	0.527
	1961–70	8.238	5.765	2.473
	1971–81	7.523	8.765	−1.242
United Kingdom	1961–81	7.977	9.079	−1.102
	1961–70	5.709	4.064	1.645
	1971–81	10.040	13.639	−3.599
United States	1961–81	5.992	5.553	0.439
	1961–70	4.350	2.764	1.586
	1971–81	7.485	8.088	−0.603

[1] The variables $\bar{i}$, $\bar{\pi}$, and $\bar{r}$ denote average nominal short-term interest rate, average inflation, and average real interest rate, respectively. Inflation is measured as $\pi_t = [(P_t/P_{t-4}) - 1] \cdot 100$, where P_t is the quarterly average consumer price index.

Table 6. Eight Industrial Countries: Two-Stage Least-Squares Estimation of Impact of Inflation on Short-Term Interest Rates, 1961–81[1]

$$(1) \quad \pi_t = \alpha + \sum_{i=1}^{8} \delta_i \pi_{t-i} + \sum_{j=1}^{8} \gamma_j \mu_{t-j} + \varepsilon_t$$

$$(2) \quad i_t = \beta_0 + \beta_1 \pi_t + u_t$$

Country	$\sum_{i=1}^{8} \delta_i$	$\sum_{i=1}^{8} \gamma_i$	β_0	β_1	$\overline{R}^2$	D-W
Canada	0.913 (10.143)	0.001 (0.293)	9.681 (3.316)	−0.068 (−0.987)	0.913	1.648[b]
France	0.917 (11.615)	0.040 (0.583)	1.477 (1.526)	0.799 (6.847)	0.662	1.871[b]
Germany, Fed. Rep	0.844 (8.636)	−0.002 (−0.040)	7.029 (6.306)	−0.079 (−2.283)	0.848	2.052[b]
Italy	0.890 (9.761)	0.325 (2.299)	13.443 (5.677)	0.022 (0.508)	0.870	1.857[b]
Japan	0.660 (3.015)	−0.041 (−0.326)	6.772 (6.061)	−0.051 (−1.133)	0.624	1.828[a]
Netherlands	0.771 (7.216)	0.116 (1.920)	7.961 (10.136)	−0.023 (−1.196)	0.835	1.706[b]
United Kingdom	0.468 (2.361)	0.430 (2.050)	9.482 (4.927)	−0.009 (−0.465)	0.899	1.901[b]
United States	0.738 (10 .720)	0.331 (3.535)	6.908 (3.757)	0.101 (1.118)	0.906	1.795[b]

[1] The two instrumental variables are $\sum_{i=1}^{8} \pi_{t-i}$ and $\sum_{j=1}^{8} \mu_{t-j}$, where the latter is the rate of growth of M_1; the t-values are in parentheses. The error term is autoregressive with one and two lags (superscripts a and b, respectively).

Table 7. Eight Industrial Countries: Estimation of Speed of Adjustment, September 1973–July 1982[1]

$$(\hat{i}_t^2 - \hat{i}_t^1) = \alpha + \beta(\hat{i}_{t-1}^2 - \hat{i}_{t-1}^1) + u_t$$

Country	α	β	$\overline{R}^2$	D-W	δ^2
Canada	0.030 (0.064)	0.766 (0.064)	0.582	1.530	3.200
France	0.150 (0.248)	0.387 (0.090)	0.141	2.033	4.948
Germany, Fed. Rep.	0.125 (0.085)	0.600 (0.077)	0.357	1.910	2.658
Italy	−0.181 (0.269)	0.369 (0.095)	0.121	0.950	11.900
Japan[3]	0.205 (0.133)	0.694 (0.083)	0.478	2.262	1.906
Netherlands	0.132 (0.109)	0.672 (0.072)	0.450	1.804	2.071
United Kingdom	0.096 (0.139)	0.547 (0.078)	0.311	2.047	3.148
United States	0.102 (0.083)	0.757 (0.064)	0.564	2.033	1.453

[1] The variables $\hat{i}^1$ and $\hat{i}^2$ represent 1-month and 12-month Eurocurrency deposit rates, respectively. Estimated standard errors are in parentheses; the technique of estimation is ordinary least squares.
[2] The speed of adjustment is $\delta = -12 \log \beta$.
[3] November 1975–March 1982.

Table 8. Six Industrial Countries: Response of Short-Term Interest Rates to Expected Inflation, September 1973–July 1982[1]

$$i_t = \beta_0 + \beta_1 \pi_t^e + u_t$$

Country	β_0	β_1	$\overline{R}^2$	D-W
France	−4.636	1.481	0.798	1.983
	(1.152)	(0.094)		
Germany, Fed. Rep.	0.615	1.143	0.931	1.881
	(0.389)	(0.063)		
Japan[2]	−4.290	1.477	0.930	1.937
	(0.566)	(0.077)		
Netherlands	−1.237	1.232	0.889	1.821
	(0.725)	(0.090)		
United Kingdom	−5.076	1.197	0.819	2.055
	(1.521)	(0.099)		
United States	−0.876	1.154	0.964	1.990
	(0.571)	(0.054)		

[1] The variable π^e is derived by the Frankel procedure from term structure of interest rates. One-lag autoregressive error term is adjusted by the Cochrane-Orcutt procedure; estimated standard errors are in parentheses.

[2] November 1975–March 1982.

Table 9. Eight Industrial Countries: Inflation and Long-Term Interest Rates, 1961–81[1]

$$i_t = \beta_0 + \beta\pi_t + u_t$$

Country/Period	β_0		β_1		$\overline{R}^2$	D-W
Canada						
1961–81	27.43	(2.30)	0.172	(1.84)	0.951	1.90
1961–70	3.58	(4.35)	0.250	(4.22)	0.969	1.87
1971–81	30.41	(2.10)	0.103	(0.691)	0.900	1.89
France						
1961–81	20.63	(2.12)	0.225	(3.47)	0.977	1.97
1961–70	11.51	(2.85)	0.35	(0.476)	0.929	1.98
1971–81	11.90	(2.16)	0.324	(3.33)	0.953	1.94
Germany, Fed. Rep.						
1961–81	7.78	(13.33)	0.023	(0.37)	0.912	1.78
1961–70	7.30	(16.25)	−0.045	(−1.08)	0.903	1.80
1971–81	6.65	(6.61)	0.229	(1.76)	0.887	1.80
Italy						
1961–81	34.58	(2.26)	0.100	(2.82)	0.983	1.76
1961–70	7.33	(13.88)	−0.069	(−1.49)	0.920	1.88
1971–81	31.05	(2.22)	0.121	(2.53)	0.972	1.74
Japan						
1961–81	10.64	(5.13)	0.012	(0.308)	0.959	1.93
1961–70	8.21	(6.06)	0.012	(0.59)	0.978	1.89
1971–81	9.62	(5.79)	0.094	(0.706)	0.841	1.94
Netherlands						
1968–81	7.36	(15.72)	0.062	(2.70)	0.900	2.05
1968–70	8.04	(18.57)	−0.0008	(−0.83)	0.980	1.54
1971–81	7.36	(13.20)	0.077	(2.71)	0.892	2.04
United Kingdom						
1961–81	15.25	(3.54)	0.037	(0.840)	0.960	1.96
1961–70	9.286	(3.66)	0.132	(2.42)	0.951	1.77
1971–81	13.28	(8.36)	0.036	(0.565)	0.839	1.99
United States						
1961–81	3.61	(4.18)	0.136	(2.55)	0.976	1.98
1961–70	3.43	(31.24)	0.528	(16.45)	0.953	2.03
1971–81	33.35	(2.61)	0.133	(1.55)	0.939	1.95

[1] The t-values are in parentheses. The Durbin-Watson statistics are adjusted for serial correlation by the Cochrane-Orcutt procedure.

**Table 10. Six Industrial Countries: Expected Inflation and Long-Term
Interest Rates, September 1973–July 1982[1]**

$$i_t = \beta_0 + \beta_1 \pi_t^e + u_t$$

Country	β_0	β_1	$\bar{R}^2$	D-W
France	14.45 (3.09)	0.58 (3.59)	0.957	2.17
Germany, Fed. Rep.	5.178 (8.44)	0.177 (8.72)	0.960	1.90
Japan[2]	4.92 (10.70)	0.141 (6.82)	0.888	1.97
Netherlands	6.90 (14.57)	0.112 (9.09)	0.947	1.97
United Kingdom	8.184 (6.88)	0.126 (4.84)	0.658	1.99
United States	13.13 (3.33)	0.925 (8.39)	0.978	1.76

[1] The t-values are in parentheses; the Durbin-Watson statistics are adjusted for serial correlation.
[2] First quarter of 1976 to first quarter of 1982.

Table 11. Eight Industrial Countries: Regression of Short-Term Interest Rates on Inflation, 1961–70 and 1971–81[1]

$$i_t = \beta_0 + \beta_1\pi_t + u_t$$

Country	Period	β_0	β_1	$\bar{R}^2$	D-W
Canada	1961–70	3.017	0.653	0.892	1.970[b]
		(5.876)	(4.452)		
	1971–81	8.124	0.270	0.893	1.638[b]
		(2.018)	(0.877)		
France	1961–70	7.401	0.150	0.933	1.325[a]
		(2.786)	(1.134)		
	1971–81	1.315	0.788	0.868	1.823[b]
		(0.865)	(5.492)		
Germany, Fed. Rep.	1961–70	5.806	0.176	0.724	2.030[b]
		(3.516)	(0.877)		
	1971–81	0.711	1.303	0.859	1.248[a]
		(0.286)	(3.407)		
Italy	1971–81	5.104	0.533	0.900	1.922[b]
		(2.281)	(4.444)		
Japan	1961–70	7.011	0.050	0.917	2.038[b]
		(4.501)	(0.737)		
	1971–81	4.961	0.292	0.892	1.461[a]
		(4.239)	(4.797)		
Netherlands	1961–70	7.270	0.064	0.918	1.956[a]
		(3.672)	(0.945)		
	1971–81	6.192	0.159	0.906	2.286[b]
		(5.947)	(2.420)		
United Kingdom	1961–70	5.744	0.099	0.822	1.530[a]
		(5.631)	(0.887)		
	1971–81	11.262	0.060	0.813	1.284[a]
		(3.911)	(0.625)		
United States	1961–70	2.754	0.622	0.940	1.776[b]
		(6.119)	(4.708)		
	1971–81	0.949	0.808	0.868	1.800[b]
		(0.602)	(4.634)		

[1] Inflation is defined as $\pi_t = [(P_t/P_{t-4}) - 1] \cdot 100$. Superscripts a and b represent one-lag and two-lag autoregressive error structures, respectively, adjusted by the Cochrane-Orcutt procedure; the t-values are in parentheses.

Table 12. Seven Industrial Countries: Regression of Short-Term Interest Rates on Inflation for Two Subperiods, 1961–70 and 1971–81[1]

$$i_t = \beta_0 + \beta_1 \pi_{t1} D + \beta_2 \pi_{t2}(1 - D) + u_t$$

Country	β_0	β_1	β_2	$\bar{R}^2$	$D\text{-}W^2$
Canada	4.278 (2.977)	0.440 (1.552)	0.512 (3.158)	0.922	1.720[b]
France	3.001 (3.328)	0.589 (3.431)	0.627 (6.455)	0.918	1.824[b]
Germany, Fed. Rep.	4.613 (3.167)	0.450 (2.064)	0.544 (2.381)	0.844	1.455[a]
Japan	6.822 (3.941)	0.018 (0.084)	−0.091 (−0.386)	0.618	1.806[a]
Netherlands	6.621 (8.398)	0.119 (1.690)	0.169 (2.769)	0.860	1.675[b]
United Kingdom	8.432 (5.131)	0.008 (0.065)	0.071 (0.946)	0.899	1.899[b]
United States	2.127 (3.110)	0.772 (4.758)	0.680 (7.406)	0.913	1.794[b]

[1] Inflation is defined as $\pi_t = [(P_t/P_{t-4}) - 1] \cdot 100$; D denotes dummy variable $D = 1$ for $t2 = 1971–81$; the t-values are in parentheses.

[2] The one-lag and two-lag autoregressive error structures are represented by superscripts a and b, which are both adjusted by the Cochrane-Orcutt procedure.

Table 13. Eight Industrial Countries: Regression of Short-Term Interest Rates on Inflation for Two Subperiods, January 1961–September 1979 and October 1979–March 1982[1]

$$i_t = \beta_0 + \beta_1\pi_{t1}D + \beta_2\pi_{t2}(1 - D) + u_t$$

Country	β_0	β_1	β_2	$\overline{R}^2$	D-W
Canada	10.189	−0.055 (0.121)	0.142 (0.139)	0.979	1.886[b]
France	4.508	0.512 (0.184)	0.551 (0.179)	0.952	1.948[b]
Germany, Fed. Rep.	5.416	0.408 (0.184)	0.552 (0.196)	0.964	1.231[a]
Italy	9.885	0.270 (0.092)	0.302 (0.093)	0.975	1.989[b]
Japan	7.105	−0.010 (0.024)	−0.044 (0.061)	0.745	1.980[b]
Netherlands	7.472	−0.001 (0.002)	−0.006 (0.005)	0.973	2.099[b]
United Kingdom	10.293	0.040 (0.065)	0.014 (0.069)	0.960	1.956[b]
United States	4.618	0.367 (0.150)	0.515 (0.149)	0.939	1.858[b]

[1] Monthly data are used. The standard errors of coefficients are in parentheses. For the period $t2$ = October 1979–March 1982, $D = 1$. Superscripts a and b represent one-lag and two-lag autocorrelated error terms, respectively, adjusted by the Cochrane-Orcutt procedure.

Table 14. Eight Industrial Countries: Response of Short-Term Interest Rates to Inflation, October 1979–March 1982[1]

$$i_t - \bar{r} = \beta_1 \pi_t + u_t$$

Country	$\bar{r}$	β_1		$\bar{R}^2$	D-W
Canada	3.876	0.992 (14.280)[d]	(0.069)[c]	0.843	1.993[b]
France	0.273	0.997 (10.099)	(0.099)	0.810	1.834[b]
Germany, Fed. Rep.	4.913	0.974 (6.497)	(1.150)	0.758	1.594[a]
Italy	−0.954	0.244 (2.032)	(0.120)	0.894	1.904[a]
Japan	4.139	0.917 (7.071)	(0.130)	0.134	1.850[a]
Netherlands	2.763	0.649 (4.387)	(0.148)	0.867	1.680[a]
United Kingdom	−0.744	0.239 (1.913)	(0.125)	0.784	1.493[a]
United States	1.153	1.004 (5.705)	(0.176)	0.558	1.722[b]

[1] Monthly data are used. Superscripts a and b represent one-lag and two-lag autocorrelated error terms, respectively; superscripts c and d represent standard errors of coefficients and t-values, respectively.

Table 15. Eight Industrial Countries: Statutory and Estimated Effective Tax Rates, 1971–81

(In percent)

Country	Personal Income Tax[1] (τ)	Corporate Income Tax[2] (τ_1)	Capital Gains Tax[3] (θ)
Canada	15	28	23
France	33	34	25
Germany, Fed. Rep.	34	40	36
Italy	30	25	25
Japan	7[4]	29	20
Netherlands	23	. . .	. . .
United Kingdom	24	18	30
United States	23	34	30

Sources: For personal income tax: reports from the income tax departments of individual countries. For corporate income tax in France, the Federal Republic of Germany, Japan, the United Kingdom, and the United States: Thomas Horst, *Income Taxation and Competitiveness* (Washington: National Planning Association, 1977); in Canada: Statistics Canada, *Corporation Taxation Statistics 1977* (Ottawa, March 1980).

[1] Tax rates for countries other than France and Italy represent the percentage ratio of tax paid to taxed/assessable income of "representative" taxpayers, defined as individuals whose taxable/assessable incomes constitute, say, about one third of the total taxed/assessed income in the highest-income brackets. For France and Italy, the rates are final withholding tax rates.

[2] For countries other than Canada, Italy, and the Netherlands, effective tax rates are those calculated by Thomas Horst on the basis of differences in corporate income tax rates, depreciation allowances, and tax credits. For Canada, effective tax rates represent the percentage ratio of corporate income tax assessed to taxable corporate profits; for Italy, they represent the statutory rate.

[3] Statutory rates.

[4] Average ratio of interest income tax to interest income.

References

Carlino, Gerald A., "Interest Rate Effects and Intertemporal Consumption," *Journal of Monetary Economics* (Amsterdam), Vol. 9 (March 1982), pp. 223–34.

Darby, Michael R., "The Financial and Tax Effects of Monetary Policy on Interest Rates," *Economic Inquiry* (Long Beach, California), Vol. 13 (June 1975), pp. 266–74.

Fisher, Irving, *Appreciation and Interest* (1896; New York: A.M. Kelley, reprint, 1965).

―――――, *The Theory of Interest* (New York: Macmillan, 1930).

Feldstein, Martin, "Inflation, Income Taxes, and the Rate of Interest: A Theoretical Analysis," *American Economic Review* (Nashville, Tennessee), Vol. 66 (December 1976), pp. 809–20.

Frankel, Jeffrey A. "A Technique for Extracting a Measure of Expected Inflation from the Interest Rate Term Structure," *Review of Economics and Statistics* (Cambridge, Massachusetts), Vol 64 (February 1982), pp. 135–42.

Gandolfi, Arthur E., "Inflation, Taxation and Interest Rates," *Journal of Finance* (New York), Vol. 37 (June 1982), pp. 797–807.

Keynes, John Maynard, *The General Theory of Employment, Interest, and Money* (London: Macmillan, and New York: Harcourt, Brace, 1936; reprint, New York: Harcourt, Brace, 1962).

Lahiri, Kajal, "Inflationary Expectations: Their Formation and Interest Rate Effects," *American Economic Review* (Nashville, Tennessee), Vol. 66 (March 1976), pp. 124–31.

Levi, Maurice D., and John H. Makin, "Anticipated Inflation and Interest Rates: Further Interpretation of Findings on the Fisher Equation," *American Economic Review* (Nashville, Tennessee), Vol. 68 (December 1978), pp. 801–12.

Modi, Jitendra R., "Survey of Tax Treatment of Investment Income and Payments in Selected Industrial Countries" (unpublished, Fiscal Affairs Department, International Monetary Fund, May 27, 1983).

Mundell, Robert A., "Inflation and Real Interest," *Journal of Political Economy* (Chicago), Vol. 71 (June 1963), pp. 280–83.

Nielsen, Niels Christian, "Inflation and Taxation," *Journal of Monetary Economics* (Amsterdam), Vol. 7 (March 1981), pp. 261–70.

Steuerle, Eugene, "Is Income from Capital Subject to Individual Income Taxation? ", *Public Finance Quarterly* (Beverly Hills, California), Vol. 10 (July 1982), pp. 282–303.

Summers, Lawrence H., *The Non Adjustment of Nominal Interest Rates: A Study of the Fisher Effect*, Research Paper No. 836, National Bureau of Economic Research (Cambridge, Massachusetts, January 1982).

Tanzi, Vito, "Inflation, Indexation, and Interest Income Taxation," *Quarterly Review*, Banca Nazionale del Lavoro (Rome), No. 116 (March 1976), pp. 64–76.

————, "Inflationary Expectations, Economic Activity, Taxes, and Interest Rates," *American Economic Review* (Nashville, Tennessee), Vol. 70 (March 1980), pp. 12–21.

————, "Inflationary Expectations, Economic Activity, Taxes, and Interest Rates: Reply," *American Economic Review* (Nashville, Tennessee), Vol. 72, (September 1982), pp. 860–63.

Thornton, Henry, "An Enquiry into the Nature and Effects of the Paper Credit of Great Britain" (London: J. Hatchard, 1802).

Tobin, James, "Money and Economic Growth," *Econometrica* (Evanston, Illinois), Vol. 33 (October 1965), pp. 671–84.

8

Financial Market
Taxation and
International Capital Flows

MARIO I. BLEJER

Extensive literature exists on the various relationships between inflation, interest rates, and exchange rates and on their interconnections
in an integrated international capital market. Very little of this literature, however, deals with the impact of taxes and the effects that
differential taxation across countries have on international financial
markets.

I. THEORETICAL BACKGROUND

In a world without taxes, theory suggests the simultaneous holding
of the Fisher effect (linking domestic inflation and interest rates),
purchasing power parity (relating the exchange rate to domestic and
foreign inflation), and interest rate parity (linking domestic and foreign interest rates).[1] The introduction of taxes tends to prevent the
simultaneous fulfillment of these three propositions. The nature and
direction of the departures from these propositions, as well as their
consequences, can be traced to the type of taxes imposed and to their
relationships across countries. However, most of the specific analyses
of taxation have centered on the effects of taxes on the Fisher equation
within the framework of a closed economy. Darby (1975) and Tanzi
(1976) modified the Fisher relationship and established that, when
taxes are considered, nominal interest rates tend to be affected more
than proportionally by changes in the expected rate of inflation.[2]
Although Makin (1978) extended the treatment by Tanzi and Darby

---

[1] See, for example, Roll and Solnik (1979).
[2] Extensions of the Darby-Tanzi treatment are presented by Gandolfi (1982) and
Miles (1983). For a recent empirical implementation supporting the revised Fisher
effect, see Peek (1982).

to an open economy, most of the empirical and theoretical studies on interest rate parity and on purchasing power parity have ignored the effects of taxes on international financial equilibrium. The omission of taxes from the analysis can be justified by assuming that capital flows are not affected by taxation or, alternatively, that taxes affect both sides of interest rate parity proportionally. However, tax practices in Western countries appear to contradict both of these implicit assumptions.[3]

The importance of differences in taxation practices for the analysis of international financial relationships and some of the implications of incorporating tax factors in the context of an open economy are studied by Levi (1977).[4] He considers the tax rules of Canada and of the United States regarding foreign-generated income and also the tax treatment of capital gains. His analysis proves that differential taxation plays a central role in explaining deviations from pretax interest rate parity. Levi's study also sheds light on the motivation for what seems, in the absence of tax factors, "abnormal" capital movements, such as two-way capital flows.

In a related paper, Hartman (1979) adds to the analysis the effects of inflation. He is particularly concerned with the effects of different tax arrangements applying to income that is generated domestically and to income that is generated abroad. In his model, taxation leads to the reallocation of real capital stock across countries.

Other recent contributions in this area include Tanzi and Blejer (1982), in which tax considerations are used to explain capital movements between developing and developed countries, and Ben-Zion and Weinblatt (1982), where it is shown that tax differentials may provide a significant incentive for short-term capital flows that may affect real interest rates and real exchange rates. Similar nonneutralities arising from variations in the rate of inflation are obtained by Howard and Johnson (1982). They explain those effects as arising from the taxation of nominal, instead of real, interest income.

These contributions are indicative of the importance of considering taxes specifically in the context of open and integrated economies. These elements are incorporated below into a unified analytical framework that deals with the interactions between the modified Fisher effect, purchasing power parity, and interest rate parity and that

---

[3] As the tax practices of major industrial countries with respect to interest income and payments, as well as dividends and capital gains (including foreign exchange gains), are very different, it is difficult to generalize regarding their points of contact and differences. For a review, see Modi (1983).

[4] See Chapter 3 (paper by Ben-Zion) for a survey of the literature dealing with the effects of taxation on the international capital market.

provides a starting point for the study of the implications of alternative assumptions about the tax treatment of financial instruments.

II. ANALYTICAL FRAMEWORK

To assess the nature of the nonneutralities arising from alternative tax treatments of financial assets, a simple analytical framework is considered, so that it is possible to evaluate the conditions under which these nonneutralities arise, as well as their expected consequences and implications. Within this framework, a number of simplifying assumptions are made in order to center the discussion around the main influence that taxation has on domestic capital markets as well as on international capital movements.

A two-country setting is assumed, where neither country is large with respect to the other. It is assumed that the whole spectrum of financial assets available in each country can be subsumed by a characteristic asset, called here a bond, and that these bonds are perfect substitutes across countries in the sense that they are identical in all respects except for the currency of denomination. This assumption rules out the presence of country-specific financial risks, with the exception of differential exchange risks. However, in order to concentrate on the effects of taxation, the role of exchange risk premiums is not considered. Instead, it is assumed that all operations can be covered in the forward exchange market or, alternatively, that expectations about the future course of the exchange rate are held with perfect certainty.[5] It is also assumed that marginal tax rates can be described by a single characteristic rate that applies in each country to the characteristic financial asset described above. Finally, the actual and expected rates of inflation are taken as exogenous, and transaction costs are ignored.

The following notation is used for the analytical framework:

i_A = nominal interest rate on Country A bonds
i_B = nominal interest rate on Country B bonds
π_a = expected rate of inflation in Country A
π_b = expected rate of inflation in Country B
t_a = marginal tax rate on interest income in Country A
t_b = marginal tax rate on interest income in Country B

---

[5] When both alternative assumptions coincide, there is no risk premium in the forward exchange market—that is, the forward rate and the expected future exchange rate are the same.

r_a^* = real after-tax rate of interest in Country A[6]

r_b^* = real after-tax rate of interest in Country B

R^A = nominal after-tax rate of return on Country A bonds for residents of Country A

R_B^A = nominal after-tax rate of return on Country B bonds for residents of Country A

R^B = nominal after-tax rate of return on Country B bonds for residents of Country B

R_A^B = nominal after-tax rate of return on Country A bonds for residents of Country B

e = expected rate of devaluation[7]

With respect to the structure of taxation, three specific assumptions are made: (1) tax treaties assure that residents of each country pay taxes only in their own country, (2) the same tax rate applies to interest income generated by domestic and by foreign instruments, and (3) capital gains, other than exchange gains, are not taxed in either of the two countries. These three assumptions are made in order to limit the number of cases discussed, but the impact of changing these assumptions can be easily analyzed within the same framework.

The two building blocks of the analysis are the Fisher equation and the interest rate parity hypothesis. Although they are reduced forms derived from unspecified behavioral relationships, they are widely taken as a representation of equilibrium conditions consistent with a variety of adjustment models.

As nominal interest is fully taxed (but there is no taxation on capital gains), the Fisher equation, as modified by Tanzi (1976) and Darby (1975), indicates that expected inflation is bound to affect the nominal interest rate more than proportionally in order to leave the real after-tax rate of return unchanged:

$$i_A = (r_a^* + \pi_a)/(1 - t_a) \tag{1}$$

$$i_B = (r_b^* + \pi_b)/(1 - t_b) \tag{2}$$

In the open economy, however, domestic interest rates may be affected also by the level of foreign exchange rates, because they are interconnected across countries by the interest rate parity condition. If there are no interferences to the free international flow of capital,

---

[6] The after-tax real rate of interest is defined as $r^* = (1-t)i - \pi$. As π is the expected rate of inflation, r^* refers to the ex ante or expected real rate of return.

[7] The exchange rate is expressed in terms of units of the currency of Country A per unit of the currency of Country B. Therefore, e stands for the expected percentage change of the value of Country A's currency in terms of Country B's currency.

portfolio considerations require that

$$R^A = R^A_B \tag{3}$$

$$R^B = R^B_A \tag{4}$$

Equations (3) and (4) indicate that, in equilibrium, the after-tax nominal returns of domestic and foreign assets should be equal within each country.

The third element, closing the system formed by equations (1) through (4), is the exchange rate rule. It is postulated here that there are two alternative patterns of exchange rate behavior: (1) the exchange rate follows purchasing power parity, and (2) the exchange rate adjusts in order to ensure the fulfillment of the interest rate parity conditions.[8]

The analysis is conducted under two different assumptions about the tax treatment of gains and losses arising from foreign currency transactions. First, it is assumed that all foreign exchange gains and losses are treated as regular revenue and therefore are subjected to the same tax treatment (i.e., t_a and t_b apply to foreign exchange gains and losses as well as to interest income). Second, it is assumed that foreign exchange gains and losses are taxed at a lower rate than interest income. Also considered is the case in which an additional asymmetry arises when tax deductions for foreign exchange losses are fully claimed while foreign exchange gains are effectively tax exempt owing to widespread tax evasion.

Equal tax treatment of interest income and foreign exchange transactions[9]

Considering first the case in which foreign exchange gains and losses are treated as regular revenue for tax purposes, portfolio equi-

---

[8] The first assumption is based on the premise that the volume of trade and commodity prices are the main determinants of exchange rates, even in the short run, while the second considers the capital account as the main force driving exchange rates.

[9] Japan, the Netherlands, and some other industrial countries do not distinguish for tax purposes between regular income and foreign exchange gains. The United States, Canada, and the United Kingdom apply the tax rates of capital gains to foreign exchange transactions (and therefore these rates differ from income tax rates). The assumption here of equal tax treatment of interest income and capital gains transactions is, therefore, appropriate for the first group of countries while the assumption of differential tax treatment of interest income and foreign exchange transactions is relevant for the second group. An additional distinction refers to the timing of taxation. While most countries tax foreign exchange gains and losses when they are realized, the United States, Japan, Canada, and the United Kingdom also tax accrued gains and losses. In the Federal Republic of Germany, unrealized gains are not taxable until they are realized whereas unrealized losses are deductible as they are incurred.

librium becomes, as expressed in equations (3) and (4),

$$i_A(1 - t_a) = (i_B + e)(1 - t_a) \tag{5}$$

$$i_B(1 - t_b) = (i_A - e)(1 - t_b) \tag{6}$$

Purchasing power parity

Under purchasing power parity, the rate of change of the exchange rate is determined by the differential rate of inflation and, therefore, the expected rate of devaluation will follow:

$$e = \pi_a - \pi_b \tag{7}$$

Using equations (1), (2), and (7), the interest rate parity conditions, as represented by equations (5) and (6), require that

$$(r_a^* + t_a\pi_a)/(1 - t_a) = (r_b^* + t_b\pi_b)/(1 - t_b) \tag{8}$$

Clearly, unless $t_a = t_b$ and $\pi_a = \pi_b$, the simultaneous emergence of purchasing power parity, interest rate parity, and the revised Fisher relationship will imply different real rates of interest across countries. Consider an initial equilibrium position in which $t_a = t_b$, $\pi_a = \pi_b$, and $r_a^* = r_b^*$ (and, therefore, $i_A = i_B$ and $e = 0$). If the income tax rate in Country A, t_a, is now increased above t_b, this will result in a higher after-tax nominal return on Country A's bonds for residents of both countries. The difference in relative return, as obtained from equations (1), (2), (5), and (6), is

$$R^A - R_B^A = [(1 - t_b)r_a^* - (1 - t_a)r_b^*]/(1 - t_b) + t_a(\pi_a - \pi_b)$$
$$+ [(t_a - t_b)/(1 - t_b)]\pi_b > 0 \tag{9}$$

$$R_A^B - R^B = [(1 - t_b)r_a^* - (1 - t_a)r_b^*]/(1 - t_a) + t_b(\pi_a - \pi_b)$$
$$+ [(t_a - t_b)/(1 - t_a)]\pi_a > 0 \tag{10}$$

The above differentials indicate that the increase in the rate of interest income tax in Country A creates an incentive for capital flows from the lower-income-tax Country B to the higher-income-tax Country A. These flows will result in a reduction in the after-tax real interest rate of Country A and an increase in the corresponding rate of Country B. Equilibrium will be restored when real rates have changed sufficiently to satisfy[10]

$$r_a^* = [(1 - t_a)/(1 - t_b)]r_b^* - [(t_a - t_b)/(1 - t_b)]\pi_b \tag{11}$$

---

[10] Replacement of r_a^* in equations (9) and (10) by the equilibrium value in equation (11) results in $R^A = R_B^A$ and $R^B = R_A^B$.

The transfer of capital and the changes in real interest rates will be larger, the higher the difference is between tax rates in the two countries and the higher the rates of inflation (equal across countries) are. Furthermore, from equations (9) and (10) it is clear that, under differential taxation, an equal increase in the rate of expected inflation in both countries will not be neutral with respect to the level of real interest rates but will tend to reduce the real interest rate in the higher-tax country and increase it in the lower-tax country.

From equations (9) and (10), it is also seen that differential rates of inflation give rise to capital flows, even if the rates of income tax across countries are identical. An increase of π_a over π_b raises the expected rate of devaluation according to purchasing power parity and, with $t_a = t_b$, yields $R^A > R_B^A$ and $R_A^B > R^B$, inducing capital flows from Country B to Country A. Thus, the real rate of interest falls in the higher-inflation Country A and increases in the lower-inflation Country B. Equilibrium is restored as the difference between real rates is fulfilled:

$$r_b^* - r_a^* = t_j(\pi_a - \pi_b), \text{ where } j = a,b \tag{12}$$

Clearly, the differential in real returns will be larger, the larger the differential is in expected inflation rates and the higher the common rate of income tax is. However, the extent to which r_a^* falls and r_b^* increases and the magnitude of the capital flows are functions of the elasticities of the capital flows to relative returns in each country.

Interest rate parity

If the exchange rate is determined by the interest rate parity condition, its rate of change, as obtained from equations (1), (2), (5), and (6), is

$$e = [(1 - t_b)(r_a^* + \pi_a) - (1 - t_a)(r_b^* + \pi_b)]/ \tag{13}$$
$$[(1 - t_a)(1 - t_b)]$$

Equation (13) indicates that for equal after-tax real interest rates, the exchange rate that preserves portfolio equilibrium will generally depart from purchasing power parity if rates of taxation and/or rates of inflation differ across countries. If $r_a^* = r_b^*$, equation (13) can be rewritten as

$$e = [(t_a - t_b)/(1 - t_a)(1 - t_b)]r_j^* + (1 - t_a)^{-1} \pi_a \tag{13'}$$
$$- (1 - t_b)^{-1} \pi_b, \text{ where } j = a,b$$

When both countries experience the same rate of inflation, equation (13′) becomes

$$e = [(t_a - t_b)/(1 - t_a)(1 - t_b)](r_j^* + \pi_j),$$

$$\text{where } j = a,b$$ (13″)

indicating that, even if rates of inflation are identical, the exchange rate will devalue in the higher-tax country (unless r_j^* or π_j is negative). The extent of the exchange rate devaluation will depend on the level of (equal) inflation and real interest rates, as well as on the difference between tax rates.

From equation (13′) it is also observed that equality of tax rates does not eliminate the nonneutrality with respect to the exchange rate. In the presence of differential inflation and with $t_a = t_b$, the equilibrating exchange rate is

$$e = (1 - t_j)^{-1}(\pi_a - \pi_b), \text{ where } j = a,b$$

Thus, if $\pi_a > \pi_b$, the exchange rate depreciates more than conventional purchasing power parity, with the extent of the depreciation being inversely proportional to the rate of the tax on interest income.

In general, for $\pi_a \neq \pi_b$ and $t_a \neq t_b$, the exchange rate may depreciate more or less than indicated by purchasing power parity. However, e will vary less (or be exactly equal) than implied by purchasing power parity only when the higher-inflation country has the lower tax rate.[11] As a whole, for given changes in inflationary expectations, taxation will lead to an exchange rate that displays more variability than it does under purchasing power parity, and the degree of variability will be larger, the higher the rates of taxation are in both countries.

Differential tax treatment of interest income and foreign exchange transactions

Next, consider the case in which interest income is taxed at a higher rate than foreign exchange gains and losses. For simplicity, the tax rate on foreign exchange gains is normalized to zero; however, the conclusions apply to all the cases where this rate is lower than the regular tax on interest income. Given this assumption, the interest

---

[11] The condition for the exchange rate to follow purchasing power parity (i.e., $e = \pi_a - \pi_b$ in equation (13′)) is that $r_j^* = [t_b(1 - t_a)\pi_b - t_a(1 - t_b)\pi_a]/(t_a - t_b)$. For a positive real after-tax interest rate, if $t_a > t_b$, $r_j^* > 0$ requires $\pi_b > \pi_a$.

rate parity conditions, as expressed in equations (3) and (4), result in

$$i_A(1 - t_a) = i_B(1 - t_a) + e \tag{14}$$

$$i_B(1 - t_b) = i_A(1 - t_b) - e \tag{15}$$

Once again, in order to evaluate the effects of taxation on the standard equilibrium propositions, the two alternative exchange rate rules should be imposed, as discussed below.

Purchasing power parity

Imposing $e = \pi_a - \pi_b$ on equations (14) and (15) and substituting equations (1) and (2) into those equations, the difference between domestic and foreign yields in each country that would give rise to capital flows can be written as follows:

$$R^A - R_B^A = [(1 - t_b)r_a^* - (1 - t_a)r_a^* + (t_a - t_b)\pi_b](1 - t_b)^{-1} \tag{16}$$

$$R_A^B - R^B = [(1 - t_b)r_b^* - (1 - t_a)r_b^* + (t_a - t_b)\pi_a](1 - t_a)^{-1} \tag{17}$$

Equations (16) and (17) indicate that, in the presence of differential taxation ($t_a \neq t_b$), the Fisher relationship and purchasing power parity are not consistent with the absence of capital flows or with the simultaneous holding of interest rate parity in both countries unless both are experiencing the same rate of inflation. Consider, for example, an initial equilibrium position in which $t_a = t_b$ and $\pi_a > \pi_b$. This implies a higher nominal interest rate in the higher-inflation country ($i_A > i_B$), the difference being matched by an equivalent devaluation. Therefore, real after-tax interest rates are equalized ($r_a^* = r_b^*$), and parity conditions hold. Assume now an increase in t_a, such as $t_a > t_b$. Clearly, incentives for capital flows from Country B to Country A are generated in both countries ($R^A > R_B^A$ and $R_A^B > R^B$), because equations (16) and (17) become

$$R_A - R_B^A = [(t_a - t_b)/(1 - t_b)](r_j^* + \pi_b), \text{where} j = a,b \tag{16'}$$

$$R_A^B - R^B = [(t_a - t_b)/(1 - t_a)](r_j^* + \pi_a), \text{where} j = a,b \tag{17'}$$

The capital flow generated by the tax differential tends to depress the real interest rate of the higher-tax country and to raise that of the lower-tax country. To satisfy parity conditions in Country A, it is observed from equation (16) that the new level of real after-tax interest rate in that country has to fulfill

$$r_a^* = [(1 - t_a)r_b^* - (t_a - t_b)\pi_b](1 - t_b)^{-1} \tag{18}$$

However, given $\pi_a > \pi_b$, the volume of capital flows and the consequent change in real interest rates that equalize domestic and foreign returns for residents in Country A will not be sufficient to eliminate the return differential for residents of Country B. From equation (17), it is observed that $R^B = R_A^B$ when

$$r_a^* = [(1 - t_a)r_b^* - (t_a - t_b)\pi_a](1 - t_b)^{-1} \qquad (19)$$

If, however, capital flows out from Country B to Country A to satisfy equation (19)—instead of equation (18)—an inverse incentive would arise in Country A, since the lower relative level of r_a^* would imply that $R^A < R_B^A$.

Thus, the nonharmonization of taxes (across countries and domestically in terms of income and foreign exchange gains taxes) gives rise, in the presence of purchasing power parity and with differential inflation, to incentives for two-way capital flows of the nature discussed by Levi (1977). The new equilibrium position requires r_a^* to fall relative to r_b^* by more than the reduction indicated by equation (18) but by less than that implied by equation (19), with capital flows in both directions and offsetting each other. It should be noted that, in the example above, two-way capital flows arise from an equilibrium in which capital is exported from both countries ($R_A < R_B^A$ and $R_B < R_A^B$). Assuming that $\pi_a < \pi_b$, the new equilibrium position will induce capital imports in both countries ($R_A > R_B^A$ and $R_B > R_A^B$). However, in both cases, the real rate of interest in the higher-tax country has to fall and the real rate of interest in the lower-tax country has to increase in order to restore equilibrium. Moreover, when $\pi_a = \pi_b$ and therefore equations (18) and (19) are identical, ensuring that two-way capital flows do not take place, the unidirectional capital flows arising from differential taxation result in the same type of relationship between relative taxation and real interest rates: the higher-tax country will, in equilibrium, have a lower real after-tax interest rate.

Interest rate parity

When the exchange rate adjusts to maintain interest rate parity, the variation required to equalize, within Country A, the returns on domestic and foreign bonds is, from equations (1), (2), and (14),

$$e = [(1 - t_b)r_a^* - (1 - t_a)r_b^* - (1 - t_a)\pi_b](1 - t_b)^{-1} + \pi_a \qquad (20)$$

However, from equations (1), (2), and (15), interest rate parity in Country B requires

$$e = [(1 - t_b)r_a^* - (1 - t_a)r_b^* + (1 - t_b)\pi_a](1 - t_a)^{-1} - \pi_b \qquad (21)$$

Two observations can be made from equations (20) and (21). As in the case of symmetrical taxation of interest and exchange gains, the exchange rate departs more from purchasing power parity as differences between taxes across countries become greater. In addition, it is clear that, even when inflation rates are equal, differential taxation induces capital flows and changes in real interest rates. That is true because, unless $t_a = t_b$, equations (20) and (21) cannot hold simultaneously for $r_a^* = r_b^*$.[12]

Assuming again an initial equilibrium where $r_a^* = r_b^*$ and $t_a = t_b$, the Fisher effect, interest rate parity, and purchasing power parity will hold simultaneously, regardless of the relative rates of inflation. If t_a is set higher than t_b, the exchange rate will, according to both equations (20) and (21), devalue more (or appreciate less) than purchasing power parity. Assuming that the exchange rate adjusts according to equation (20), its value may be replaced in equations (14) and (15), and, as obtained from equations (1) and (2),

$$R^A - R_B^A = 0 \tag{22}$$

$$R_A^B - R^B = [(t_a - t_b)^2/(1 - t_a)(1 - t_b)]r_j^* \tag{23}$$
$$+ (t_a - t_b)[\pi_a(1 - t_a)^{-1} - \pi_b(1 - t_b)^{-1}], \text{ where } j = a,b$$

Thus, the exchange rate change required to preserve portfolio equilibrium in Country A does not maintain interest rate parity in Country B as long as $t_a \neq t_b$. If $\pi_a \geq \pi_b$, the returns on foreign investments for residents in Country B are higher than the returns on domestic investments, and capital will flow from Country B to Country A, reducing r_a^* and increasing r_b^* until incentives for portfolio shifts in Country B are eliminated (i.e., $R_A^B = R_B$).[13] From equation (23) the new relationship between real after-tax interest rates that will equalize returns for residents of Country B is obtained as[14]

$$r_a^* = (r_b^* + \pi_b)(1 - t_a)(1 - t_b)^{-1} - \pi_a \tag{24}$$

---

[12] For $r_a^* = r_b^*$ and $\pi_a = \pi_b$, equations (20) and (21) result in

$$e = [(t_a - t_b)/(1 - t_b)](r_j^* + \pi_j), \text{ where } j = a,b \tag{20'}$$

$$e = [(t_a - t_b)/(1 - t_a)](r_j^* + \pi_j), \text{ where } j = a,b \tag{21'}$$

Clearly, unless $t_a = t_b$, the exchange rate change required by equation (20') differs from that required by equation (21').

[13] It should be noted that, if $\pi_b > [(t_a - t_b)r_j^* + (1 - t_b)\pi_a](1 - t_a)^{-1}$, the exchange rate adjustment implied by equation (20) will induce capital imports from Country A into Country B. This type of capital flow tends to widen the differential in relative returns, giving rise to the possibilities of an unstable result. Therefore, from stability considerations, that case should be ruled out.

[14] When real rates differ across countries, equation (23) becomes

$$R_A^B - R^B = (t_a - t_b)[(r_a^* + \pi_a)(1 - t_a)^{-1} - (r_b^* + \pi_b)(1 - t_b)^{-1}] \tag{23'}$$

By substituting equation (24) into equations (20) or (21), $e = 0$ is obtained in both equations. Substituting equation (24) into equation (1) and using equations (14) and (15), it is observed that, when $e = 0$, parity conditions are maintained in both countries. This result indicates that, under differential taxation and differential treatment of interest and exchange gains, interest rate parity in both countries is only consistent with a constant exchange rate and therefore requires equality of *nominal* rates of interest. When inflation rates differ, equalization of nominal rates is attained by changes in the after-tax real rates that are brought about by international capital flows. This mechanism of equalization of nominal interest rates through capital mobility has a number of implications. For example, an acceleration in Country A's inflation induces a capital inflow into Country A, raising the real interest rate in Country B and reducing its own real rate. Such an effect will be magnified by increases in the tax rate of the inflationary country.

Tax evasion on exchange gains

The results obtained above in relation to differential tax treatment of interest income and foreign exchange transactions are based on the assumption that both countries differentiate in their tax treatment between interest income and the value changes arising from exchange fluctuations. It can be shown that similar qualitative results arise from the alternative assumption that exchange variations and interest income are formally taxed at the same rate within each country, but, while tax deductions for foreign exchange losses are fully claimed, the effective tax rate on foreign exchange gains is much lower (or zero) because of the widespread incidence of tax evasion. This assumption imposes an additional asymmetry on the system—between devaluing and revaluing countries—which, although not based on legal considerations, appears to be an economic fact widely observed in practice.

With this assumption, interest rate parity conditions, as expressed by equations (3) and (4), result in

$$i_A(1 - t_a) = i_b(1 - t_a) + e(1 - \lambda t_a) \tag{25}$$

$$i_B(1 - t_b) = i_a(1 - t_b) + e(1 - \lambda t_b) \tag{26}$$

where

$$\lambda = 1 \text{ for } e < 0$$
$$\lambda = 0 \text{ for } e > 0$$

Imposing purchasing power parity and using equations (1) and (2), the differential in returns within each country between domestic and foreign bonds becomes, assuming $\pi_a > \pi_b$, or $e > 0$,

$$R^A - R^A_B = [(1 - t_b)r^*_a - (1 - t_a)r^*_b](1 - t_b)^{-1} \tag{27}$$

$$+ \pi_a - (1 - t_a)(1 - t_b)^{-1}\pi_b$$

$$R^B_A - R^B = [(1 - t_b)r^*_a - (1 - t_a)r^*_b](1 - t_a)^{-1} \tag{28}$$

$$+ (t_a - t_b)(1 - t_a)^{-1}\pi_a + t_b(\pi_a - \pi_b)$$

Again, as under previous assumptions, purchasing power parity and the presence of taxation result in incentives for two-way capital flows and changes in the real rates of interest. If inflation rates differ, this result will emerge even if $t_a = t_b$. Consider the case where $\pi_a > \pi_b$. From equations (27) and (28), it is observed that capital will flow from Country B to Country A and the real after-tax interest rate in the higher-inflation country will therefore tend to fall. The differential in real rates that will restore portfolio equilibrium in Country A is equal to the rate of devaluation:

$$r^*_b - r^*_a = \pi_a - \pi_b = e \tag{29}$$

This differential, however, provides an incentive in Country B for capital flows in the opposite direction, since, by substituting into equation (28) the equilibrium condition for Country A obtained in equation (29), the result is

$$R^B_A - R^B = -(1 - t_b)(\pi_a - \pi_b) \tag{30}$$

which implies that $R^B > R^B_A$. Clearly, equilibrium will require capital flows in both directions, with a reduction in r^*_a and an increase in r^*_b smaller than that implied by equation (29). This outcome will be strengthened if the higher-inflation country also has a higher tax rate ($t_a > t_b$), but it can be offset by $t_b > t_a$. These results are similar to the ones obtained in the preceding subsection under full tax exemption of foreign exchange gains and losses.[15]

III. SUMMARY AND CONCLUSIONS

The Fisher effect, purchasing power parity, and interest rate parity are equilibrium relationships that are taken to hold simultaneously in the absence of exogenous interferences. Taxation in the financial

---

[15] It can also be shown that, as in the previous case, if the exchange rate adjusts in order to maintain interest rate parity, real after-tax interest rates will change, so that $e = 0$ will be the only exchange rate change consistent with interest rate parity in both countries.

market constitutes one such interference, because it may introduce a wedge between the returns on domestic and foreign assets (when the various components of those assets are taxed differently) and/or between the returns of a given asset according to the residence of the holder (when taxation differs across countries). Therefore, taxation often prevents the simultaneous emergence of the three basic propositions and induces departures from their conventional formulations.

This paper has considered the nature of these departures and has discussed their implications. The basic premise of the analysis is that the introduction of taxes induces portfolio shifts aimed at restoring equality between the returns on domestic and foreign assets. These shifts result in interest rate and exchange rate nonneutralities that can be traced to the types and the combinations of taxes used. Some conclusions obtained from the analysis can be summarized as follows:

(1) Identical rates of taxation across countries will not prevent the emergence of nonneutralities when rates of inflation differ and interest income and foreign exchange gains are taxed at the same rate. Differences in inflation rates (with equal tax rates across countries) do *not* result in international capital flows, with the consequent changes in real interest rates and/or in departures from purchasing power parity, only in the case where exchange gains are not taxed at the same rate as interest income.

(2) Differences in tax rates between countries are conducive to differentials in real after-tax rates of interest (except when the exchange rate can depart from purchasing power parity in order to maintain interest rate parity and equal taxation applies to interest income and foreign exchange changes). In general, higher tax rates result in lower real interest rates, even if rates of inflation are identical.

(3) Under purchasing power parity, increases in the rate of inflation of a high-tax country result in a capital inflow and in a reduction of its real rate of interest. If the increase in inflation is not matched by an equivalent increase in other countries, the new equilibrium will induce two-way capital flows when exchange gains are taxed at a lower rate than interest income.

(4) When the exchange rate is determined by interest rate parity, the departures from purchasing power parity and the variability of the exchange rate are proportional to the differences between tax rates. However, when foreign exchange gains are not taxed, interest rate parity is consistent only with constant exchange rates, which implies equality of nominal interest rates. Such an equality in nominal rates is brought about by capital flows from the low-tax country to the high-tax country, with consequent adjustment in real after-tax rates.

Although some of the conclusions obtained here are dependent on the assumptions made, it is clear that the introduction of tax considerations provides an additional dimension to the analysis of interest rate determination in an open economy. One of the aspects of that dimension relates to the relationships between domestic inflation and the real rate of interest. The effects of expected inflation on the real rate of interest have been extensively analyzed in the context of a closed economy as arising from the domestic substitutions between real and nominal assets (the Mundell and Tobin effects). In an open economy, the presence of taxation appears to provide an additional rationale for the relationship between inflation and real rates—a rationale based on the response of capital flows to differential inflation and the consequent relocation of the international capital stock.

References

Ben-Zion, Uri, and J. Weinblatt, "Purchasing Power, Interest Rate Parity and the Modified Fisher Effect in the Presence of Tax Agreements" (unpublished, August 1982).

Darby, Michael R., "The Financial and Tax Effects of Monetary Policy on Interest Rates," *Economic Inquiry* (Long Beach, California), Vol. 13 (June 1975), pp. 266–74.

Gandolfi, Arthur E., "Inflation, Taxation, and Interest Rates," *Journal of Finance* (New York), Vol. 37 (June 1982), pp. 797–807.

Hartman, David G., "Taxation and the Effects of Inflation on the Real Capital Stock in an Open Economy," *International Economic Review* (Osaka, Japan), Vol. 20 (June 1979), pp. 417–25.

Howard, David H., and Karen H. Johnson, "Interest Rates, Inflation, and Taxes: The Foreign Connection," *Economics Letters* (Amsterdam), Vol. 9, No. 2 (1982), pp. 181–84.

Levi, Maurice D., "Taxation and 'Abnormal' International Capital Flows," *Journal of Political Economy* (Chicago), Vol. 85 (June 1977), pp. 635–46.

Makin, John H., "Anticipated Inflation and Interest Rates in an Open Economy," *Journal of Money, Credit and Banking* (Columbus, Ohio), Vol. 10 (August 1978) pp. 275–89.

Miles, James A., "Taxes and the Fisher Effect: A Clarifying Analysis," *Journal of Finance* (New York), Vol. 38 (March 1983), pp. 67–77.

Modi, Jitendra R., "Survey of Tax Treatment of Investment Income and Payments in Selected Industrial Countries" (unpublished, Fiscal Affairs Department, International Monetary Fund, May 27, 1983).

Peek, Joe, "Interest Rates, Income Taxes, and Anticipated Inflation," *American Economic Review* (Nashville, Tennessee), Vol. 72 (December 1982), pp. 980–91.

Roll, Richard, and Bruno Solnik, "On Some Parity Conditions Encountered Frequently in International Economics," *Journal of Macroeconomics* (Detroit, Michigan), Vol. 1 (Summer 1979), pp. 267–83.

Tanzi, Vito, "Inflation, Indexation, and Interest Income Taxation," *Quarterly Review*, Banca Nazionale del Lavoro (Rome), No. 116 (March 1976), pp. 64–76.

————, and Mario I. Blejer, "Inflation, Interest Rate Policy, and Currency Substitution in Developing Economies: A Discussion of Some Major Issues," *World Development* (Oxford, England), Vol. 10 (September 1982), pp. 781–89.

9

Impact of Taxation
on International Capital Flows:
Some Empirical Results

MENACHEM KATZ

In recent years, only a few studies taking into account the impact of taxation have been added to the large body of literature on international finance. These studies have attempted to show analytically how the introduction of taxation can affect the interrelationships among interest rates, inflation rates, and exchange rates. This paper aims to demonstrate empirically the impact of tax factors on international capital flows.

The interrelationships among interest rate differentials, expected inflation differentials, and expected exchange rate movements, which are also known as the interest rate parity and the purchasing power parity, have been shown in theoretical papers (Aliber (1973) and Hodjera (1973)) to hold simultaneously in equilibrium. However, empirical studies have found deviations between interest rate differentials and forward exchange rate premiums, on the one hand, and between these and expected inflation differentials, on the other. These deviations have been explained by transaction costs, degrees of political risks, government interventions, and varying degrees of exchange controls; tax factors have not been suggested as a possible explanation (Aliber (1975); Frenkel and Levich (1975)). Thus, it can be argued that these studies have implicitly assumed that tax factors do not affect these differentials or, alternatively, that tax factors affect all relevant variables proportionally so that the net effect is neutral.

The recent studies introducing tax considerations have demonstrated that differences in tax practices among countries may affect the relationships between interest rate parity and purchasing power parity (Ben-Zion and Weinblatt (1982) and Blejer).[1] In addition, they

---

[1] See Chapter 8 (paper by Blejer).

have shown how taxes may affect the direction of capital flows (for example, capital can flow simultaneously in opposite directions (Levi (1977)) and how taxes introduce nonneutrality in that a change in expected inflation in one country affects the expected real rate of interest or the path of the real exchange rate in a two-country setting (Hartman (1979); Howard and Johnson (1982)).

The first section of this paper provides empirical evidence on the impact of tax factors on the relationship between interest rate differentials and expected inflation differentials for the United States and each of seven other industrial countries—Canada, France, the Federal Republic of Germany, Italy, Japan, the Netherlands, and the United Kingdom, based on quarterly time series data over the period 1972–80.

The second section focuses on the potential for "abnormal" simultaneous capital flows in opposite directions between the United States and each of the seven industrial countries, based on Levi's methodology, and shows to what extent such flows are significant.

I. TAXATION AND INTEREST RATE DIFFERENTIALS

International capital flows arise from interest rate differentials across countries when investors choose securities yielding the highest return. In times of exchange rate uncertainty, investors in foreign-denominated securities can hedge against the risk of fluctuations in the value of foreign currencies by buying a contract to sell the foreign exchange in the forward market upon redemption of the foreign-denominated securities. Consider a two-country case: Country A and Country B. Residents of Country A can buy domestic securities and receive a yield, i_A, or they can buy foreign securities whose yield is composed of two components—the foreign interest, i_B, and the expected foreign exchange gain (or loss), $\dot{s}^e$, which is defined as the expected percentage change of the spot exchange rates and is denominated in units of domestic currency per unit of foreign currency. From the point of view of the residents of Country A, portfolio equilibrium will exist when

$$i_A = i_B + \dot{s}^e \tag{1}$$

Viewed differently, the expected change in the exchange rate is equivalent to the differential in expected inflation, or

$$i_A - i_B = \pi_A^e - \pi_B^e \tag{2}$$

where π^e is the rate of expected inflation.

The first is known as the interest rate parity, while the second is the purchasing power parity. A third relationship can be established by applying the Fisher equation to a two-country setting.

$$i_A = r_A^e + \pi_A^e \tag{3}$$

$$i_B = r_B^e + \pi_B^e \tag{4}$$

where r^e is the expected real rate of interest.

Thus, subtraction of equation (4) from equation (3) yields

$$i_A - i_B = (r_A^e - r_B^e) + (\pi_A^e - \pi_B^e) \tag{5}$$

Equation (2) differs from equation (5) in that it assumes that there is no difference in expected real rates of interest (actual real rates of interest can diverge because of differences in productivity of capital). In other words, equation (5) assumes that a Mundell effect may exist in a two-country case operating in a similar manner to the Mundell effect in a single-country case. Namely, a change in the differential of expected inflation between two countries may affect the differential of expected real interest rates.

Before introducing tax factors into the analysis, it would be useful to describe briefly how industrial countries tax income arising from international transactions. The treatment of taxation on interest income and capital gains arising from foreign exchange transactions varies across countries. As the tax laws in industrial countries generally do not contain explicit provisions about the treatment of foreign exchange gains, practices tend to reflect accounting and legal practices. For example, taxes on foreign exchange gains are payable on an accrual basis in Canada and France. Furthermore, foreign exchange gains are taxed at the capital gains tax rate rather than at the income tax rate in Canada, the United Kingdom, and the United States. With the exception of these countries, all other countries in the sample allow deductions for unrealized foreign exchange losses. Moreover, the eight industrial countries studied have tax treaties allowing for reduced tax rates on withholding taxes that apply to interest income of nonresidents. This does not necessarily mean that investors abroad enjoy lower tax rates; the general practice has been that the withholding tax paid on interest income abroad is deducted from total domestic income tax payments. Thus, investors continue to pay on the basis of domestic tax rates. In effect, tax treaties divide tax revenue between the capital-exporting and capital-importing countries.

Of the eight countries, only Canada, the United Kingdom, and the United States apply capital gains tax rates that are lower than the tax rates on interest income or company income. And only in Canada and the United Kingdom do these capital gains tax rates apply to short-term gains. In the United States, the capital gains tax is applied only on gains realized after 12 months; short-term gains are taxed as normal income.

The introduction of taxation into the Fisher equation in the single-country case results in a modified Fisher effect, as has been demonstrated theoretically by Darby (1975) and Tanzi (1976), and empirically for eight industrial countries.[2]

Consider the introduction of tax factors into the analysis. Suppose a tax rate, τ_A, is applied to interest income of residents of Country A earned in any of the countries. If the tax applies to interest income while capital gains are exempt, the relationship in equation (1) will be modified as follows:

$$i_A(1 - \tau_A) = i_B(1 - \tau_A) + \dot{s}^e \tag{6}$$

or

$$i_A - i_B = \left(\frac{1}{1 - \tau_A}\right) \dot{s}^e \tag{7}$$

If the tax applied to capital gains, θ_A, is equal to the tax rate on interest income, then equation (6) reverts to equation (1). However, if there is no capital gains tax ($\theta_A = 0$), then equation (7) remains intact.

If a reduced capital gains tax, $\theta_A < \tau_A$, applies, then equation (6) becomes

$$i_A - i_B = \left(\frac{1 - \theta_A}{1 - \tau_A}\right) \dot{s}^e \tag{8}$$

and similar considerations apply to residents of Country B.

When the expected rate of change of the exchange rate is replaced by the differential of expected inflation rates, the introduction of tax factors viewed in terms of the portfolio equilibrium requirements of residents of Country A would require equating the net-of-tax interest rate differential to the differential of expected inflation. If capital gains tax rates are equal to interest income tax rates, then equation (2) will not be affected by the introduction of tax factors:

$$i_A(1 - \tau_A) - i_B(1 - \tau_A) = (1 - \tau_A)(\pi_A^e - \pi_B^e) \tag{9}$$

---

[2] See Chapter 7 (paper by Katz).

If, however, foreign exchange gains are not subject to any tax or if foreign exchange gains tax does not apply to unrealized gains, then equation (2) becomes

$$i_A - i_B = \left(\frac{1}{1 - \tau_A}\right)(\pi_A^e - \pi_B^e). \tag{10}$$

Alternatively, if foreign exchange gains are subject to a reduced capital gains tax, $\theta < \tau$, then equation (10) becomes

$$i_A - i_B = \left(\frac{1 - \theta_A}{1 - \tau_A}\right)(\pi_A^e - \pi_B^e) \tag{11}$$

As the United States applies a capital gains tax of 30 percent on foreign exchange gains to individuals realized after at least 12 months, it would be expected that this would affect the relationship between the differentials for interest rates and expected inflation rates. In order to verify this hypothesis, the following tests were conducted:

$$i_{At}^s - i_{Bt}^s = \alpha^s + \beta^s(\pi_A^e - \pi_B^e) \tag{12}$$

$$i_{At}^L - i_{Bt}^L = \alpha^L + \beta^L(\pi_A^e - \pi_B^e) \tag{12'}$$

where superscripts s and L represent short-term (3 months) and long-term (12 months) maturities, respectively. In order to account for a possible two-country Mundell effect, an alternative formulation to equation (12) is considered. This alternative formulation constrains the constants, α^s, and α^L, to the actual ex post differential of real interest rates, $(r_A - r_B)$.

$$(i_{At}^s - i_{Bt}^s) - (\bar{r}_A - \bar{r}_B) = \beta^s(\pi_{At}^e - \pi_{st}^e) \tag{13}$$

$$(i_{At}^L - i_{Bt}^L) - (\bar{r}_A - \bar{r}_B) = \beta^L(\pi_{At}^e - \pi_{st}^e). \tag{13'}$$

The time series for expected inflation were derived from the term structure of interest rates using the Frankel (1982) method.[3]

To the extent that the differential tax treatment of foreign exchange gains on short-term and long-term flows on the part of the United States affects the link between interest rate and expected inflation differentials, this can be demonstrated in coefficients of equations (12) and (13). If short-term foreign exchange gains are not realized, for tax purposes, it would be expected that β^s in both formulations—(12) and (13)—would be greater than β^L, as the first reflects $1/(1 - \tau_A)$, while the latter reflects $(1 - \theta_A)/(1 - \tau_A)(>1$ if $\theta_A < \tau_A)$.

---

[3] An application of this method to single-country Fisher effects appears in Chapter 7 (paper by Katz).

If, however, short-term foreign exchange gains are realized and taxed as income, β^s could be smaller than β^L.

The results of the estimations as summarized in Table 1 demonstrate that β^s is significantly greater than β^L for all differentials between the United States and each of the seven countries. These indicate that the relationship between interest rate differentials and expected inflation differentials is affected by tax considerations. The results also demonstrate that the two alternative formulations do not result in substantially different coefficients.

II. TAXATION AND DIRECTION OF CAPITAL FLOWS

Section I empirically demonstrates how tax factors affect the relationship between interest rate differentials and expected inflation differentials. Section II studies to what extent tax factors may lead to simultaneous movements of capital in opposite directions between two countries.

The following investigation is an extension of Levi's (1977) framework (which relates to flows between the United States and Canada) to flows that occur between the United States and each of six additional industrial countries.

Levi's demonstration of abnormal capital flows is based on a differential tax treatment of interest income and capital gains.

Table 1. United States and Seven Industrial Countries: Short-Term and Long-Term Interest Rate Differentials and Expected Inflation Differentials, 1972–80

Country	β^s	β^L	β^s	β^L
	Without adjustment for real interest rates[1]		With adjustment for real interest rates[2]	
Canada	1.517	1.029	1.515	1.024
France	1.333	1.075	1.248	1.069
Germany, Fed. Rep.	1.184	1.022	1.142	1.023
Italy	0.231	0.123	0.231	0.121
Japan[3]	1.349	1.012	1.265	1.005
Netherlands	1.413	1.078	1.421	1.090
United Kingdom	1.213	1.017	1.038	1.003

[1] Based on Tables 3 and 4 in the Appendix.
[2] Based on Tables 5 and 6 in the Appendix.
[3] Data for the second quarter of 1977 through the fourth quarter of 1980.

Suppose there is a pretax advantage of investing in Country A

$$i_A - i_B + (1 + i_B)\left(\frac{F - S}{S}\right) > 0 \tag{14}$$

where S and F are the spot and forward exchange rates denominated in units of domestic currency per unit of foreign currency.

Residents of Country A are subject to interest income tax, τ_A, and capital gains tax, θ_A, where $\theta_A < \tau_A$; residents of Country B are subject to income tax, τ_B, and no capital gains tax. Residents of Country A will prefer to buy securities of Country B when the foreign currency is at a premium because the exchange gain component of their earnings is taxed at a lower rate. Residents of Country B will prefer to buy securities of Country A because of their higher yield.

This situation arises when

$$i_B(1 - \tau_A) + \left[(1 + i_B)\left(\frac{F - S}{S}\right)(1 - \theta_A)\right] > i_A(1 - \tau_A) \tag{15}$$

or

$$\left(\frac{i_A - i_B}{1 + i_B}\right)\left(\frac{1 - \tau_A}{1 - \theta_A}\right) < \frac{F - S}{S} \tag{16}$$

where

$$\frac{F - S}{S} > 0 \text{ and } \tau_A > \theta_A.$$

Such a situation may result in capital flows in both directions as residents of both countries buy each other's securities. Because only Canada and the United Kingdom apply differential tax rates on interest income and foreign exchange gains on short-term securities having maturities of less than 12 months, the frequency of such potential occurrences for these two countries vis-à-vis other countries can be measured. Canada applies a corporate income tax rate of $\tau_A = 0.46$ and a capital gains tax of $\theta_A = 0.23$. Let Canada be Country A and the United States Country B. Canadians will buy short-term U.S. securities and U.S. residents will buy Canadian securities simultaneously when

$$1 > \left(\frac{F - S}{S}\right)\Big/\left(\frac{i_A - i_B}{1 + i_B}\right) > \frac{1 - \tau_A}{1 - \theta_A} = 0.7 \tag{17}$$

During 1972–80, using weekly data on three-month treasury bills and three-month forward exchange rates with annualized premiums, such a potential existed during 3.2 percent of the weekly observations (14 out of 436). The frequency of abnormal capital flows arrived at by Levi is considerably higher. This may be due to the fact that he does not use annualized three-month forward exchange rate premia. When three-month Eurocurrency deposit rates were used, no such observations were recorded (Table 2). Similarly, with three-month treasury bills, a potential for simultaneous flows between the United Kingdom and the United States existed in 2 out of 437 weekly observations.

Because the United States applies lower foreign exchange gains tax rates for realized gains of at least 12 months, such an exercise can be conducted on differentials between the United States and other countries using 12-month Eurocurrency deposit rates. Consider the U.S. tax treatment of interest income and capital gains arising from foreign exchange gains. U.S. corporations are subject to a 48 percent tax rate that applies to interest income ($\tau_B = 0.48$) and to a 30 percent capital

Table 2. United States and Seven Industrial Countries: Frequency of Abnormal Capital Flows, 1972–80

Country and Rate	Number of Observations When U.S. Dollar at Forward Premium	Number of Observations When U.S. Dollar at Forward Discount	Total Number of Observations
Canada			
3-month treasury bill rate	14	1	436
3-month Eurocurrency deposit rate	0	6	423
12-month Eurocurrency deposit rate	15	1	406
France			
12-month Eurocurrency deposit rate	13	2	431
Germany, Fed. Rep.			
12-month Eurocurrency deposit rate	0	0	436
Italy			
12-month Eurocurrency deposit rate	12	0	390
Japan			
12-month Eurocurrency deposit rate	0	1	262
Netherlands			
12-month Eurocurrency deposit rate	3	1	435
United Kingdom			
3-month treasury bill rate	2	1	437
3-month Eurocurrency deposit rate	0	0	433
12-month Eurocurrency deposit rate	82	8	430

gains tax ($\theta_B = 0.30$) that applies to foreign exchange gains realized after at least 12 months. Denote the foreign country as Country A and the United States as Country B. Suppose there is a pretax advantage to investing in U.S. securities:

$$i_B - \left[i_A + (1 + i_A)\frac{S - F}{F}\right] > 0 \tag{18}$$

where i_A and i_B are 12-month Eurocurrency deposit rates, and $\frac{S-F}{F}$, which is derived from $\frac{1/F - 1/S}{1/S}$, is the 12-month forward premium of the foreign currency vis-à-vis the U.S. dollar. Without taxes, U.S. residents will clearly prefer to buy securities denominated in U.S. dollars, as will residents of Country A. With the introduction of taxes on interest and foreign exchange gains on U.S. residents, the above relationship becomes

$$i_B(1 - \tau_B) - \left[i_A(1 - \tau_B) + (1 + i_A)\frac{S - F}{F}(1 - \theta_B)\right] \tag{19}$$

Under certain conditions, the pretax advantage of buying U.S. securities can be reversed and U.S. residents will prefer to buy foreign securities on which the exchange gain component of their earnings is taxed at a lower rate. Algebraically,

$$i_A(1 - \tau_B) + (1 + i_A)\frac{S - F}{F}(1 - \theta_B) > i_B(1 - \tau_B) \tag{20}$$

$$\frac{S - F}{F} > \left(\frac{i_B - i_A}{1 + i_A}\right)\left(\frac{1 - \tau_B}{1 - \theta_B}\right) > 1 \tag{21}$$

or

$$1 > \left(\frac{S - F}{F}\right)\bigg/\left(\frac{i_B - i_A}{1 + i_A}\right) > \left(\frac{1 - \tau_B}{1 - \theta_B}\right) = 0.74 \tag{22}$$

As far as residents of Country A are concerned and as long as there is no distinction between interest income tax and foreign exchange gains tax, they will prefer U.S. securities when equation (17) obtains. Thus, if equation (22) obtains, U.S. residents will prefer buying foreign securities and residents of France, the Federal Republic of Germany, and Japan, inter alia, will prefer buying U.S. securities, thus giving rise to simultaneous capital flows in opposite directions. The frequencies of a potential for occurrences such as those in column 2 of Table 2 are very low for all of the above countries. Such a situation may or may not arise regarding Canada and the United Kingdom, which apply differential tax treatment to foreign exchange gains. Because Canada and the United Kingdom also apply lower foreign exchange gains tax rates, the existence of equation (22) will result in capital flows to the country with the lower pretax yields.

It is possible to conceive of situations in which U.S. residents will prefer buying U.S. securities while foreign residents will prefer buying their own securities. Such situations may arise when the U.S. dollar is at a forward premium and equation (22) obtains. Suppose there is a pretax advantage to buying foreign securities. Under such conditions, U.S. residents will borrow in foreign currency in order to invest in securities denominated in U.S. dollars. Because the U.S. dollar is at a forward premium, the foreign exchange gain is treated as a capital gain that will more than compensate for any higher foreign interest cost. Every dollar lost through the high foreign interest cost will represent a net tax loss of $0.52 but every exchange gain will represent a net tax gain of $0.70. The frequencies of a potential for such occurrences, which are shown in column 1 of Table 2, are low, with the exception of the United Kingdom. Therefore, it can be argued that, while the concept of abnormal capital flows is appealing because it can explain simultaneous flows in opposite directions, the fact is that during 1972–80 such flows rarely took place.

III. CONCLUSIONS

This paper empirically examines two ways in which tax factors may affect the flow of international capital.

The first method is designed to test whether tax factors affect the relationship between the differentials of interest rates and expected inflation rates. The empirical tests show that the coefficients of the regression of long-term interest rate differentials on expected inflation differentials are smaller than those for short-term interest rates. These findings suggest that if the difference in the coefficients is wholly attributable to tax factors, then short-term foreign exchange gains are effectively taxed at lower rates than long-term gains. This is a surprising conclusion, which would bear further analysis.

The second, which is an application of the Levi (1977) method, demonstrates how differential tax treatment by the United States of interest income and foreign exchange gains realized after 12 months can lead to simultaneous capital flows in opposite directions. Under certain conditions and when the U.S. dollar is at a forward discount, U.S. residents will be inclined to buy foreign securities while residents of the foreign country will be inclined to buy U.S. securities; in the opposite case, and when the U.S. dollar is at a forward premium, residents of both countries will be inclined to buy their own securities. In practice, however, the frequency of a potential for such flows is shown to be very low.

Appendix

Table 3. United States and Seven Industrial Countries: Short-Term Interest Rate Differentials and Expected Inflation Differentials, 1972–80[1]

$$i^s_{At} - i^s_{Bt} = \alpha^s + \beta^s(\pi^e_{At} - \pi^e_{Bt}) + u_t$$

Country	α^s	β^s	$\bar{R}^2$	D-W
Canada	0.393	1.517	0.944	1.78
	(0.134)	(0.091)		
France	0.856	1.333	0.901	1.96
	(0.356)	(0.102)		
Germany, Fed. Rep.	−0.008*	1.184	0.862	1.88
	(0.341)	(0.094)		
Italy	−5.021	0.232	0.849	2.05
	(1.871)	(0.022)		
Japan[2]	−2.571	1.349	0.886	1.89
	(0.405)	(0.141)		
Netherlands	0.971	1.413	0.677	1.77
	(0.336)	(0.186)		
United Kingdom	3.851	1.213	0.910	1.96
	(0.532)	(0.080)		

[1] Short-term interest rates are three-month Eurocurrency deposit rates; * represents insignificant coefficients; standard errors are in parentheses.
[2] Data for the second quarter of 1977 through the fourth quarter of 1980.

Table 4. United States and Seven Industrial Countries: Long-Term Interest Rate Differentials and Expected Inflation Differentials, 1972–80[1]

$$i^L_{At} - i^L_{Bt} = \alpha^L + \beta^L(\pi^e_{At} - \pi^e_{Bt}) + u_t$$

Country	α^L	β^L	$\bar{R}^2$	D-W
Canada	0.194 (0.039)	1.029 (0.025)	0.989	2.12
France	0.210* (0.121)	1.075 (0.288)	0.990	2.01
Germany, Fed. Rep.	−0.123* (0.065)	1.022 (0.016)	0.995	1.84
Italy	−5.707 (1.908)	0.123 (0.023)	0.761	1.98
Japan[2]	0.333 (0.025)	1.012 (0.054)	0.999	1.88
Netherlands	0.846 (0.121)	1.078 (0.058)	0.935	1.78
United Kingdom	2.829 (0.042)	1.017 (0.006)	0.999	2.06

[1] Long-term interest rates are 12-month Eurocurrency deposit rates; standard errors are in parentheses; * represents insignificant coefficients.
[2] Data from the second quarter of 1977 through the fourth quarter of 1980.

Table 5. United States and Seven Industrial Countries: Short-Term Interest Rate Differentials and Expected Inflation Differentials, 1972–80[1]

$$(i^s_{At} - i^s_{Bt}) - (\bar{r}_A - \bar{r}_B) = \beta^s(\pi^e_{At} - \pi^e_{Bt}) + u_t$$

Country	β^s	$\bar{R}^2$	D-W
Canada	1.515 (0.100)	0.941	1.83
France	1.248 (0.101)	0.891	2.02
Germany, Fed. Rep.	1.142 (0.053)	0.865	1.86
Italy	0.231 (0.022)	0.838	2.11
Japan[2]	1.265 (0.110)	0.888	1.83
Netherlands	1.421 (0.170)	0.687	1.77
United Kingdom	1.038 (0.029)	0.901	1.85

[1] Short-term interest rates are three-month Eurocurrency deposit rates; standard errors are in parentheses; $\bar{r}_A$ and $\bar{r}_B$ represent real ex post interest rates.
[2] Data for the second quarter of 1977 through the fourth quarter of 1980.

Table 6. United States and Seven Industrial Countries: Long-Term Interest Rate Differentials and Expected Inflation Differentials, 1972–80[1]

$$(i^L_{At} - i^L_{Bt}) - (\bar{r}_A - \bar{r}_B) = \beta^L(\pi^e_{At} - \pi^e_{Bt}) + u_t$$

Country	β^L	$\bar{R}^2$	D-W
Canada	1.024 (0.026)	0.987	2.12
France	1.069 (0.029)	0.990	2.10
Germany, Fed. Rep.	1.023 (0.010)	0.996	1.84
Italy	0.121 (0.022)	0.739	2.06
Japan[2]	1.005 (0.003)	0.999	1.90
Netherlands	1.090 (0.053)	0.937	1.77
United Kingdom	1.003 (0.002)	0.999	1.86

[1] Long-term interest rates are 12-month Eurocurrency deposit rates; standard errors are in parentheses; r_A and r_B represent real ex post interest rates.
[2] Data for the second quarter of 1977 through the fourth quarter of 1980.

References

Aliber, Robert Z., "The Interest Parity Theorem: A Reinterpretation," *Journal of Political Economy* (Chicago), Vol. 81 (November/December 1973), pp. 1451–59.

————, "Exchange Risk, Political Risk, and Investor Demand for External Currency Deposits," *Journal of Money, Credit and Banking* (Columbus, Ohio), Vol. 7 (May 1975), pp. 161–80.

Ben-Zion, Uri, and James Weinblatt, "Purchasing Power, Interest Rate Parity, and the Modified Fisher Effect in the Presence of Tax Agreements" (unpublished, August 1982).

Darby, Michael R., "The Financial and Tax Effects of Monetary Policy on Interest Rates," *Economic Inquiry* (Long Beach, California), Vol. 13 (June 1975), pp. 266–74.

Frankel, Jeffrey A., "A Technique for Extracting a Measure of Expected Inflation from the Interest Rate Term Structure," *Review of Economics and Statistics* (Cambridge, Massachusetts), Vol. 64 (February 1982), pp. 135–42.

Frenkel, Jacob A., and Richard M. Levich, "Covered Interest Arbitrage: Unexploited Profits? ", *Journal of Political Economy* (Chicago), Vol. 83 (April 1975), pp. 325–38.

Hartman, David G., "Taxation and the Effects of Inflation on the Real Capital Stock in an Open Economy," *International Economic Review* (Osaka, Japan), Vol. 20 (June 1979), pp. 417–25.

Hodjera, Zoran, "International Short-Term Capital Movements: A Survey of Theory and Empirical Analysis," *Staff Papers*, International Monetary Fund (Washington), Vol. 20 (November 1973), pp. 683–740.

Howard, David H., and Karen H. Johnson, "Interest Rates, Inflation and Taxes: The Foreign Connection," *Economics Letters* (Amsterdam), Vol. 9, No. 2 (1982), pp. 181–84.

Levi, Maurice D., "Taxation and 'Abnormal' International Capital Flows," *Journal of Political Economy* (Chicago),Vol. 85 (June 1977), pp. 634–46.

Modi, Jitendra R., "Survey of Tax Treatment of Investment Income and Payments in Selected Industrial Countries" (unpublished, Fiscal Affairs Department, International Monetary Fund, May 27, 1983).

Tanzi, Vito, "Inflation, Indexation, and Interest Income Taxation," *Quarterly Review*, Banca Nazionale del Lavoro (Rome), No. 116 (March 1976), pp. 64–76.

INDEX

Author Index

Subject Index[1]

---

[1] Letters are used as follows: c for chart and t for table.